The Proof of the External World

The Proof of the External World

Cartesian Theism and the Possibility of Knowledge

Steven M. Duncan

WIPF & STOCK · Eugene, Oregon

THE PROOF OF THE EXTERNAL WORLD
Cartesian Theism and the Possibility of Knowledge

Copyright © 2008 Steven M. Duncan. All rights reserved. Except for brief quotations in critical publications or reviews, no part of this book may be reproduced in any manner without prior written permission from the publisher. Write: Permissions, Wipf & Stock, 199 W. 8th Ave., Suite 3, Eugene, OR 97401.

ISBN 13: 978-1-55635-109-9

Manufactured in the U.S.A.

Contents

Preface vii

1 The Perils of Methodological Doubt 1

2 The Deceiver Hypothesis 27

3 Skepticism and the *Cogito* 56

4 Thinking 68

5 Being 96

6 How Can God Be Apprehended? 112

7 The Cartesian Cosmological Argument 126

8 The Concept of God 143

9 God and Knowledge in the *Meditations* 174

10 Descartes' Arguments for God's Existence: A Vindication 203

Bibliography 229

Preface

DESCARTES' FIRST *Meditation* was the first philosophical text I ever read and I credit it, more than anything else, with making a philosopher out of me. My initial reaction on finishing the text was one of amazement at how quickly and easily Descartes appeared to be able to completely undermine the common-sense picture of the world that all of us take for granted in everyday life, using compelling and seemingly unanswerable arguments. The condition of giddiness described by Descartes at the beginning of the second *Meditation* certainly described my state of mind after having read the first, and led me to the continued reflection on the questions of epistemology that, after the space of nearly forty years, has finally produced this book.

The path I traveled during those years was hardly a straight and narrow one, however. I eagerly investigated and tried out every position that offered any hope of providing a way to evade the Cartesian problematic—neo-Thomism, direct realism, perspective realism, ordinary language philosophy, and even the early versions of externalist epistemology—all to no avail. A number of influences, including personal contact with Laurence BonJour during my years as a graduate student at the University of Washington (with whom I did a tutorial on the philosophy of perception) and the writings of Barry Stroud[1] persuaded me that I could not honestly evade the Cartesian problematic. More than this, I became convinced that the only possible solution to the challenge of skepticism was the very one that Descartes had attempted in the *Meditations*; however, like everyone else, I was equally convinced that the Cartesian strategy to rescue knowledge from the jaws of skepticism simply could not be made to work.

Although my interest in epistemological issues continued unabated, a parallel interest in the philosophy of religion led to my discovery of the writings of Austin Farrer and to my dissertation, *Transcendence and Image:*

---

1. Especially his *The Significance of Philosophical Skepticism*, New York, Oxford University Press, 1984.

Austin Farrer on the Existence of God.² Although Farrer is not entirely unknown, even to analytic philosophers, he remains a very minor figure in twentieth century thought; perhaps his sole distinction is his contention (shared with many English religious thinkers of the 1940's who were reeling under the onslaught of logical positivism) that God's existence is apprehended rather than inferred and that the traditional arguments for God's existence, while all defective as demonstrations for God's existence, may nevertheless serve as the catalyst for an intellectual intuition of God mediated by creatures, most directly by reflection on my own nature. I was fascinated by the novelty of this approach to the question of our knowledge of God's existence and did my best to make sense of Farrer's complex and difficult thoughts. I was only partially successful in my own eyes and left my study of his major work—*Finite and Infinite*³—less than fully convinced that Farrer's approach would work. I was soon looking into other, more mainstream defenses of theism, such as those initiated in the 1970s and '80s by Swinburne and Plantinga.

A few years ago, I began lecturing on the *Meditations* once again, after a space of some years. My conviction that Descartes had hit upon the only possible strategy to defeat skepticism—in particular, the skepticism of the "egocentric predicament" that gives rise to the problem of the external world—was, if anything, deepened by my reading of the text; more than this, it seemed to me that I was beginning to see a glimmer of how the Cartesian project might be made to work. I recalled something about *Finite and Infinite* that had struck me as odd at the time I was first reading it. Although Farrer was generally classified as a neo-Thomist—he himself stated that when he wrote *Finite and Infinite* he was "imbued with the Thomist vision and could not think it false"—when he initially turns to his characterization of the basic elements of theism as a metaphysical system, it is not to Thomas Aquinas that he turns, but rather to Descartes.⁴ Indeed, Farrer explicitly rejects the traditional Thomist proofs for God's existence that arrive at God only as a transcendent theoretical entity posited to explain some otherwise mysterious feature of the observable world, on the ground that the notion of "cause" employed in such proofs is equivocal and, as such, cannot be brought under any common principle of causal explanation. It remains, then, that God's existence must be some-

---

2. University of Washington, 1987, Thesis 34772.
3. London, Dacre Press, 1943; reprinted by Seabury, 1979.
4. See *Finite and Infinite*, 6–8.

how apprehended rather than inferred; Farrer turns to the *Meditations* for a simple sketch or outline of the approach he recommends.

The plan I adopted was to reconstruct the project of the *Meditations* along the lines suggested by Farrer, placing Descartes squarely in the medieval *itineram mentis* tradition pioneered by Augustine of Hippo. God is to be found, not by contemplation of the created world, but instead by turning inward and discovering Him in oneself by discovering one's self as the image and likeness of God through which God reveals Himself to us as that upon which we immediately depend for our existence and as the infinite expression of being to which our finite essence aspires. In so doing, I hope also to complete Descartes' project by establishing one of the most controverted claims made by Descartes, i.e. that I have a clear and distinct innate idea of God as a perfect being, a claim both necessary for his proofs for God's existence (and which, having been apprehended, makes those proofs largely superfluous) and for his subsequent proof of the existence of the external world.

In saying that I hope to complete Descartes' project through construing it in a particular way, I do not necessarily mean to be attributing the views I shall here defend to Descartes himself. I am not a Descartes scholar. Since I read neither Latin nor French, I am disqualified from discussing exegetical questions concerning either Descartes' texts or his intentions; despite this fact, I have not found it entirely possible to avoid taking stands on some controversial issues within Descartes scholarship. However, I have consulted what I regard to be the best available translations and have endeavored to acquaint myself with the major works on Descartes available in English.[5] Although I have learned a great deal from these scholars, I have not, of course, been able to read everything on Descartes which I might have read, nor have I been able to make use of everything that I did read in what follows. No doubt there are many worthy scholars whose works I have not read and from whom I would have profited; to those scholars I can but tend my sincere regrets and plead the shortness of human life that bids us make an end to every project at some point on pain of never finishing it at all. Nor do I even wish to suggest that Descartes would agree with every claim I have made here, or ought to have done so. As it turns out, I myself disagree with a number of claims that I am persuaded Descartes accepted or was committed to. To the extent that I deviate from or am indifferent to Descartes' views, it is only because I think the truth is to be found elsewhere; that does not prevent me from thinking—or being right in thinking—that in Descartes we find important and substantial truths.

5. See my bibliography.

Preface

This project has, like the *Meditations* themselves, been a largely solitary venture; my only conversation partners have been the aforementioned scholars who have helped me grasp Descartes' texts. While I do not regard solitary meditation as a profitable way of doing philosophy in general, it is perhaps more excusable in this context than others; at any rate, I do not have any objections and replies to append to the text I have written. I would like to acknowledge the assistance of my mother, Lydia Duncan, and Mitchell Erickson of Philosophers on Holiday, in proof-reading my manuscript. They managed to save me from many serious errors and infelicities; no doubt many more remain for which they bear no responsibility. It is to my mother that this book is dedicated.

1

The Perils of Methodological Doubt

RECENT SCHOLARSHIP has noted that Descartes was the first to use the traditional skeptical arguments to call into question our knowledge of the external world, something that we find absent both in classical skepticism and in the skeptical revival that began in the Renaissance.[1] Less often is there any discussion of the reason why Descartes applies the skeptical arguments in this way. For my part, I believe that answering this question is the key to understanding the dialectical strategy of the first *Meditation* both with regard to its target and the way in which the various skeptical arguments used by Descartes are intended to be understood. As I understand it, the Cartesian project in the first *Meditation* is to present a critique of Aristotelianism, and in particular the Aristotelian version of common-sense empiricism and that this is the basis for understanding how Descartes intended his skeptical arguments to function within the overall economy of the *Meditations* as a whole.[2] To claim that Descartes desires to critique the foundations of Aristotelian physics is perhaps not very surprising or novel. It is well known that Descartes was an ardent enthusiast for the so-called New Physics, to which his friend Isaac Beeckman introduced him in 1618. Although Descartes achieved his greatest fame as a philosopher and arguably made his most signal contributions to the advance of human knowledge as a mathematician, natural science was Descartes' peculiar and abiding interest, to which his other studies were at best mere preliminaries. The bulk of Descartes' works are on topics that today we would recognize as belonging to natural science; his unpublished system of physics and astronomy, *Le Monde*, was completed years before the *Discourse on Method* and the publication of the *Meditations* and nearly

---

1. On the Greek skeptics, see Myles Burnyeat, "Idealism and Greek Philosophy: What Descartes Saw and Berkeley Missed," 3–40. See also Charles Larmore, "Skepticism" in the *Cambridge History of Seventeenth-Century Philosophy*, 1146.

2. In particular, I will argue that this is the key to understanding the extent to which a deceiving God is capable of imposing false beliefs on us by interfering with the operation of our cognitive faculties.

three-fourths of the *Principles of Philosophy* concerns substantive topics in physics and the other sciences. It was in solving the problems of physics that he hoped to find the vindication of his philosophical principles, as the *Dioptrics*, *Meteorology*, and *Geometry*, attached as appendices to the *Discourse*, were self-consciously intended to demonstrate.[3]

However, the critique of the then-dominant Aristotelian paradigm was no small matter in Descartes' time. The traditional story, which most of us still believe despite the deflationary studies of more recent historians of science, is that the confrontation between the Aristotelian and Galilean physical paradigms was one in which the superiority of the New Physics was obvious from the very first to every competent judge due to the fact that Galilean physics outperformed its Aristotelian counterpart in every way in which they could be compared, such that only academic inertia and the threat of ecclesiastical persecution could retard its progress through the learned world.[4] However, if I am right, there is at least one area in which the New Physics was decidedly inferior to its Aristotelian competitor and that Descartes was, however inchoately and implicitly, aware of this fact. Further, this disadvantage of the New Physics was so great that it threatened to undermine its credibility even before it could find a hearing. Essentially, I shall argue that the difficulty with the New Physics is that it is self-undermining in such a way that the substantive truth of the theory makes it impossible that we should ever be able to know that it is true about reality.[5] As such, the truth of the New Physics rules out that we could ever have any justification for believing that it is so, at least if we adopt the perspective of scientific realism. By contrast, the Aristotelian paradigm, as we shall see, does not generate this particular problem, whatever its defects as a foundation for empirical science as we now understand the term. As such, the New Physics is in a decidedly inferior position, epistemically speaking, to its Aristotelian competitor and widespread appreciation of

---

3. For an account of Descartes' scientific opinions and their influence, see Stephen Gaukroger, *Descartes System of Natural Philosophy*, New York, Cambridge University Press, 2002 and Daniel Garber, *Descartes' Metaphysical Physics*, Chicago, IL, University of Chicago Press, 1992.

4. The works of Draper, White, et al., though no longer much read and long since discredited, nevertheless capture what most educated people still believe—or at any rate would like to believe—about the "warfare" of science and religion.

5. Incidentally, although I will not argue this here, I believe that this problem has not been solved or bypassed by the success of modern science. It is a testament to the success of Descartes' rhetorical strategy in the first meditation that this problem has not even so much as been faced by modern science, let alone taken seriously.

this fact would certainly have slowed down and even possibly prevented its acceptance by the learned world.

Descartes' strategy for dealing with this problem is not to try to resolve it from within the perspective of the New Physics itself. This is just as well, since, as I shall argue, the problem is not soluble within that framework. Instead, Descartes attempts to show that the Aristotelian paradigm does not ultimately escape the problem by showing that it is a perfectly general epistemological problem, one that can be generated from the very assumptions of common-sense empiricism that underlie the Aristotelian paradigm. This problem, *the problem of the external world*, becomes the central problem in a new philosophical enterprise, theory of knowledge or epistemology, that will dominate philosophy for the next 350 years. By converting the problem as it arises within the New Science into a general epistemological problem that afflicts every scientific paradigm, Descartes was successful in deflecting any criticism of the New Science capable of being constructed by reference to that problem and thus helped advance the acceptance of that new physical paradigm. Ironically, it also made problem of the external world apparently dismissible on the part of those exponents of the New Science who accept scientific realism and the autonomy of science thesis, i.e. the claim that the methods and results of scientific inquiry cannot be critiqued from any perspective external to that of the natural sciences. The problem of the external world, now made abstract and general rather than internal to the perspective of the New Science arising from its ontological commitments, becomes just another idling "philosophical problem" the solution of which has only academic interest. However, as I will also shortly argue, Descartes cannot generate the sort of skepticism he needs to undermine the Aristotelian paradigm without adopting some fairly radical means: in particular, only the Deceiver hypothesis introduced at the end of the first *Meditation* is sufficient to accomplish his goal. The question then arises whether or not Descartes has gone too far and left himself without any means of escape from methodological doubt. I shall argue that Descartes can, in fact, escape skepticism without arguing in a circle, whether or not he does in fact do so in the text of the *Meditations* itself. Further, I will argue that he could have done this in a manner consistent with his main ideas, though not perhaps as he would have understood them. This project will occupy us for the next two chapters. To begin with, we need to review the general outlines of the Galilean paradigm, the centerpiece of which is a view I shall call *Galilean Physicalism*.

Placing the Cartesian Project in *Meditation I*
The Ontology of Galilean Physicalism

Historians of philosophy and science generally trace the notorious primary/secondary quality distinction to Galileo's *Dedicatory Letter* to his patron, Cardinal Cesarini, introducing *Il Saggiatore* ("The Assayer"), a treatise on comets.[6] According to this distinction, all the qualitative properties we attribute to external bodies based on sense-perception, such a color, taste, smell, texture, sound, heat, and cold exist as we experience them only in consciousness and in the things themselves only as dispositional properties they possess due to the configurations of the matter-in-motion out of which they are composed by which it is possible for them to cause us to have certain ideas. These are what Locke will call *secondary qualities* of body which, as they exist in bodies themselves, are reducible to combinations of what Locke will call *primary qualities*, the quantitative, measurable properties of bodies attributed to them in accordance with the New Physics, such as size, shape, solidity, extension, and motion/rest. Only the primary qualities belong to the bodies inherently and non-dispositionally, i.e. independently of reference to a perceiving subject. By contrast, secondary qualities, considered as the causal effects of concatenations of the primary qualities of bodies existing in consciousness, make inevitable reference to perceiving subjects and thus depend on such subjects in order to exist.

Galileo, of course, has no proof or evidence for the existence of these two sets of properties or for attributing one set of them to bodies and the other only to minds beyond using the *a priori* argument, familiar to students of Locke, that the primary qualities are inseparable from the concept of body, hence essential to it. Galileo's drawing of this distinction is motivated by his fundamental commitment to *physicalism*, i.e., the view that nothing exists—in the external, non-mental, world at any rate—except those entities and properties of entities that would be attributed to them by a completed theory of physics; we might therefore describe Galilean physicalism as physicalism about the external world, of everything other than consciousness and its contents. On this view, physics is both *omnicompetent* to describe the external world and thus capable in principle of *exhaustively* describing it. Since the purely qualitative qualities of bodies—what we might call their observable surface properties—cannot be accommodated by the New Physics except by reduction to the quantitative properties required for its

---

6. See the Galileo selections in Michael Matthews, *The Scientific Background to Modern Philosophy*, 56–86.

mathematical laws to be descriptive of external reality, those properties as we experience them must be banished from the external world and deposited in another realm, the mind or soul (where conscious experience takes place) and treated as fundamentally subjective and non-physical because qualitative and incapable of mathematical description. Descartes' commitment to this view is surely beyond serious doubt.

Galilean physicalism, as described above, is fully committed to the view known nowadays as *scientific realism*, the philosophical position which asserts that the well-confirmed theses of natural science (of which the laws of physics are a part, and constitute perhaps the most fundamental part) describe the world as it in itself, or the way it really is and thus are objectively true or (at any rate) possess a high degree of verisimilitude. According to scientific realism, the goal of natural science is to discover the truth about the physical universe and the use of the scientific method (that collection of techniques and procedures used by working scientists to formulate, address and answer questions about that universe) is the only effective means of accomplishing this end. Physicalism and scientific realism are compatible but not equivalent; one can be a scientific realist but not a physicalist simply by declining the omnicompetence thesis, i.e., the claim the external world is exhaustively described by the categories of mathematical physics. Aristotelians, for example, also embraced scientific realism but not physicalism, since they maintained that the qualitative properties of bodies were just as real and objective as their purely quantitative ones and irreducible to them. However, for Galileo, Descartes and other exponents of physicalism both ancient and modern, the doctrine of physicalism is an ontological thesis about the way the world is, hence an essentially metaphysical one underwriting the realist interpretation of modern physical theory as the truth about the nature of external reality.

It is just here, however, that the primary difficulty for any form of physicalism, including Galileo's, arises. On the one hand, we will only have a good reason for supposing that physicalism is true if we are confident about scientific realism. However, as it turns out, physicalism undermines all of the evidence we think we have for scientific realism, so that if physicalism is true, we would never have any reason to think that it is—or, at any rate, no scientific reason for so thinking. So, paradoxically, the truth of physicalism is incompatible with our having any reason that will pass scientific muster for thinking that it is. As such, physicalism is self-refuting inasmuch as it is self-undermining. Let me now illustrate in detail just how this is the case.

The Epistemic Consequences of Galilean Physicalism

No one familiar with history of modern philosophy needs to be informed of the epistemic consequences of the causal theory of perception generated by the foregoing views. However, since perhaps not all the consequences of these theoretical commitments have been properly appreciated from within the perspective of the New Science itself, it will be worth our while to review those consequences here. Essentially, Galilean physicalism, with its commitment to scientific realism, purports to be describing the external world as it exists in and of itself, independently of our experience of it. At the same time, it implies that the immediate objects of our experience (*qualia*, sense-data, ideas—call them what you will) are merely subjective, mind-dependent contents of consciousness that are at best the causal products of certain physical processes occurring in the external world. Although these immediate objects of our experience are said to represent external objects to us, there is in fact no resemblance whatsoever between ideas or sense-data on the one hand the objects in the external world as described by the New Physics, thus making it very difficult to see how it could possibly be the case that the immediate objects of our experience could represent such objects or possess intentionality sufficient to allow us to even conceive of their existence. Although Descartes formulates this problem as a general epistemological difficulty, let us here consider these implications from within the perspective of the New Science itself.

Suppose that the Galilean physicalist picture is true and the immediate objects of awareness are all, so far as we know, subjective and mind-dependent. Given this, we are immediately landed in what Ralph Barton Perry called *the egocentric predicament* and are trapped in the charmed circle of our own ideas.[7] Due to this, we are completely cut off from any sort of direct contact with the external world; at best, our ideas represent that external world to us. The egocentric predicament appears to entail representational realism in the philosophy of perception, according to which we infer from our ideas, the immediate objects of experience, to the existence and nature of external objects.[8] Yet, as the history of philosophy testifies, it is notoriously difficult to justify such an inference and virtually impossible to do so if we restrict ourselves solely to data of consciousness. The philosophies of Malebranche, Leibniz, Berkeley, Hume, and Kant thoroughly demonstrate the difficulties here in ways that will be generally familiar to philosophers.

7. See Ralph Barton Perry, "The Egocentric Predicament," 5–14.
8. Some scholars have denied this, e.g. John Y. Yolton, *Perceptual Acquaintance from Descartes to Reid*; I do not have space here to consider Yolton's arguments and merely note in passing that it is and remains very much a minority view.

Given the foregoing, however, it is easy to see how Galilean physicalism undermines itself. Galilean physicalism's commitment to scientific realism results in its offering itself as the true picture of the external world as it exists in and of itself or *noumenally* as Kant would put it. However, the epistemic implications of the New Science place that external world beyond our grasp; it transcends our experience in such a way that it can at best be a theoretical entity or *posit* for us. But not only does the external world wholly transcend our perceptual experience; the egocentric predicament leaves us without the resources necessary to justify belief in that external world, either by inference or as a theoretical postulate, and thereby to justify any specific knowledge-claims about that world. Now we are only going to be able to embrace the New Physics as the true view about the world as it exists independently of our experience of it if it is possible for us to have some rational justification for believing that there is such a world and that the substantive theses of that theory are true of it. However, given that the epistemic implications of the truth of physicalism rule out (at least the practical) possibility of our possessing any such rational justification, it would appear that physicalism, of the Galilean or any other sort, is self-undermining: on the assumption that it is true, we can have no reason to think that it is so and thus no justification for making that assumption in the first place. This does not prove that Galilean physicalism is false, but it certainly puts it at a disadvantage to any theory, such as Aristotelian physics, that does not generate the same difficulty.

It is to be emphasized here that the self-undermining character of the New Science as interpreted by the Galilean physicalist arises from within that interpretation itself, not from some perspective external to that theory, such as Descartes' methodological skepticism, some version of historicism, post-modernism or contemporary anti-realism. Quine was quite correct to say the problems of modern epistemology were produced by the scientific revolution.[9] Nevertheless, the enormous success of the New Science in relieving our curiosity about the nature of the external world and providing us with powerful tools of prediction, control, and technological development have largely helped suppress our awareness of this problem. Instead, we prefer to think of it as merely a "philosophical" problem motivated by only the most hyperbolic considerations. Descartes, as we shall see, is largely responsible for creating this appearance, but as must be clear by now, this is an illusion that can be sustained only by inadvertence or self-deception. Nor, given the subsequent history of philosophy, does there

---

9. See Quine, "Epistemology Naturalized," in *Ontological Relativity and Other Essays*, 69–90.

appear any way for the unreconstructed Galilean physicalist to escape the difficulty here. So imbued are we with the tradition of modern science that it is barely conceivable to us that it could be false, let alone self-refuting. However, it would not have been difficult for people of Descartes' time to have seen this had it been pointed out to them nor would the advantages of the New Science been so palpable at that point that they would have been able to disguise this problem from themselves. It would have been perceived as a major stumbling block to the acceptance of that theory and either prevented or further retarded its acceptance. However, due to Descartes' generalization of the problem and its conversion into a general epistemological problem, he was able to prevent this problem from arising for the New Physics, whether or not this was his conscious intention.

Of course, we can always abandon the realist interpretation of the New Science, as Malebranche, Berkeley, Hume, Kant, Dewey and many others, especially in the latter half of the twentieth century, have been wont to do. Descartes, however, was loath to do so and attempted to provide a foundation for knowledge that would restore the external world to us in a way that makes it amenable to belief in the New Science. Before we turn to this, however, let us consider how the Aristotelian alternative avoids the sort of self-refutation inherent in Galilean physicalism.

Apprehending the External World: The Aristotelian Alternative

For the Aristotelian, the external world is a very different place from that world as conceived of by the Galilean physicalist. Though no less committed to representational realism than Galileo and Descartes, Aristotle's substantive metaphysics and cognitive theory[10] avoid the difficulties inherent in representational realism when yoked to Galilean physicalism. This episode in the history of the theory of knowledge—here using this term to include philosophical theories of cognition as well as epistemology proper as we understand it today—is unfamiliar enough to most

---

10. Although the roots of this theory can arguably be traced to Aristotle—see Joseph Owens, *The Doctrine of Being in Aristotle's Metaphysics*, 386–95 and fn., 444—it remains only a tantalizing sketch in Aristotle himself, receiving continuous development at the hands of the scholastics and, later, the neo-Scholastics. The theory as presented here is actually the product of twentieth-century neo-Thomism and formulated precisely with the modern alternative deriving from Descartes in mind; see, for example, Joseph Owens' *Cognition*. For an extension of this version of cognitive theory to the philosophy of language, see Mortimer J. Adler, *Some Questions about Language*, Chicago, IL, Open Court Publishing, 1965.

philosophers to require that it be briefly presented so that its difference and advantages can be appreciated.

For Aristotle, external things are a composite of two principles, *form* and *matter*. Form exists in things as its structural principle of organization and development. It is due to the presence of form that an external thing is actualized as a particular of one kind rather than another; thus, it is due to form that an external thing possesses its occurrent and dispositional properties, among which are included its powers and liabilities to be changed by the operation of external causes. Indeed, it is due to form, or what is sometimes called substantial form, that a thing is the kind of thing that it is, such as a vase, a knife or a human being. Matter, by contrast, has no inherent structure *as such*; matter is merely that which receives form, whatever that is. Further, form and matter are relative terms; form is whatever structures matter, whereas matter is simply whatever receives form. It is quite possible, then, for something (e.g., flesh and bones) which is itself a form/matter composite to be the matter for some further substance (e.g., an animal) due to the imposition of a further form (e.g., the soul). Matter at most serves as the principle of individuation for external bodies, i.e., that by means of which it acquires a unique set of spatial and temporal locations.

More important for our purposes here, form is the *principle of intelligibility* in things. Since matter, considered *as such* or as *prime* matter, has no determinate nature, features or properties, it is not intelligible to us except in relation to the form imposed upon it. It is nothing more than "what would be left over" if its nature and all its determinate properties were removed, a completely indeterminate, characterless "stuff" which is, strictly speaking, intelligible only as a limiting or regulative idea. Matter as such, then, cannot be an object of knowledge for us in its own right. By contrast, form, whether as nature or essence ("human being," "giraffe," "triangle") or as an accident inhering in a thing ("red," "six feet long," "is to the left of") is intelligible to us insofar as it is apprehensible to us in sense-perception, cognizable by us in abstract concepts, the object of lexical definition, and capable of being synthesized with other concepts to produce propositions and to facilitate immediate and mediated inferences. Knowledge of external things, then, can only be acquired by reference their forms, not their matter.

Unlike Plato and Descartes, who characterize knowledge as justified, true belief and regard theoretical knowledge as the product of methodical, free inquiry, Aristotle defines knowledge as the conformity of belief to its object. Aristotle regards knowledge as the product of a largely automatic causal process over which we have no direct control, to which we make very little contribution and largely consists of mechanisms whose operations underlie (and thus are not accessible to) consciousness. Since it is form that is the principle of intelligibility in things, not matter, form must play the central role in accounting for the fact of knowledge. Thus, the process of acquiring knowledge must be one in which the knower is becomes informed *about* the object by being literally *informed by* it. Knowledge, con*form*ity of belief to its object, requires that the mind of the knower literally take on the form of what it knows and thus become that very thing formally and intentionally. The knowing faculty, or intellect, is thus conceived of as potency for the reception of all forms, not as their proper matter such that the form becomes its nature or essence, but instead as an abstract concept or idea. The process by means of which this conformity is established is the subject of cognitive theory, which we might describe as the account of the process of in*form*ation by things through which means we acquire information about those things.

According to this theory, the form of a thing (for our purposes here, we will follow the Scholastics and consider only substantial form) exists in the thing itself as its essence or nature, making that thing to be what it is according to its kind and endowing it with its characteristic (natural) powers and liabilities through which it acquires accidental properties, each of which is also a form inhering in that thing. Although the form inheres in the external thing and is inseparable in existence from it *as* its essence or nature, it is also capable of existing in a different manner as a *species*, as inherent in something other than its proper matter without becoming the essence or nature of what it informs. Thus, as a *species in medio* the form of an external thing informs the air between the knower and the known; the air transfers that form, thus takes it on without that form becoming its essence or nature, from the external thing to the body of the knower. The air can do this because, given its own essence or nature, it has the capacity to take on the forms of other things in this way. In turn, the body of the knower has the capacity to receive that form by means of the senses as a *sensible species*, which is usually understood as an actual state of the sense-organ itself, a bodily effect/modification produced by the direct causal influence of the external thing on the organ of sense subsequent to its being conveyed there by the medium. At this point, the immaterial *agent intellect* enters the picture, using a process called abstraction to convert the sensible species (or perhaps several instances of sensible species of the same form) into an *intelligible species* existing in the *passive intellect* (something like memory as understood by St. Augustine). The closest we have to the notion of intelligible species is perhaps something like the notion of a concept as understood by Frege except that concepts are not abstract entities existing independently of minds, but rather in them as objects of thought: these abstract concepts, once acquired, become the subject of mental operations such as definition, synthesis with other concepts into categorical propositions and, functioning as class-names, as terms in deductive and inductive inferences. These processes are capable of self-conscious direction on the part of the intellect; logic is the branch of philosophy that provides us with the method for doing this efficiently and effectively in order to organize our knowledge systematically. For Aristotle, logic is the only *organon*; since the intellect automatically produces knowledge, there is no need for that curious preoccupation of the renaissance critics of Aristotle, the so-called *ars inviendi* or "logic of discovery."

Aristotle's theory of cognition is based neither on empirical science nor on any sort of introspective phenomenology. In particular, consciousness plays no role whatever in the Aristotelian knowledge-acquisition process. Aristotle has no occurrent notion of consciousness and no interest in conscious awareness as an object of theoretical inquiry. While the Scholastics occasionally advert to certain features of consciousness and conscious experience in their discussion of cognition, consciousness, especially perceptual awareness, makes no essential contribution to our understanding of the phenomenon of knowledge from the Scholastic point of view.[11] If neither science nor conscious experience makes any contribution to Aristotelian cognitive theory, where does the theory come from? The answer seems to be that this theory is an *a priori* construct intended to account for the fact of knowledge in terms of Aristotle's fundamental metaphysical commitments, in particular his form/matter doctrine. The justification for the theory resides in the recognition that, given the assumptions of the theory, this is the only possible way that things could work. For this reason, the Scholastics, lacking all but the most rudimentary knowledge of the actual physical processes at work in perception, are likewise lacking in any details about how the various stages or the entities/states that figure in that theory are actually constituted. More than this, they show a remarkable lack of interest in the details of this account. It is not surprising, then, that critics of Scholasticism were able to parody the view and pass that parody off as Aristotle's theory.[12]

---

11. For a contemporary defense of Thomistic views about the soul, which contrasts the Aristotelian and Cartesian accounts of mind and cognition to the disadvantage of the latter while rejecting the theoretical significance of consciousness, see Ric Machuga, *In Defense of the Soul*, Grand Rapids, MI, Baker Publishing, 2002.

12. Descartes explicitly rejects this theory of perception precisely as parodied as the view that the surface-images of objects detach themselves from their originals and fly through

Even so, it is clear that Aristotle and his followers would not be at all bothered by the sort of problem that afflicts the Galilean physicalist. Aristotle's account of knowledge does not undermine itself in the way that the doctrines of the New Physics appear to do. To the contrary, the Aristotelian approach consistently accounts, despite its representationalism and reliance on external causal processes in the knowledge-acquisition process, for the fact of knowledge, explaining both the intentionality of our concepts and the manner in which our ideas/concepts of things are capable of representing them. In both cases, the explanation turns on the notion that, despite the mediating factors present in the process of acquiring knowledge, the upshot of that process is that the thing itself is present to the knowing subject *by means of its form after the manner of an idea or concept*. The knower is thus *formally and intentionally identical* with what it knows due to the fact that numerically one and the same form existing in the thing itself as its essence or nature comes to exist, simultaneously but in a different manner, in the mind of the knower as the form of his or her intellect. The species by means of which I know that object, then, is no mere idea in the Lockean or Cartesian sense, nor is it merely the causal product of some purely mechanical causal process at best externally related to the object that produces it after the manner of a copy. Finally, given that there is no reason to think otherwise, Aristotle and his followers undoubtedly supposed that the world as it exists in itself is qualitatively largely identical with the way it appears to us in perception, something which Galilean physicalism, with its theory-driven ontology, is forced to deny.[13]

Even if this last point is abandoned, however, there can be no doubt that Aristotelianism is in a far superior position from the epistemic point of view in relation to the New Science. In fact, the crippling epistemic difficulties afflicting the New Science as interpreted through the categories of Galilean physicalism would seem to prevent it from ever even getting off the ground as a research program in natural science. Even so, my intention here is not argue for a restoration of Aristotelian physics or the bankruptcy of modern natural science. Here my only concern is to see the extent to which Descartes' first *Meditation* is profitably read as an attempt

---

the air, where they enter the eye and become a material species; see *Optics* in *CSM*, Vol. I, 153–4. For another version of this same critique, see Arthur Collier, *Clavis Universalis*, 83–87, originally published in 1713.

13. Of course, we must not present the above as the "Medieval" view as though this were a monolithic consensus among all scholastics thinkers. For an idea of the variations and complexity of the views on offer here, see Robert Pasnau, *Theories of Cognition in the Later Middle Ages*, Cambridge, Cambridge University Press, 1997.

to devise a critique of Aristotelian science that robs it of the single advantage that it possesses over its competitor. I shall interpret the text of the first *Meditation* as a sort of dialogue between Descartes' early, Aristotelian self and his current, Galilean physicalist, self with each of his three main skeptical arguments as devices intended to show that Aristotelians cannot escape the net of the classical skeptic. After dispatching the Aristotelians, Descartes, having motivated the general epistemological problem of the external world, will then offer his own method of introspective meditation as the only possible response to this problem.

Descartes' Initial Critique of the Senses in *Meditation*[14]

The first *Meditation* famously begins with a brief sketch of our epistemic predicament and Descartes' proposal as to how we might overcome it.[15] It has been many years, he says, since he discovered that many of his beliefs were false and that he has no certain means of distinguishing true from false beliefs.[16] He therefore proposes to seek the foundations of human knowledge by calling into question everything that he has previously be-

---

14. All references to Descartes, unless otherwise noted, are from John Cottingham, Robert Stoothoff and Dugald Murdoch, eds., *The Philosophical Writings of Descartes*, 3 volumes—hereafter *CSM*; volume 3, edited in collaboration with Anthony Kenny, will be designated *CSMK*. I have also consulted the translations by Haldane and Ross, Lawrence LaFleur and Donald H. Cress—see bibliography. Since I do not read Latin or French, I have not consulted the standard critical edition by Adam et Tannery or used the standard AT numbers for my citations.

15. Although Descartes scholars have recently raised some questions about who the meditator is supposed to be in the first meditation, I take it that it is Descartes himself conceived of as an instance of an ideal type, i.e. a contemporary intellectual who is well aware of the current unsettled state of European intellectual life but not yet a committed skeptic. See Janet Broughton's discussion in *Descartes's Method of Doubt*, 21–32, especially 26–28 and references. Her main target is John Carriero's contention that the meditator is a scholastic philosopher; see his "The First Meditation," in Vere Chappell. ed., *Descartes Meditations: Critical Essays*, 1–31. On Descartes' complex relation to scholasticism, see Marjorie Grene, *Descartes among the Scholastics*, Milwaukee, WI, Marquette University Press, 1991; Roger Ariew, *Descartes and the Last Scholastics*, Ithaca, NY, Cornell University Press, 1999 and Dennis Des Chene's trilogy *Physiologia* (1996), *Life's Form* (2000) and *Spirits and Clocks* (2001), all published by Cornell University Press.

16. *CSM*, Vol. II, p. 12 (the opening paragraph of the first *Meditation*). Note Descartes' caveat regarding the principles of revealed religion and morality in Part III of the *Discourse on Method*, *CSM*, Vol. I, 122–126. Compare with the opening paragraphs of the *Principles of Philosophy*, op. cit., Vol. I, 193, paragraphs 1–3 and the apple-basket analogy used in the *Response* to Bourdin's Seventh set of *Objections*, *CSM*, Vol. II, 324.

lieved by resolving to doubt any proposition that even might possibly be false.[17] This is Descartes' famous *methodological doubt*, by means of which he hopes to discover the indubitable foundations for knowledge by carrying through the skeptical project to its radical completion in the discovery of something which even the skeptic cannot call into question, thereby overcoming the skeptical challenge.

Descartes realizes that he cannot hope to identify and call into question all of his beliefs individually; he therefore proposes to undermine them in large groups. In particular, he says, most of what he has previously believed he has derived from the senses; as such, it will be sufficient for advancing his purpose if he is able to find general reasons for distrusting the senses themselves as sources of knowledge.[18] Although this seems practical enough, in adopting this strategy Descartes is, in fact, taking a very dangerous tack. For in attacking the senses directly, rather than particular beliefs, or classes of beliefs drawn from the senses, Descartes is proposing to undermine one of his cognitive faculties itself: that is to say, he challenges the source of his beliefs rather than merely the beliefs themselves by suggesting that there might be something systematically and irremediably flawed about the operation of the senses themselves. The danger involved in this strategy may not at first be apparent, but it is clearly there: to the extent that I am able to undermine my cognitive faculties in this way, the fewer will be my resources for undertaking and successfully completing the task of reconstructing human knowledge. If I find substantial reasons for thinking that this is possible for all of my cognitive faculties, I will find myself completely without resources for doing so. As we shall see, Descartes arguably puts himself in just such a position, though his project can be interpreted in such a way as to avoid this.

Nevertheless, it is easy to see why Descartes would want to promote skepticism about the senses. First of all, his inherent Christian Platonism naturally bids us turn away from the senses and seek inward for the truth. Not surprisingly, skeptical arguments against the veracity of the senses help to advance this project.[19] Secondly, Descartes' nascent rationalism naturally

17. *CSM*, Vol. II, p. 12 (the opening paragraph of the first Meditation). Note Descartes' *caveat* regarding the principles of revealed religion and morality in Part III of the *Discourse on Method*, *CSM*, Vol. I, 122–126. Compare with the opening paragraphs of the *Principles of Philosophy*, op. cit., Vol. I, 193, paragraphs 1–3 and the apple-basket analogy used in the *Response* to Bourdin's Seventh set of *Objections*, *CSM*, Vol. II, 324.

18. See *CSM*, loc cit.

19. Malebranche, clearly following Descartes here, takes this admonition to extremes in his *Dialogues on Metaphysics and Religion*, Nicholas Jolley and David Scott, eds., 3–5.

suggests to him the necessity of undermining the senses in order to establish those of pure intellect or intuitive reason as the primary means to the attainment of theoretical truth. Thirdly, Descartes' anti-Aristotelian polemic will be greatly advanced if the senses can be discredited, since commonsense Aristotelian metaphysics and natural science takes uncritical acceptance of the senses as a source of knowledge for its starting-point. Fourthly, his positive commitment to the New Science, according to which external bodies are vastly different than they appear to the senses, provides strong motivation for a critique of the senses as the primary source of knowledge about external bodies in favor of an account according to which it is scientific theory, the product of reason and theoretical imagination, which truly reveals the nature of those bodies to us. Fifthly and perhaps most important of all, Descartes needs to strongly motivate his cutting-edge approach to philosophy by showing that there is, in fact, a deep, abiding and unsolved problem about the nature of human knowledge which gives rise to skepticism and threatens not just our pretensions to theoretical knowledge but the claims of religion, morality and politics as well. Thus, Descartes feels driven to depict our current epistemic situation as very grave indeed, in order to motivate our acceptance of his solution to that problem as the last, best hope on behalf of human knowledge.

Skepticism about the Senses and the Perils of Methodological Doubt

One of the most impressive features of the first *Meditation* for the casual reader is the apparent ease with which Descartes refutes our customary, easy-going reliance on the senses as a source of true belief about the existence and nature of the external world. Barely six pages in length, one can read the entire text in less than half an hour; even so, its contents are so intellectually earth-shaking that hardly any modern reader goes away unchanged.[20] At the same time, however, a closer examination of the strategy of Descartes' first *Meditation* reveals that it is rather more difficult to undermine the senses than

---

20. This was apparently not so in Descartes' own day. Of his major critics, only Bourdin devotes any time to a critical (if rather light-minded) examination of Descartes' methodological doubt and a closer look at this discussion may well yield fruit once scholars get past Bourdin's polemical style. So familiar were skeptical arguments to his contemporaries that Hobbes expresses amazement that Descartes would even consider publishing this "ancient material," while the authors of the Second Objections note Descartes' lack of originality in the first two *Meditations*. On this point, see Stephen Menn, *Descartes and Augustine*, Cambridge, 220, n. 15 and Roger Ariew, "Pierre Bourdin and the Seventh Objections" in Roger Ariew and Marjorie Grene, eds., *Descartes and his Contemporaries*, 208–25.

a cursory reading of the text makes it appear. In fact, in order to motivate the radical skepticism about the senses Descartes needs in order to pursue the all of the aims I have listed above, Descartes is driven to ever more extreme and hyperbolic suppositions culminating in the notion of the *malin genie*, which, no matter how much Descartes attempts to soft-pedal it, threatens to undermine his entire project.[21] While it is natural to read the text as presenting three fairly independent, stand-alone arguments for skepticism about the senses, a careful reading of the text reveals that the arguments presented by Descartes, in fact, form a continuous chain each link of which is needed to win through to the final conclusion that the senses cannot be trusted as a source of knowledge about the external world. A brief review of those arguments will help to make this clear to the reader, but before turning to the arguments themselves one might well ask why Descartes feels compelled to go so far in his critique of the senses.

The answer, as we have seen, is that Descartes' commitment to the New Science requires him to accept Galilean physicalism and thus deny that the senses reveal to us the natures of external things. Galilean physicalism also seems to require the Representational Realist account of the nature of perception which, in turn, generates the problem of the external world and thus threatens to undermine the New Science, both epistemologically and metaphysically. As such, it is in this respect clearly inferior to the reigning Aristotelian scientific tradition, which takes the senses at face value and simply assumes that external bodies are, for the most part, just as they appear to us in perception.[22] Thus, Aristotelian philosophy and its physics appear to avoid a problem which has apparently fatal consequences for the New Physics. In order to defend the New Science, then,

---

21. Menn (op. cit., p. 220) suggests that the four main arguments for skepticism touched on by Descartes have their probable source in Cicero's dialogue *Academica*, Translated by H. Rackham, 399–659.

22. In saying this, I do not mean to suggest that Aristotle was a direct realist. Aristotle was most likely a representationalist, as were his medieval followers. On this point, see Robert Pasnau, *Theories of Cognition in the Later Middle Ages*, e.g. 86. However, since he (and they) lived before the time of the New Science, the epistemic problems of representationalism, which loom so large for thinkers of the Early Modern period, such as the problem of the external world, are merely unmotivated epistemic possibilities, since the medievals assume (having no reason to doubt it) that the world as it exists independently of consciousness is largely just as it appears to us in perception. Indeed, as Pasnau unwittingly demonstrates, to a large extent the Aristotelians lack even the concepts required to formulate the questions which, after Descartes, become centrally important in epistemology, the philosophy of mind and the philosophy of perception, which is to say that even if we would class Aristotle as a representationalist, he would not have been able to do so himself.

Descartes has to show how we can generate the problem of the external world from purely philosophical considerations and thus undermine the Aristotelian confidence in the senses and its consequent epistemic superiority to Galilean physics in this regard, thus making skepticism about the external world an ineliminable feature of our epistemic situation. To do this, however, requires that the classical skeptical arguments be required to carry more weight than they were designed to bear, forcing Descartes to ever more desperate and hyperbolic considerations in order to achieve this end. As we shall see, Descartes cannot do this without putting the rest of his cognitive faculties at risk as well.

The Argument from Perceptual Error

The first and most well-established of the skeptical arguments against the senses is the argument from perceptual error, closely allied to the argument from perceptual relativity, the stock-in-trade of the ancient skeptics whether Pyrrhonist or Academic. According to this argument, the senses sometimes deceive us in the sense that they present us with appearances which, if taken as literally descriptive of external objects, will generate false judgments/beliefs about those external objects. For example, a stick submerged part way in water gives the appearance to the eye of being bent, when in fact it is straight (a fact which can be confirmed by the sense of touch). Likewise, a square tower seen straight on from a significant distance appears to be round, and so on. Optical illusions, mirages such as the *fata morgana*, hallucinations and so on present other cases in which the senses present us with deceptive appearances. In the twentieth century, arguments of this sort have been used to justify the claim that we are never directly aware of external objects in sense-perception, but only of ideas which represent those objects to us and critics of this sort of argument have striven to resist this interpretation of the perceptual facts.[23] Despite being clearly committed to representationalism, Descartes does not use this argument in this way. Instead, he concludes quite modestly that the

---

23. For a good representative collection of twentieth-century papers on the philosophy of perception and the debate between representationalism and direct realism, see R. J. Swartz, ed., *Perceiving, Sensing and Knowing*, Garden City, N.Y., Anchor Books, 1965. Notable defenders of representationalism include A. J. Ayer, *Foundations of Empirical Knowledge*, London, Macmillan and Co., 1941, H. H. Price, *Perception*, London, Methuen, 1954 and Frank Jackson, *Perception: A Representative Theory*, Cambridge, Cambridge University Press, 1977. Opponents of representationalism include J. L. Austin, *Sense and Sensibilia*, London, Oxford University Press, 1962 and more recently Michael Huemer, *Skepticism and the Veil of Perception*, Lanham, MD, Rowman & Littlefield, 2001 and A. D. Smith, *The Problem of Perception*, Cambridge, MA, Harvard University Press, 2002.

most that follows from this argument is that "it is prudent never to trust completely those who have deceived us even once."[24]

The problem with this conclusion is that it does not yield any strong skeptical implications, as Descartes himself realizes. It does not follow from the fact that my senses sometimes deceive me that it is possible that my senses always deceive me, since such an argument is plainly invalid, as the following argument demonstrates:

> Some paintings are forgeries.
> _____
> Therefore, possibly all paintings are forgeries.[25]

Nor does it even follow that it is possible on any particular occasion that the senses might be deceiving me. To the contrary, as Descartes immediately goes on to point out, perceptual errors resulting from sense-deception are vanishingly rare and most are easily detectable from within sense-experience itself. This, then, yields no strong reason for thinking that the senses are not generally reliable; more importantly, the suggestion that we can in fact discover from within sense-experience itself (without the help of natural science or any other cognitive faculty) that such situations occur strongly suggests that the senses are self-correcting, hence free from any systematic flaw or defect which would ground any general skeptical attitude toward the operation of the senses. Descartes apparently agrees, since he simply lets the argument drop without any further comment. The argument from perceptual error does not yield the kind of skepticism required to motivate the project of the *Meditations*.

Am I Crazy?

A second classical skeptical argument concerns the possibility that I might be insane. Insane people, as we know from observation, believe all sorts of bizarre and obviously false propositions (such as that their bodies are made of glass, their heads are pumpkins, that they are kings or possess great wealth when in fact they are in rags, and so on) with absolute conviction despite the presence of easily accessible evidence to refute these beliefs. Descartes briefly considers the possibility that he might be insane as a basis for his skeptical doubts about the senses. However, he just as quickly dismisses it out of hand, remarking that he would indeed be crazy if he were to seriously consider this possibility.

---

24. See *CSM*, loc. cit.

25. This example is taken from Jay F. Rosenberg, *The Practice of Philosophy*, Englewood Cliffs, NJ, Prentice-Hall, 1978, 15. However, the point is taken from Bernard Williams, *Descartes*, New York, Routledge, 2003, 38–39, originally published by Penguin in 1978.

Is Descartes really justified in dismissing this skeptical possibility so quickly?[26] After all, it is not logically impossible that he is insane and his conviction that he is in fact sane is perfectly compatible with that possibility; indeed, it seems to be standard features of most forms of mania that those afflicted have no awareness that they are mad or that there is any defect in their cognitive structure.[27] Presumably, if it were the case that Descartes was mad, it is at least possible that he would be unable to determine that this was so. So, then, how can Descartes be so sure that he is not crazy?

Obviously, one reason that Descartes would want to resist this possibility is that it clearly goes too far. For me to seriously consider the possibility that I am insane would put me in an epistemic position in which it would be impossible for me to trust any of my cognitive faculties and thus leave me with no resources for resolving the question of whether or not I am sane. This result would affect the skeptic no less than Descartes, since on the supposition that the skeptic is insane any reason that the skeptic might give for embracing skepticism—including the possibility of his own madness—counts for no more from the rational point of view than the witless ravings of a lunatic. To put it a different way, my ability to rationally weigh and consider arguments for any position, including skepticism, requires that my cognitive faculties be reliable; in turn, a necessary condition for this to be the case is that I not be insane. Therefore, to the extent that I am able to recognize the possibility of my own madness as a ground for doubting the reliability of my cognitive faculties and embracing skepticism, I am to that extent assured that I am not insane and thus am not justified in embracing skepticism on the basis of that possibility. On the other hand, to the extent that I am insane, I am thereby disqualified from employing my cognitive faculties in the evaluation of reasons for and against skepticism and thus, given my current situation, cannot embrace skepticism on the basis of any

---

26. Broughton, *Descartes's Method of Doubt*, p. 65 n.3, claims that Descartes does not in fact reject this possibility out of hand as incompatible with the possibility of rational inquiry and makes reference to a forthcoming article that I have not seen. In what follows I attempt to defend the claim that Descartes is right to reject this hypothesis and that the same reasons will justify some restrictions on the power of the Evil Genius. The same will hold of the worry raised by some scholars about the possibility that God may have created me with flawed cognitive powers; see Lex Newman and Alan Nelson, "Circumventing Cartesian Circles," *Noûs*, 33 (1999), 370–404.

27. According to one interview, mathematician John Nash, who spent years in the mental hospital suffering from schizophrenia before eventually recovering, says that when he was crazy his delusions had the same sort of compelling, *a priori* certainty about them that mathematical truths have for him when he is lucid.

of those reasons, including the supposition that I might be insane. In neither case, then, does the possibility that I am insane provide a reason for questioning the reliability of my cognitive faculties and embracing skepticism on that ground. Finally, to the extent that I am sane and rational enough to follow the argument currently under consideration, I am right to agree with Descartes that I would be as crazy as the madmen he describes if I were to seriously consider this possibility. Indeed, more than this, it is literally impossible for me to consider it in the fashion intended since one of the necessary conditions for doing so is that I am not mad.

Descartes, then, is right to dismiss this consideration out of hand despite the fact that the logical possibility of his own insanity cannot be excluded by any argument or evidence.[28] The possibility of his own madness does not provide any reason for embracing skepticism or doubting the reliability of his cognitive faculties and could not do so without undermining the very supposition intended to motivate it. By the same token, such an argument provides no reason for doubting the senses as a source of knowledge about the external world. As such, we have still not discovered compelling, non-scientific grounds for doubting the reliability of sense-perception. Yet another argument, it seems, is needed.

The Dream Argument

Immediately after dismissing the possibility that he might be mad, Descartes pulls himself up short and notes that he is subject to fits of dreaming, the contents of which are every bit (and sometimes even more) bizarre than the waking delusions of the mad. At the same time, says Descartes, my dreams can be very pedestrian in content in such a way as to be indistinguishable in content from waking experience. Indeed, says Descartes, have I not sometimes mistakenly believed that I was awake and, e.g., reading in front of the fire when I was in fact asleep in bed and dreaming? If so, is it not at least possible that I might be dreaming now and only think that I am awake, and given this, that everything I am inclined to believe on the basis of sense-experience at the current moment might merely be the false

---

28. The same would apply to the generalized version of Descartes' suggestion that my cognitive faculties may be irremediably flawed in some fundamental way discussed by Hatfield, *Descartes and the Meditations*, 228–31. Again, on the supposition that I am in a position to examine this hypothesis and evaluate it as an argument for skepticism, it has to be false; on the supposition that the hypothesis is true, I am in no position to trust my cognitive faculties, even far enough to consider that this hypothesis might be so, and this regardless of whether or not it is. So no argument for skepticism can be generated from such a supposition and it cannot be used to undermine my confidence in whatever, on reflection, is clearly and distinctly apprehended by me to be so.

production of my imagination? Here at last it seems we have an argument that succeeds in providing a completely general ground for doubting the senses as a source of knowledge about the external world, since the same consideration could be applied to any moment at which I am conscious.

It is to be noted here that Descartes evidently thought that this skeptical consideration could not be dismissed on the same grounds that one could arguably dismiss the suggestion that I might be mad. Apparently, Descartes takes it to be the case that the possibility that I might be dreaming now is compatible with my full and proper exercise of my cognitive faculties with regard to their objects. This suggests that Descartes, at least in this context, is committed to a homuncular theory of consciousness involving what D. C. Dennett has called the *Cartesian theater* and an inner spectator or *homunculus* who witnesses the contents of consciousness like a theater patron witnesses the images projected on a movie screen. On this view, the sleeping subject has the same cognitive powers as a waking one, and is fully capable of formulating judgments, affirming beliefs and arriving at knowledge as one who is fully awake.[29] The only difference between the waking and sleeping subjects is that, in the case of the waking subject the images on the screen in the Cartesian theater are produced by external objects, whereas in the case of the dreamer they are produced by the imagination and thus do not represent actually existing external objects or situations. Since, in this case, my powers of reasoning remain intact and unaffected, it is only the senses that are fooled in a manner that lies beyond my power to correct using either the senses themselves or any

---

29. *Contra* Dennett, there is no reason to postulate a separate homunculus in addition to the intentional field of consciousness in which mental contents arise or appear, as I have explained elsewhere. However, the naturalness of the Cartesian picture is suggested by the fact that all of Descartes' critics acquiesce in the Cartesian account of dream-experience. Only Bourdin, in the seventh set of *Objections*, challenges Descartes' view by suggesting that all of the contents our dreams, including our acts of perception and judgment, are merely part of the dream rather than independent conscious operations over mental contents of the same sort we exercise when awake; see Cottingham, et al., 334–5 and 337–8. Bourdin fails to develop this point, however. The preferred solution of some moderns, such as Norman Malcolm, as presented in his article "Dreaming and Skepticism," reprinted in Sesonske and Fleming, 5–25, his book *Dreaming*, Routledge and Kegan Paul, 1960 and endorsed by Daniel Dennett (see his "Are Dreams Experiences?" Philosophical Review (85) (1975), 304–24, reprinted in *Brainstorms*, 129–48) is obviously false on phenomenological grounds and as such unacceptable. However, for a critique of Malcolm, see E. M. Curley, "Dreaming and Conceptual Revision," *Australasian Journal of Philosophy*, 53 (1975), 119–41; Curley defends the dream argument in his *Descartes Against the Skeptics*, Cambridge, MA, Harvard University Press, 1978, 46–69 and provides scientific evidence for the contention that dreams are experiences, which claims are disputed by Dennett (above).

of my other cognitive faculties. The dream argument, then, apparently manages to provide a strong argument for skepticism about the senses without undermining my ability to evaluate that argument and embrace its conclusion.

Or does it? Consider the following formulation of the dream argument as it occurs in Descartes' text:

1. I am subject to episodes of dreaming.
2. Any experience I can have while I am awake I can have while I am dreaming, including the experience of believing that I am awake.
3. Therefore, there are no certain marks to distinguish dreaming from waking experience.
4. Therefore, it is possible that I am dreaming now.
5. If I am dreaming now, then none of my putative sense-experiences are veridical.
6. Therefore, it is possible that none of my current sense-experiences are veridical.
7. Therefore, I have genuine grounds for doubt that my senses are veridical.
8. Therefore, I ought to suspend judgment with regard to the deliverances of my senses, i.e., I ought to embrace skepticism about the senses.

The problem with this argument is that it does not begin, as does the madness suggestion, from a pure possibility. Instead, it begins from a pair of contingent, factual assertions that Descartes apparently claims to know to be the case, namely, that he sometimes dreams and that any experience he has while awake he can also have while he is asleep. From these claims he deduces the further claim that there is no way to distinguish dreaming from waking experience. It is only after having established this further claim that he is able to introduce the possibility, which is not otherwise motivated, that it is possible that I am dreaming right now and only mistakenly believe that I am awake. However, one is surely entitled to ask here how it is that Descartes can know the initial facts about dreaming, as well as the further claims about dreaming that he makes (such as that dreams are produced by the imagination and as such do not veridically reflect external reality) if his first intermediate conclusion (premise three in the above reconstruction) is true. If there are, *in fact*, no certain marks distinguishing dreaming from waking experience, then it is difficult to fathom how Descartes, or anyone else, could have so much information about the

The Perils of Methodological Doubt

nature of dream-experience or, indeed, even the concept of dreaming itself as something distinct from and opposed to waking experience. As such, if Descartes can know that the first two premises of his argument are true, then it follows that the third premise of his argument must be false and as such we cannot deduce from it the possibility that I am dreaming now and only think that I am awake. Indeed, once again, it seems that a necessary condition for affirming that possibility requires that I possess knowledge which undercuts the grounds for affirming that possibility whenever I contemplate it.[30]

The argument derives its apparent strength from its tendency to focus on experiential content as the source of our knowledge of the distinction between sleeping and waking. Thus, premises two and three above, if rewritten, might be read as follows:

2. Any experiential content I can have when I am awake I can have when I am dreaming.

3. Therefore, there are no certain marks to distinguish the content of waking experience from dream experience.

These claims seem uncontroversial, but they presuppose the truth of another claim not in evidence, i.e.:

---

30. I am here thus siding with W. H. Walsh on this issue; see his *Metaphysics*, 91–92. Margaret Wilson, *Descartes*, London, Routledge, 1978, 22–3 reformulates the dream argument without relying on the premise I am attacking here; however, her version of the argument seems to me to lack any significant skeptical bite. For discussion of her proposal, see Gareth Matthews, *Thought's Ego*, 70–72. Curley and Stroud reject the notion that Descartes's argument requires that he actually *know* that he dreams, maintaining in their different ways that it can succeed with some weaker premise; see E. M. Curley, *Descartes Against the Skeptics*, 47–61 and Barry Stroud, *The Significance of Philosophical Skepticism*, 11–23. Curley points to the fact that I have had experiences that I believed were actually occurring at the time but which I later decided were the illusory products of dreaming even though I could not tell that they were illusory experiences at the time I was having them. However, if my "having decided" that this is the case it to have any epistemic import, then it cannot be the case that it is altogether impossible for me to subsequently distinguish putative dreaming from putative waking experiences and hence to distinguish them *simpliciter*, at least under some conditions, something that Curley tacitly admits. Stroud maintains that it is sufficient to get Descartes's conclusion simply by relying on the *possibility* that I might be dreaming now; however, this appeal to possibility will be unmotivated unless I have some reason for affirming it, such as that I have good reason to believe that I have actually dreamed in the past; that it is *merely possible* that I have dreamed in the past and could not at that time tell that this was the case provides no reason, in and of itself, for the claim that I might be dreaming now in such a manner; that I have such a reason requires that I be able to distinguish putative dream-experiences from putative waking ones, which will be impossible if they are in no way distinguishable from each other. See also what follows in the main text.

C: The only way in which dreaming and waking experience could possibly be distinguished from each other is by reference to their distinct contents.

Descartes has given no argument for this claim whatsoever, nor does there seem to be any prospect of providing such an argument. Once again, in order to know that claim C is true, it seems that we would have to be able to compare examples of dreaming and waking experience in order to demonstrate their conformity to the facts, which implies that, in order to know that these claims are true, we must have some other way of distinguishing dreaming from waking experience than simply by reference to their experiential contents. Thus, if we know that claims 2' and 3' are true, as it certainly appears that we do, there must be some way of knowing this without depending solely on the contents of dreaming and waking experience, which entails that claim C is false. Thus, the possibility that I am dreaming now and simply don't know it is not entailed by the truth of 2' and 3' as above interpreted; quite the contrary, my putative knowledge that these claims are true implies I am in fact able to distinguish dreaming and waking experience in some fashion other than by reference to their content.

Indeed, it seems impossible in principle to suppose that we could distinguish dreaming from waking from dreaming experience solely by reference to content alone. Suppose that there is some experiential content, call it E, which occurs only in one form of experience and not the other. This would give us a clear mark distinguishing one form of experience from the other by giving us a unique content which always occurs only in the one and not the other. Still, how would this help us determine which of these was waking experience and which was dreaming experience? Suppose, for example, that a running caption appeared at the bottom of my visual field saying "You are now dreaming . . . this is all just a dream . . . this is not really happening . . . " and so on. How would I know that this is really a dream, rather than merely a waking hallucination? Again, it seems that I would not, at least with anything like the Cartesian certainty needed to persuade the skeptic.

What this suggests, then, is that the qualities that distinguish dreaming from waking experience are *global qualities* of the states themselves, corresponding to intrinsic differences in levels of conscious awareness, rather than features of the content as such. The suggestion here is that the difference between being awake and being asleep corresponds to differences in the sort of conscious awareness accompanying these distinct episodes in our conscious lives that gives them a unique "feel" which, being ubiquitous to those states, is not isolable as a distinct phenomenological content and can be appreciated only by contrast to one another, in much the same way that consciousness and unconsciousness can be appreciated only by contrast to one another. Furthermore, these degrees of consciousness correspond to different degrees of awareness, ability to employ our cognitive powers and causal connectedness to the external world, such that some levels are higher, freer and more engaged than others.[31] Such a proposal can be made consistent with the apparent fact that I can sometimes believe that I am awake when I am dreaming by supposing that, given the relatively low level of conscious awareness that accompanies dream-experience, that the vividness of certain dream-experiences can induce the false belief that I am awake, which is at least consistent with the supposition that when I am actually awake my level of conscious awareness is generally such that I can immediately apprehend that fact. Thus, on this account, it does not follow from the fact that I can sometimes falsely believe that I am awake when I am dreaming that I cannot know with absolute certainty that I am awake when I am awake.[32] If so, then I could claim to know that I am awake now with apodictic certainty if I am actually awake and thus rule out the possibility that I am dreaming now and only think that I am awake. Obviously, I have no space to develop any such account here, nor need I do so. The mere possibility of such an account is sufficient to block the inference from any of the putative facts presented here to any strong reasons for accepting the conclusion of the dream argument as presented above.

As such, I make no claim here to have proven that the possibility that I am dreaming now and falsely believe that I am awake can be known by me to be false, only that the putative facts about dreaming do not provide me with any reason for believing that this is the case. To the contrary, a consideration of the relevant facts strongly suggests that I could not have

---

31. See Farrer, *Finite and Infinite*, London, 45–48 for discussion of the idea of an interior scale of phenomenologically distinct levels of consciousness ranging from a total absence of consciousness to full-blown waking experience enjoyed at the highest degree of concentration. Austin may be onto something similar when he discusses the idea of a global "dreamlike quality" that distinguishes dreaming from waking experience and that certain novelists have attempted to convey; see *Sense and Sensibilia*, 48–49.

32. This point is made more forcefully by Williams, *Descartes*, 298–301. One may as well argue that, since I cannot know that I am unconscious when I am in fact unconscious, that I can't know that I'm conscious when I am in fact conscious or (even more absurdly) that since—on some views, anyway—I cannot know that I am dead if I am dead, that I cannot know that I am alive if I am alive. There are disanalogies here, of course, but the point is simply a logical one—it simply does not follow that if I can mistakenly believe that I am awake when I am asleep and dreaming that I cannot know with complete certainty that I am awake when I am awake. As such, if I am awake now, I can know that this is the case and thus that I am not dreaming.

any reason to believe that this is possible unless I at the same time had it within my power to know whether or not that possibility were realized. As such, I am once again justified in rejecting this possibility despite the fact that I cannot exclude its truth. However, in a certain sense, the foregoing discussion is off the topic and irrelevant to our main concern here, inasmuch as Descartes himself is dissatisfied with this argument, though for entirely different reasons. It is high time we returned to Descartes and our main topic.

According to Descartes, one of the things we know about dreams is that dreams are the products of the imagination, and as such, derive their contents from sense-experience, having been constructed from the elements of sensory images on hand in St. Augustine's great store-house of memory. Even the most bizarre nightmare monster is ultimately fadged together from shapes, colors, etc., derived from the images representing putatively real things—only the combination of elements is novel. As such, the dream argument does not suffice, in Descartes' own terms, to wholly undermine the senses as a source of knowledge about the external world. For even if I am able to deny that my ideas of external objects (like my material body) and their parts (heads, hands, and so on) represent anything existing independently of my mind, it nevertheless remains that both the qualitative (colors, shapes, etc.) and quantitative properties of bodies studied by arithmetic, geometry and so on remain unaffected and demand for their explanation some external source that accounts for their presence in consciousness. As Descartes notes, whereas the sciences of bodies (such as medicine and astronomy) may be undercut by the dream argument, the more basic sciences of arithmetic, geometry and mathematical physics escape unscathed, at least as hypothetical constructs. The very possibility of dreaming, then, presupposes that there exists an external world that is the source of the contents of my dreams, at a bare minimum the simple ideas of sensation and the truths of mathematics. This is certainly less knowledge than we believe we possess, but it is not negligible and it does not demonstrate that the Aristotelian worldview is self-undermining in the way that the New Science turns out to be. Descartes therefore requires some further argument to completely discredit the senses and motivate the problem of the external world. He finds such an argument in the Deceiver hypothesis. Let us now turn to that hypothesis.

2

The Deceiver Hypothesis

EVEN IF Descartes has been successful in undermining the senses by means of his first two skeptical arguments—and I have argued that he has not—he has still not completely succeeded in undermining the Aristotelian world-picture. The very possibility of dream-deception requires that there exist an external source for the contents of my dreams; at a bare minimum, the simple ideas of sensation must have an external cause. Further, there are certain truths, such as the claims that $2+3=5$ and that *every square has four sides*, that remain true even in a dream and about which I can be certain quite independently of whether I am awake or asleep. In order to undermine the senses as a source this sort of basic knowledge requires that Descartes be able to offer some alternate account of the origin of these ideas in consciousness, one that does not require the existence of the external world and which cannot be discovered to befalse by the use of the senses alone. It is not required that this alternate hypothesis be likely to be true or even remotely plausible, simply that it be possibly true, since under the aegis of methodological doubt Descartes is resolved to doubt anything that could conceivably be false regardless of its likelihood of being true.

Descartes finds this alternative in a more radical skeptical scenario. Descartes notes that he has a conception of a God who is all-powerful, such that even the truths of logic and mathematics are products of His will and dependent upon that will for their existence and their truth. Surely, he says, it would be no trouble at all for such a being to completely undermine my senses as a source of knowledge, in either of two ways. First of all, he could have created me such that my cognitive faculties were systematically defective in such a way that I am unable to use those faculties to arrive at the truth no matter how carefully I attempt to use them. Secondly, God could simply interfere with the operation of my cognitive processes on every occasion that I use them, such that I always arrive at an erroneous result. Thus, in one notorious passage,[1] Descartes envisages the possibility that a deceiving God could bring it about that I am always mistaken whenever I add 2 and 3 or count the sides of a square.[2] In this case, Descartes is calling into question the truth of even mathematical and logical statements when accepted on the basis of sense-dependent or at any rate temporally extended processes such as counting, adding or inference, operations that we know from experience can result in erroneous beliefs. However, in this case, we would not be able to use those faculties to check themselves and thereby discover our errors, since they would be produced systematically by the deceiving God in such a way that the error could never be detected by anyone.

Further, atheism, the denial of God's existence, does not offer us a way out of this unfortunate situation. Descartes notes that some would rather deny God's existence rather than admit that a being with such extensive powers might exist. In this case, says Descartes, I must conceive of myself and my cognitive faculties as produced by mere chance or some chain of merely physical causes operating without end or purpose, in which case I have even less reason to trust the reliability of my cognitive faculties. The notion that my cognitive powers would have developed in such a way as to make it possible for me to discover the theoretical truth about reality as the result of a purely random process seems too improbable to take seriously. Although I cannot discuss this matter here, it seems to me that Descartes is almost certainly right about this, the fact of evolution notwithstanding.[3]

1. See Hide Ishiguro, "The Status of Necessity and Possibility in Descartes," in Emily Oskenberg Rorty, ed., *Essays on Descartes' Meditations*, 459–71 and Menn, *Descartes and Augustine*, 337–52. Both Ishiguro and Menn maintain that Descartes' view was that God could have made 2+2 not equal to 4, but, being immutable and once having decided to make 2+2=4, this truth is eternal and unchangeable as well. Further, God has imprinted these eternal truths on our minds so that, when we contemplate them, we apprehend them as self-evident and thus as known *a priori* with absolute certainty.

2. See *CSM*, Vol. II, 14; note that Descartes does not reiterate this claim about the Evil Genius.

3. Most contemporary readers will be satisfied to make some sort of vague appeal to evolution as the explanation for how our cognitive faculties have developed so as to track the way the world is: see, for example, Quine's famous article "Epistemology Naturalized" in *Ontological Relativity and Other Essays*, 69–90. However, the idea that our capacity for theoretical knowledge might have evolved is highly unlikely, given that it has only a very indirect connection to differential reproduction, the generally accepted standard for evolutionary "success." Nineteenth century evolutionists, such as Chauncey Wright and John Fiske, recognized this and postulated that our capacity for theoretical knowledge developed as a byproduct of the development of other, non-cognitive brain capacities, creating an "overplus" which became available for the pursuit of theoretical knowledge only when human beings had largely conquered the day-to-day problems of survival. This

The Deceiver Hypothesis

Descartes recognizes that his standard idea of God includes the notion of benevolence and veracity, hence that it would be blasphemous to suppose that God could be either incompetent or a deceiver.[4] He therefore suggests that, instead of a deceiving God that we instead conceive of a very powerful though not perfect being called the Evil Genius (*malin genie*), a demon who exerts every effort to deceive me, i.e., induces me to commit errors when I exercise my cognitive faculties. Such a being, says Descartes, could simply destroy the external world and directly produce the contents of my consciousness, thus preserving the illusion that such a world exists. In that case, there would be no way to discover the deception, since there would be no way to use the senses to discover which of these two possible explanations, the external world or Evil Genius-deception, is true. By hypothesis, our conscious experience will be just as it is now, of a putative external world composed of extramental objects, only on the first possibility there really is such a realm and such things and on the other there is and are not. Here we find a scenario that completely trumps the senses and thus undermines them as a source of knowledge about reality, at least in their own right. The skeptic wins and the only rational course is to doubt all the deliverances of the senses in accordance with the methodological commitments of the first *Meditation*. Further, only such a supposition seems sufficient to finally undermine the senses as a source of knowledge about the world in such a way as to finally overthrow common-sense, the Aristotelian system that rests on common sense, and to prepare the way for the initially counterintuitive claims of the New Science.

---

idea may be true, but it remains highly speculative; at any rate, so far as I am aware there is no positive reason to believe it. However, given that this is the case, the epistemic status of the theory of evolution itself, which after all is the product of the exercise of these faculties, is called into question. Ultimately, it may be that only design can rescue us from the self-undermining scientific paradigm to which atheistic naturalism commits us. On this, see Alvin Plantinga, "Is Naturalism Irrational?" in *Warrant and Proper Function*, 316–337 as well as the large body of secondary literature engendered by Plantinga's argument—e.g., James Bielby, *Naturalism Defeated?*, New York, Oxford University Press, 2002. Even more impressive is Stephen Stitch's article "Could Man be an Irrational Animal?" in Hilary Korrnblith, ed., *Naturalizing Epistemology*, 338–57, in which he presents cases in which cases of animal behaviors, if expressed as grounded in cognitive beliefs, would be false yet still (presumably) have proven to have survival value to the species that possess them.

4. Later, Descartes will be able to exclude the deceiving God hypothesis by showing it to be self-contradictory; see below.

The Epistemic Status of the Evil Genius Hypothesis

Descartes himself seems anxious to soft-pedal the Evil Genius hypothesis from the very first. In the first *Meditation*, Descartes writes as though the Evil Genius hypothesis were merely a convenient device for preventing him from slipping back into his preconceived ideas and fixing firmly in his mind the skeptical results of his inquiry up to that point.[5] Throughout the rest of the *Meditations* and *Replies* he refers to this hypothesis as merely metaphysical and hyperbolic, not a serious ground for actual doubt. Indeed, Descartes insists that, whenever I am actually perceiving or conceiving anything clearly and distinctly that I cannot doubt the truth of what I clearly and distinctly perceive or conceive. Instead, it is only when I am not actually doing so, and merely remembering that I did so in the past, that the Evil Genius hypothesis provides any grounds, and then only of the most exaggerated sort, for doubting the deliverances of my cognitive faculties.[6] Nor does this appear to be merely a psychological observation. After all, if my cognitive faculties are working properly and there is no Evil Genius, my psychological inability to doubt that which I clearly and distinctly perceive is clearly going to be produced by my apprehension of the self-evidence of the content of my act of clear and distinct perception.

Nevertheless, in discussing the cognitive situation of the atheist, Descartes wants to insist that the atheist can never have certain knowledge of any proposition, including mathematical and logical truths. This is not because (*a là* Karl Barth) the unredeemed cognitive faculties of the nonbeliever do not permit him or her to grasp the truths that are self-evident to those who have been granted the gift of faith. Presumably, the operation of the cognitive faculties of the atheist with regard to, e.g., the truths of arithmetic is identical to those of the believer. Rather, it is simply that, without knowledge of God's existence, one cannot altogether eliminate all possible grounds of doubt and thus can never claim to know with absolute certainty that any of these propositions are true, since we can never claim to know anything which might be brought into doubt in any set of circumstances.[7] The atheist is in an irremediable state of cognitive dissonance, in which he or she is both, at one and the same time, convinced on the basis of the deliverances of his or her cognitive faculties that 2+3=5 is necessarily true and indubitable on the basis of clear and distinct perception but

---

5. *CSM*, Vol. II, 15.

6. *CSM*, Vol. II, 100. Descartes reiterates this claim in many other places as well, both in the replies to the objections and his letters.

7. *CSM*, Vol. II, 101.

also unable to wholly exclude the possibility that an Evil Genius might be deceiving him or her about this fact. The believer, however, armed with knowledge of God's existence and the incompatibility of that existence with the existence of an Evil Genius, rests confidently in the deliverances of his cognitive faculties. The suggestion (which Descartes never explicitly states) is that this state of cognitive dissonance, in which apparently indubitable self-evident truth is juxtaposed to the possibility of a deceiving God whose power to deceive extends even to apparently self-evident truth, can only be alleviated by confronting that possibility with an indubitable self-evident truth whose content excludes it.[8] This, of course, is the claim that God, a perfect and veracious being, exists. Such a course is not open to the atheist, who is therefore condemned to the outer epistemic darkness where there is wailing and gnashing of cognitive teeth.

Of course, Descartes can only proceed if there are cognitive resources left to him to accomplish the task of proving God's existence and most philosophers, not even his own believing contemporaries, are willing to grant him this. I shall deal with these qualms in due course and argue that Descartes does in fact manage to avoid undercutting his own position and arguing in a circle. For the present, however, let me just consider what sort of epistemic threat the Deceiver hypothesis represents.

Conceivability, Possibility, and the Deceiver

It seems clear enough that Descartes accepted the conceivability criterion for possibility, i.e., the thesis that whatever is conceivable without contradiction is both logically possible and thus possibly existent in the real world unless somehow prevented from existing by antecedent actual conditions. By the same token, Descartes, Spinoza and Leibniz as well accepted the corollary that whatever we clearly and distinctly conceive to be self-evidently true is necessarily true and thus true of the actual world as it exists independently of consciousness. In our post-Kantian (indeed, post-modern and, it seems, soon to be post-everything) world this strikes us as breath-takingly naïve. However, we must remember that Descartes lived at a time before these matters had been thought out with the sophistication we enjoy today. We not only now distinguish various kinds of possibility and necessity but also recognize that the relation between these various sorts of possibility are com-

---

8. Descartes does say in other places that an atheist has no certain knowledge unless he knows that he was created by a non-deceiving God, which reinforces the suggestion made here, that it is the possibility of a deceiving God, not that of the Evil Genius, that threatens this possibility; see *CSM*, Vol. II, 137 and 289.

plex and subtle, resisting any simple nested classification.⁹ For our purposes here, let us consider four kinds of possibility:

Epistemic Possibility, i.e., what is possible relative to what is known by an individual or group of individuals given their current circumstances.

Logical Possibility, i.e., what is possible in the sense that it exists or occurs in some possible world, whether actual or non-actual.

Physical Possibility, i.e., what is possible relative to the laws of nature governing the actual world.

Metaphysical Possibility, i.e., what might exist, occur or obtain in the actual world as an actually existing constituent of that world.

Of course, to do a proper job we would need to define corresponding senses of impossibility and necessity for each of these as well. As there is no space to do this here, I shall simply have to dogmatically assert the conception of the relation of conceivability and possibility I think is correct and apply this account to Descartes' Deceiver hypothesis. With regard to the last form of possibility, metaphysical possibility, I will simply stipulate that anything that is both logically and physically possible will also be possible in that further sense, treating logical and physical possibility as jointly sufficient and independently necessary for metaphysical possibility.

First of all, I shall assume that the practical expression of the conceivability criterion of possibility is what we might call the *Imaginability Criterion of Possibility*, i.e., the standard for what is conceivable is, in practical terms, simply what is imaginable without contradiction by someone, or ideally, by anyone. However, since we cannot be certain that our powers of imagination (or conceivability) extend so far as to embrace the entirety of what is conceivable in principle (i.e., what would be conceivable for an infinite intellect, such as God would possess), nor prove apodictically that whatever seems, even on reflection, to be conceivable by us is, in fact, con-

---

9. While discussion of the role of conceivability in the determination of what is possible or impossible antedates even Descartes, serious contemporary consideration of the issues involved here seems to have its roots in Kripke's attempts to articulate the metaphysical implications of modal logic, culminating in his *Naming and Necessity*, Cambridge, MA, Harvard University Press, 1980. Also important is Alvin Plantinga's *The Nature of Necessity*, New York, Oxford University Press, 1974. For a recent summary of the ongoing work in this area, see Tamar Szabo Gendler and John Hawthorne, eds., *Conceivability and Possibility*, Oxford, Clarendon Press, 2002 and works cited there; note especially the article by David Chalmers, "Does Conceivability Entail Possibility?," 145–200. I have not benefited from this article as much as I might because I found it largely over my head; at any rate, my concerns are largely epistemic whereas Chalmers appears to be primarily concerned about metaphysical questions.

ceivable in principle, we shall have to interpret imaginability in this context as *Apparent* Conceivability or Imaginability. On this view, then, what counts as conceivable for us is what is coherently imaginable by us, i.e., apparently conceivable without contradiction.[10] This is, of course, quite a weak interpretation of this criterion but it is hard to see how we could demand anything more given our limited cognitive powers and situation.

Matters are yet more complicated, however. For our purposes here, we must distinguish two modes of *apparent inconceivability*. Sometimes the intuitive inconceivability of a thing or state-of-affairs is due to the incoherence of what one is attempting to conceive of; we can call this inconceivability in the conception or inconceivability *simpliciter*. For example, square circles and persons who are older or taller than themselves are inconceivable due to the fact that the very content of the conception itself is incoherent or internally self-contradictory. In such cases, the impossibility of our conceiving of what is being described is due to incoherence in the very object of our act of conception. In such case, we feel confident that we can infer from the incoherence of the conception to the logical and physical impossibility of what we are conceiving of.

There is, however, a second sort of inconceivability which does not appear to support such inferences, which I call inconceivability in the conceiving.[11] In this case, it is not what is conceived of that is incoherent or self-contradictory, but rather the act of conceiving—with that thing or state-of-affairs as its object—itself. Thus, in Anselm's version of the ontological argument, we are asked to conceive of God—a being whose essence contains existence—as non-existent and told that to do this involves an incoherence or self-contradiction.[12] Likewise, in Berkeley's *Principles of Human Knowledge*, we are asked to imagine something existing unper-

---

10. It should not be thought that my appeal to what is imaginable is a simple appeal to what is "imageable," i.e., capable of being represented by a mental image or picture. There are good reasons for doubting that imageability is a sufficient condition for imaginability in the full and proper sense in all cases. See the important but neglected article by V. C. Aldrich, "Image Mongering and Image Management," *Philosophy and Phenomenological Research*, 13, no. 1, 1962, 51–61; see especially page 54.

11. The obvious parallel here is to Kant's distinction between contradiction in the will and contradiction in the willing; see his *Grounding for the Metaphysics of Morals*, trans. by James W. Ellington, 32.

12. Anselm, *Proslogion*, Chapter II, translated by S.N. Deane; in Plantinga, *The Ontological Argument*, 2–4. When Aquinas criticizes this argument by claiming that what holds of the conceptual order need not hold of the order of external reality his objection is merely question-begging unless we construe his comments as invoking something like the distinction being developed here, i.e., that Anselm's argument involves only inconceivability in the conceiving, not in what is being conceived.

ceived yet informed that to even attempt to do this involves perceiving that object in the sense that the very act of conceiving of something brings about that the thing in question exists in relation to a mind, thus making it impossible to conceive of something existing wholly unperceived.[13] In these cases, it is not what is being conceived of (the object of conception or perception) that is intrinsically incoherent or self-contradictory but instead the act of conceiving that object itself under a certain description. The most that follows from this is that our powers of conception are limited, not that the object conceived of is either logically or physically impossible. The fact that I cannot conceive of God as non-existent under a certain description does not prove this conception of God must be instantiated or exemplified in reality. Likewise, the fact that I cannot conceive of something as existing unperceived simply because conceiving is a kind of perceiving as Berkeley defines it does not prove that nothing can exist outside of my mind. In what follows, then, I shall concern myself solely with conceivability (and inconceivability) in the conception.

Now the criterion of apparent coherent conceivability in that sense seems most closely related to epistemic possibility, since epistemic possibility is a subjective, rather than objective form of possibility, one closely tied to the actual state of one's knowledge at a particular time. However, the claim that apparent coherent conceivability is sufficient for epistemic possibility has been challenged. According to Gendler and Hawthorne, the epistemically impossible is apparently coherently conceivable in some cases.[14] For example, suppose I see that the cat is on the mat. Treating "see" as a verb of achievement, seeing that the cat is on the mat entails knowing the cat is on the mat, which in turn entails that the proposition "The cat is on the mat" is true. In that case, that proposition is epistemically necessary and its contradictory, "It is not the case that the cat is on the mat" is epistemically impossible. At the same time, the state-of-affairs of the cat's *not* being on the mat seems perfectly coherently conceivable. As such, we cannot use apparent coherent conceivability as the criterion for epistemic possibility.

But perhaps this is a bit too fast. There is a sense in which it is apparently coherently conceivable in the envisaged circumstances that the cat is not on the mat, since that proposition is clearly logically contingent, i.e., such that there is a possible world in which the cat is not on the mat. The fact that the actual world is not one of the worlds in which that is the case

---

13. Berkeley, *Principles of Human Knowledge*, Sec. 23; in the Dancy edition, p. 110. This case is discussed in John Campbell's paper, "Berkeley's Puzzle," in Gendler and Hawthorne, *Conceivability and Possibility*, 127–43.

14. See Gendler and Hawthorne, *Conceivability and Possibility*, 3–4.

The Deceiver Hypothesis

is beside the point. In another sense, however, given the epistemic necessity of the proposition that the cat is on the mat for someone properly placed in the real world, it is not coherently conceivable that the cat not be on the mat, since this would require that the same state-of-affairs in that world be both epistemically impossible and yet epistemically possible for the same person at the same time, which is a contradiction. We can perhaps sort this out by distinguishing two kinds of epistemic possibility, one of which, *intrinsic* epistemic possibility, is determined solely by the content of the mental act which constitutes the contemplation of that putative possibility and the second of which, *extrinsic* epistemic possibility, is relative to one's complete body of knowledge at a particular time. Given this distinction, the cat's not being on the mat is intrinsically epistemically possible, i.e., epistemically possible considered in itself (and hence epistemically possible in fact for anyone not in a position to determine whether or not it is the case that the cat is on the mat) but not extrinsically so for someone who sees that the cat is on the mat. On the basis of the foregoing, then, we can clarify the relation between apparent coherent conceivability and epistemic possibility as follows:

> Apparent coherent conceivability in the conception is a sufficient condition for *intrinsic* epistemic possibility.

By this revised criterion, nothing which is inconceivable in the conception is epistemically possible in either sense and everything which is conceivable in the conception is intrinsically epistemically possible but not everything that is conceivable in the conception is also extrinsically epistemically possible.

Now let us briefly consider the relation between apparent coherent conceivability and logical possibility as above defined. It does not seem to be the case that everything that is intrinsically epistemically possible is logically possible as well. As we have seen, what is intrinsically epistemically possible encompasses more than is extrinsically epistemically possible (i.e., what is epistemically possible all things considered). Among the intrinsically epistemically possible states-of-affairs which fall into these categories appear to be some which are logically impossible. Consider, for example, Goldbach's conjecture. Since Goldbach's conjecture has never been proven or refuted, it seems that both the truth and falsity of Goldbach's conjecture are apparently coherently conceivable by us and hence intrinsically epistemically possible for us. However, given that Goldbach's conjecture is a mathematical truth, it is either true in all possible worlds or false in all possible worlds. Of the two envisaged alternatives, one of them is logically necessary and the other logically impossible, though in the absence of proof we cannot know which is which, so each remains intrinsically epistemically possible considered in itself (though not extrinsically so for those who know that all mathematical truths are necessary truths). By the same token, the class of states-of-affairs that are apparently coherently conceivable for us is wider than the class of states-of-affairs that are coherently conceivable *as such* or *simpliciter*. Presumably, for an infinite intellect who knows the truth-values for all propositions, including mathematical propositions like Goldbach's conjecture, it is not conceivable in any sense that Goldbach's conjecture might be true if it is false or *vice versa*. Thus, we ought to conclude that apparent coherent conceivability is at best necessary for logical possibility; surely, nothing that is inconceivable in the conception could be logically possible. So, then, apparent coherent conceivability can be at most an epistemically necessary condition for logical possibility, and one that is defeasible in the face of evidence establishing that this putative possibility is not after all genuinely possible. Still, if some thing or state-of-affairs is apparently coherently conceivable, hence intrinsically epistemically possible, in most cases this should be sufficient to create a defeasible *presumption* in favor of the logically possibility of that thing or state-of-affairs, one which may be overcome by contrary evidence or argument. Thus, while intrinsic epistemic possibility does not entail logical possibility, it supports the attribution of logical possibility to whatever is envisaged as intrinsically epistemically possible, thus justifying our taking it to be logically possible in lieu of any positive reason to do otherwise.

Applying this to the case of the Deceiver, we can see that Descartes is not committed even to so much as the logical possibility of the existence of such a being simply on the grounds that the existence of the Deceiver is apparently coherently conceivable. The apparent coherent conceivability of such a Deceiver only establishes the intrinsic epistemic possibility of such a being and this, as we have seen, is insufficient to entail even the logical possibility of such a being, let alone its metaphysical possibility, since the former is necessary for the latter. As such, Descartes is on good ground when he claims that the Evil Genius hypothesis represents only an exaggerated or hyperbolic doubt which carries much less weight than the deliverances of those cognitive faculties that reveal to us putatively self-evident truths. Thus, given that the question of the logical possibility of the Deceiver remains an open question, we are in no position to assert this possibility dogmatically. In presenting an argument against the logical possibility of the Deceiver in the course of the *Meditations*, then, Descartes may have thought that it was not sufficient to appeal to that possibility by itself to undercut his argument.

The Deceiver Hypothesis

However, Descartes cannot have it both ways. If the Deceiver hypothesis represents a merely epistemic possibility which in no way supports the logical possibility of that hypothesis, then it will not do the skeptical work required to motivate skepticism about the senses. Further, as I have argued, intrinsic epistemic possibility is sufficient to provide at least a presumption in favor of the logical possibility of whatever is envisaged as epistemically possible in most cases, and there do not appear to be any special reasons applicable to the case of the Deceiver that would rule this out. We must concede, at least at this point, that there is a presumption in favor of the thesis that the Deceiver is a logically possible being so far forth. Yet, in so doing, we are also thereby envisaging the metaphysical possibility that such a Deceiver actually exists and possesses all the power that the hypothesis attributes to him, because logical possibility is a necessary condition for actuality and thus for metaphysical possibility; thus, given that our supposition of such a being is not ruled out by the laws of nature, we have to take seriously the metaphysical possibility that such a being really exists. Thus, Descartes cannot treat the Deceiver hypothesis as though it were merely hypothetical, as nothing more than a thought-experiment; as tenuous as the Deceiver's grip on reality may be, it cannot be altogether discounted, nor would it provide any help to the cause of skepticism if it could. At this point, then, it becomes necessary to consider the extent of the powers that Descartes attributes to the Evil Genius.

How Powerful is Descartes' Deceiver?

Obviously, if Descartes' Evil Genius is to play his necessary role in the *Meditations*, he must be powerful enough to undermine the senses as a source of knowledge by generating the problem of the external world. As we have seen, this means that he must possess sufficient power to cause us to have sense-experiences purporting to present us with an extramental external world in the absence of such a world. Does it require that we grant to such a being any more extensive powers, as is commonly done by interpreters of Descartes? Perhaps more pointedly, has Descartes let the genie (or the Genius) out of the bottle in such a way that he is powerless to resist the further expansion of the Demon's power to all of our cognitive faculties, thus leaving us without any means of escaping the skeptic's clutches? For reasons that will emerge, we cannot fully answer this question here.

However, we can at least make a preliminary feint, which we will follow up in the next chapter.[15]

Some philosophers have supposed that Descartes attributes practically unlimited powers to the Evil Genius. Descartes certainly *does* seem to attribute unlimited powers to the hypothesis of a deceiving God, who can make me believe anything simply by *force majeure*. However, given the foregoing, Descartes now has a potential "trump card" he can play against this particular skeptical scenario.[16] According to Descartes, we have a clear and distinct idea of God as a perfect being, and it is incompatible with this conception of God to suppose that God is a deceiver, since God could be a deceiver only if He were either incompetent or malicious, neither of which is consistent with the divine perfection. The notion of a deceiving God, then, is self-contradictory and thus logically impossible. To put it in my terminology: intrinsic epistemic possibility is a necessary condition for logical possibility and the concept of a deceiving God, being incoherent in the conception (like the concept of a square circle) thereby fails to be intrinsically epistemically possible. By the same token, then, it fails to be logically possible as well. Furthermore, this realization proves to be extrinsically certain for us, since its very content directly rules out the possibility that a deceiving God exists; thus, we cannot be mistaken in accepting this result.[17]

Someone might balk at this. Supposing that a deceiving God has the power that Descartes claims He has, wouldn't it lie within His power to make me think (even if only by *force majeure*) that the idea of such a being was self-contradictory, thereby deceiving me into believing that He fails to exist?[18] In that case, even an apparent self-contradiction in the notion of a

---

15. For a different analysis and critique of the Evil Genius hypothesis, see Peter Klein, *Certainty: A Refutation of Skepticism*, Minneapolis, MN, University of Minnesota Press, 1981. I do not find Klein's analysis persuasive and continue to hold to the view that Descartes's strategy is the only possible response to the Evil Genius challenge to human knowledge.

16. Descartes will not in fact play this trump card until the fourth *Meditation*; see *CSM*, Vol. II, 37. He cannot play it until the clear and distinct idea of God as a perfect being has been explicitly adverted to and its implications clearly and distinctly grasped. In fact, the notion of a deceiving God is self-contradictory and always has been so but we are not in a position to note this until this idea has been explicitly grasped and reflected upon in the third *Meditation*. Until that point, we are in the same position as someone who contemplates the Pythagorean Theorem prior to a consideration of the proof for that claim and finds it quite easy to doubt that the square of the hypotenuse *must* equal the sum of the squares of the other two sides. I will be at pains later to vindicate Descartes' claim that we do, in fact, possess an innate idea of God as a perfect being.

17. On the notion of extrinsic certainty, see below, 51.

18. Gary Hatfield appears to suggest something like this; see his *Descartes and the*

deceiving God would not be enough to secure the logical impossibility of such a being; once again the skeptic will have evaded our grasp and it will appear that we are still enmeshed in the toils of the skeptical scenario. Is the there any defense against this final, most extreme skeptical challenge?

I think there is. To construe the deceiving God hypothesis in this way is to make it equivalent to the Insanity Hypothesis we considered and dismissed earlier, such that a version of the same set of considerations will justify dismissing this alternative as well. After all, the skeptical scenario of a deceiving God will only rationally justify skepticism if it can count as a reason for supposing that such a being is logically possible, since only in that case would such a being be metaphysically possible, i.e., potentially actually existent. On the envisaged hypothesis, however, the deceiving God can make us believe anything He wishes, simply by *force majeure*. In that case, however, nothing can count as a reason for anything, not even for supposing that a deceiving God is a logically possible. Any reason that I might give for supposing that such a being is possible is one that such a being could make me accept by *force majeure*, regardless of whether or not it provided the slightest evidence for that claim. After all, God is omnipotent and thus has unlimited power over me, so that it would be easy for Him to force me to accept any putative reason, no matter how fallacious or irrelevant, as sufficient for believing that He is a logically possible being. Under these conditions, however, I can have no confidence in my judgment with respect to any such reasons, since in that case I do not have the cognitive independence required in order for me to be able to evaluate any such reasons. As such, I can never have, on the envisaged hypothesis, any reason for supposing that it is even possible, let alone true. As such, this hypothesis cannot provide me—or anyone else, including the skeptic him- or herself—with any reason for embracing skepticism, regardless of whether or not a deceiving God exists. The skeptic, then, has failed in the attempt to undermine our claims to knowledge using the envisaged hypothesis and thereby provide a rational motivation for skepticism. In that case, skepticism may be safely put aside, at least until such time as the skeptic is prepared to supply us with credible reasons for embracing this view.

However, not even this path appears to be open to the skeptic on the envisaged hypothesis. For, supposing for a moment that such reasons might become available to us, we will be in a position to examine such reasons only to the extent that we can take ourselves to possess the cognitive independence and rational acumen required to examine the deceiving God hypothesis and the reasons for skepticism it generates. To the extent

---

Meditations, 175.

that we do credit ourselves with this capacity, we are making a supposition that is contrary to the very hypothesis we are proposing to consider, since a deceiving God can make us believe whatever He wants for whatever reason He wants regardless of what happens to be the case. Thus, either we are in a position to evaluate those reasons, in which case the deceiving God hypothesis must be false, or, if after examining the skeptic's reasons we are inclined to accept the logical possibility of a deceiving God, we are buying into a scenario according to which we do not have the logical acumen to evaluate those reasons in the first place and thus cannot arrive, *via* those reasons, at the rationally justified judgment that the existence of such a being is logically possible after all. The paradox, it seems, is unavoidable and in either case the deceiving God hypothesis gives us no grounds for embracing skepticism.

Of course, even our ability to arrive at this paradox and recognize its force requires that this paradox be only apparent and not real, since if it were a genuine paradox we would not possess sufficient cognitive independence or rational acumen even to accomplish this much. We can therefore safely reject the paradox as unsound on the ground that the suposition that we can judge it to be genuine entails that it is not, since this is inconsistent with that very supposition itself! At any rate, it is profitless to consider it further and to the extent that the deceiving God hypothesis supports such a conclusion we must suppose that, as in the case of the supposition that I am mad, we have reached an epistemic dead end. It is therefore not to be so much rejected as put aside.[19]

19. It is in this spirit, I believe, that we should read the oft-quoted passage from the second *Replies* (see *CSM*, Vol. II, 103–4) in which Descartes scoffs at the notion that what is intrinsically certain for us might be "absolutely false" in the eyes of God or an angel. (Compare: "I know that the notion of a square circle is self-contradictory and that as such square circles can't exist; but how do I know that this claim might not be "absolutely false" in the eyes of God or an angel?") To such things is merely to engage in "image-mongering"/story-telling (as Descartes calls it) or to be uttering an empty form of words. To put the point less polemically, we can read Descartes here as suggesting that we ought to be interested in skeptical scenarios only to the extent that such scenarios can provide us with *reasons* for embracing skepticism. Skeptical scenarios that have neither any statable content (so that we cannot even appraise the epistemic possibility of what is being suggested—which I believe is what Descartes is referring to in this passage) or which undermine the rationality of skepticism itself—such as the madness scenario or the deceiving God scenario we are currently discussing—do not represent genuine challenges to our knowledge-claims and thus do not require an answer. It is enough that we can eliminate those skeptical challenges which we can coherently conceive. At any rate, there is no necessity in reading this passage (as many have) as asserting that Descartes is tacitly admitting that he cannot provide or is ultimately not interested in claiming absolute certainty for the central doctrines of the *Meditations*. Whatever is intrinsically certain for me is indubitable when clearly and

The foregoing does not, however, eliminate every version of the Evil Genius hypothesis. In line with Descartes' own presentation of this hypothesis, we may suppose that the Evil Genius is not omnipotent but more like the Devil as he has been conceived of in the monotheistic tradition, a powerful and malicious finite spirit who bends all of his energies to entice us into sin. The Evil Genius, of course, is only a cognitive Devil, solely intent on getting us to voluntarily ignore or misuse our cognitive faculties in such a way as to bring it about that we fall into error, which temptation we can stoutly resist by making sure that we follow Descartes' first rule of method: never accept any proposition for which we cannot give adequate justification.[20] The concept of such a being is not self-contradictory and so cannot be ruled out on the ground that the existence of such a being is intrinsically epistemically impossible. Nevertheless, on the supposition that such a being is metaphysically possible, it is quite easy to generate the problem of the external world in the way that Descartes does and thus motivate complete skepticism about the senses as a source of knowledge. This, of course, is Descartes' intention in the first *Meditation* and Evil Genius hypothesis thus represents a different challenge from that of the deceiving God. Descartes' strategy in dealing with that skeptical scenario will have to be different as well.

On Descartes' Way Out

The Cartesian response to the challenge represented by the Deceiver hypothesis is well known in outline, i.e., in the manner in which Descartes presents it. Descartes proposes to discover an Archimedean point, some-

---

distinctly conceived due to the intentional content of that act of conceiving and fails to be extrinsically certain only to the extent that the content in question fails to provide me with a positive reason for excluding the deceiving God hypothesis. When joined to the claims that God exists and is not a deceiver, it likewise becomes extrinsically certain as well. As to Descartes' contention that the appeal to God is needed only when I have forgotten the proof, etc. this seems to me to be a disingenuous and *ad hoc* response to the Circle objection that does not even seriously address it. But I cannot linger to argue this here.

20. On the supposition that the Evil Genius had the power to interfere in our cognitive processes in such a way as to directly induce false beliefs by *force majeure*, we would be right back to the epistemic dead end that we have just declined with regard to the deceiving God hypothesis. We are assuming, then, that it is possible for us to evaluate reasons for and against the logical possibility of the Evil Genius envisaged in the hypothesis under discussion; this entails, as we have seen, that the Evil Genius has limited power with respect to me: in particular, the Evil Genius cannot directly interfere with my cognitive processes in such a way to make me believe what is false by *force majeure*. On this account, then, the sole purpose of the Evil Genius is to undermine the senses as a source of knowledge about the world in the way described by Descartes.

thing which is indubitable and incorrigible for him, something about which not even God or the Evil Genius can deceive him. Descartes believes that he has discovered this in the fact of his own existence, revealed to him through the fact of his own self-conscious awareness of his mental states and acts. On this basis, he proposes to establish the existence of God and, given that God is veracious, to exclude the logical possibility of the Evil Genius, thereby eliminating the sole remaining challenge to reason as a source of knowledge about reality and establishing at last a firm foundation for the New Science and as much of common sense as can be salvaged from the wreckage of the Aristotelian worldview, such as that an external world exists.

The problems with this strategy are equally well-known. In order to provide a platform for further beliefs, Descartes embraces the principle that whatever he clearly and distinctly perceives or conceives must be true. He then claims to possess a clear and distinct idea of God as a perfect being and proceeds on that basis to establish the existence of that being by a series of arguments. Given that God exists and, being perfect, is not a deceiver, Descartes concludes that God would not permit the existence of an Evil Genius or create me in such a way that my cognitive faculties were systematically flawed in such a manner that no matter how carefully I used them I could never arrive at the truth. As such, he concludes that whatever he is led to believe by the natural light of reason must be true. Among the things Descartes claims to know as a consequence of this line of reasoning are that the essence of the soul is thought, that the essence of body is extension and that soul and body are distinct. Yet from the very beginning, Descartes has been accused of arguing in a circle, illegitimately assuming the principle that whatever he clearly and distinctly perceives or conceives is true, a principle that he can only legitimately employ after he has eliminated the logical possibility of the Evil Genius, in order to prove the existence of God and then using God's veracity to eliminate the possibility of the Evil Genius, thus justifying the principle that whatever I clearly and distinctly perceive or conceive must be true.[21] The fact that neither Descartes nor his immediate followers make any plausible response to this charge suggests that Descartes has, in fact, argued in a circle after all.[22]

---

21. See, e.g., Arnauld, fourth *Objections*, *CSM*, Vol. II, 150–1.

22. In fact, nearly all the mainstream Descartes scholars—Frankfurt, Kenny, Williams, Curley, Margaret Wilson, etc. have tried in various ways to absolve Descartes of the circularity charge; I shall also attempt this, following a suggestion made by Wolterstorff. Regardless of these attempts, they are all universally agreed that Descartes' arguments for God's existence all fail, so that the lack of circularity in his argument is ultimately neither

The Deceiver Hypothesis

My contention is that he need not have. Descartes has the resources within his system to explicate his strategy in such a way that he does not argue in a circle or commit any other invidious error in the course of eliminating the Evil Genius hypothesis. To begin with, let me outline that strategy in the manner that I think best characterizes what Descartes is up to.

In the first *Meditation*, Descartes adopts the attitude of methodological doubt, according to which he is resolved to doubt every proposition for which he can find any reason, even the most remote, for thinking that it might be false. This methodological assumption is neutral with regard to the actual truth of the propositions that Descartes calls into doubt; indeed, he thoroughly expects to be able to vindicate many of them by the end of the *Meditations*. He follows this method through the rest of that *Meditation* but in the second *Meditation* discovers a fact—his own existence—concerning which he cannot be mistaken, hence which he cannot doubt. At this point, the principle of methodological doubt is discharged as having served its purpose; at the same time, global skepticism has been refuted by showing that not everything is dubitable. Although there was no guarantee that the use of this method would lead to the discovery of anything immune to doubt, Descartes claims that it has done so in fact. Having done its work, there is no longer any reason to employ that method. However, to proceed from the fact of his own existence to any more substantive result requires that he develop or adopt some further method whose employment, though not guaranteed in advance to achieve any substantive results, promises at least that possibility. Descartes finds this in what we might call the *assumption of methodological certainty*, which investigates the certainty of the *Cogito* in order to develop a general account of the conditions for certainty which he can then apply to other cases in the hopes of arriving at something that excludes the existence of the Evil Genius and thus removes the threat of demon-based skepticism which, as we have seen, is the only really substantive ground for skepticism.

Descartes arrives at the criterion of clear and distinct perception or conception as the mark of certainty on the grounds that it was due to his having clearly and distinctly perceived his own existence that he was able to grasp that fact with certainty. He thus proposes to accept as true whatever he clearly and distinctly perceives/conceives to be true. This, as I understand it, is neither a dogmatic claim on Descartes' part nor something he proposes as a self-evident truth but instead a methodological proposal,

---

here nor there. It is here that I part company with them; I fully intend to argue that Descartes' arguments for God's existence can be vindicated and thus that his project can be completed.

a kind of hypothesis to be justified in terms of its results in application.[23] There is no guarantee in advance that such results will be attained; however, if the intended results do obtain, then our methodological procedure will have been vindicated by means of the results of its employment, i.e. by its *success* in helping us reach a significant desired result. There is nothing circular about this procedure, which proceeds by way of assumption and hypothesis; it is commonly employed in logic, mathematics and natural science, though in different ways. So, the fact that Descartes begins from the assumption that whatever he clearly and distinctly perceives/conceives is true and then concludes that he was correct in making this assumption given the results he has been able to derive from it is no more circular than adopting an hypothesis as the basis for a research program in natural science and then arguing that the hypothesis has been vindicated due to the success of that hypothesis in explaining otherwise inexplicable phenomena or through having been confirmed by observation and experiment.[24]

We can go one step further: given the manner in which the principle that *whatever I clearly and distinctly perceive/apprehend is true* has been methodologically vindicated, i.e. through our having arrived at knowledge of the existence of a veracious God, we are now in a position to affirm that this claim is *categorically true* as well. Since God would be a deceiver (or at any rate less than minimally benevolent) if I could not trust my clear and distinct perceptions, either because I was being manipulated by forces beyond my control or endowed with systematically flawed cognitive faculties, a veracious God will not permit this to happen.[25] As such, it follows

---

23. It is to be noted that in the passage in which Descartes makes this proposal, *CSM* translates the sentence as the claim that he now *seems* to be able to take it as a general rule that whatever he clearly and distinctly perceives is true, not that he knows this to be true with certainty.

24. As is noted by Nicholas Wolterstorff in *John Locke and the Ethics of Belief*, 201–2; However, Wolterstorff cashes this out in purely psychological terms and still believes that Descartes fails, since his argument for God's existence is not compelling. A similar defense of Descartes is mounted in Alan Gewirth, "The Cartesian Circle," *Philosophical Review* 50, (1941) and by Harry Frankfurt in his article "Descartes's Validation of Reason," reprinted in Willis Doney, ed., *Descartes: A Collection of Critical Essays*, 209–26 and his book *Dreams, Demons and Madmen*, 29–30. Both these sources treat the relevant distinction as one between subjective (constituted by mere inability to doubt) and objective certainty rather than, as I do, as the distinction between intrinsic and extrinsic certainty, both of which are forms of objective certainty as they construe this term.

25. It does not follow, of course, that I cannot mistakenly believe that something is clear and distinct when it is not, as Descartes seems to have done with regard, e.g., to the nature of body and the laws of motion. All that is guaranteed here is what Descartes himself demands, i.e., that any mistakes I make are due to my own negligence and in prin-

that it must be the case that whatever I clearly and distinctly perceive to be true is true, hence that the proposition to that effect, i.e., the claim that *whatever I clearly and distinctly perceive is true* is also true. Again, there is no circle here. The principle that whatever I clearly and distinctly perceive is true does not function, at its first appearance, as a premise in a proof for God's existence, but instead merely as a methodological assumption suggested by reflection on the *cogito* and provisionally employed by us in the hopes of arriving at something (in this case, knowledge of God's existence) that will eliminate the logical possibility of the Evil Genius hypothesis. To use the principle in this way does not require us to so much as even suppose that the principle in question is true, let alone clearly and distinctly known to be so; from this point of view, then, it is not the truth but rather the methodological *usefulness* of this principle that is in question and its usefulness is vindicated by its success in guiding us to an apprehension of God's existence, which in turn allows us to exclude the logical possibility of Demon-deception.[26] However, a byproduct of this happy outcome is that we can now justify the truth of the claim that *whatever I clearly and distinctly conceive is true* in the foregoing manner.

Of course, unless it were substantively true that *whatever I clearly and distinctly conceive is true* this strategy could not have succeeded, so there is a sense in which the proof for God's existence does presuppose the substantive truth of this claim. Nevertheless, once again this does not result in any invidious circularity. After all, when we assume an hypothesis for the purposes of scientific investigation, we do so with the recognition that this hypothesis will not guide us to the truth unless it is itself substantively true; it does not follow from this that we are arguing in a circle when we claim to have confirmed that hypothesis through observation or experiment, despite the fact that we could not have confirmed the hypothesis in question if it were not substantively true. In one sense, the substantive truth of an hypothesis is a necessary condition for the possibility of its confirmation, but given that it does not guarantee that the hypothesis *will be* confirmed by the course of investigation, there is no circularity in the claim that the course of investigation does in fact confirm that hypothesis.

---

ciple correctible using the very cognitive faculties I employed improperly to arrive at my erroneous views; see chapter 9 below. The principle that whatever I clearly and distinctly perceive is true must be understood within this stricture.

26. That is to say, it is not necessary that Descartes even believe that this proposition is true; it is sufficient that he simply *accept* that proposition provisionally in order to see how it plays out. On this distinction, see William P. Alston, "Belief, Acceptance and Religious Faith," in Jordan and Howard-Snyder, eds. *Faith, Freedom and Rationality*, 3–12.

The same holds in this context as well. In one sense, the substantive truth of the claim that *whatever I clearly and distinctly conceive is true* is a necessary condition of the successful employment of the strategy it recommends in arriving at the apprehension of God's existence; however, this amounts merely to the harmless form of dependence just mentioned. Since the claim that whatever I clearly and distinctly conceive is true did not have to be known to be true (nor even believed to be true, but merely accepted provisionally for the sake of inquiry) in order for us to achieve that result, our having achieved it does count as a genuine vindication of that principle and a good, non-circular confirmation of its categorical truth.

Nevertheless, our subsequent recognition that this claim is categorically true certainly helps reinforce our confidence in that claim as it functions as a methodological principle within philosophical inquiry; any objections to the principle that might be urged from the possibility that it could be categorically false have thereby been laid to rest and with it the formal possibility that Descartes inevitably argues in a circle in the *Meditations*. More than this, it actually *vindicates* our use of that method by showing that it is, in fact, sound and our initial confidence in it well-placed. Thus, once we have sorted all of this out, we can affirm without fear of begging the question both that (in a sense) the possibility of proving that God exists depends on the substantive truth of the claim that whatever I clearly and distinctly conceive is true and yet that it is only by first having proved that God exists that we can be confident that the claim that whatever I clearly and distinctly perceive is categorically true—so much, then, for the Cartesian circle! Of course, this is where the *real* work begins: we must vindicate Descartes' claim to have a clear and distinct idea of God and justify his assertions about the implications of our possession of that concept for God's existence.

Clarity and Distinctness in Relation to Certainty

To begin with, then, this matter needs to be looked into a bit further. Descartes apparently takes it to be the case that for me to clearly and distinctly perceive/conceive something is sufficient for my knowing that it is true, whereas in fact it seems to be no more than necessary. For example, no matter how clearly and distinctly I perceive, say, that I am seated at my desk typing right now, this claim is trumped by the possibility that an Evil Genius exists. The reason for this is that, given that possibility, the distinction between the experiential content by means of which I clearly and distinctly perceive that state-of-affairs and the state-of-affairs intended by that content, what we might call its *object*, is such that I could be in possession of the former even though there is nothing distinct from consciousness to which it corresponds. The Evil Genius could be directly affecting my senses (or my intentional field of consciousness) in such a way to make it appear that I am sitting at my desk typing right now when in fact no external world exists at all.

In other cases, however, it can be the case that what I am aware of clearly and distinctly is also certain for me in such a way as to exclude the possibility of demon-deception. So, suppose I describe my current experience by saying that it appears to me that I am sitting at my desk typing at the current moment. Here I am merely describing how the world appears to be to me given my clear and distinct apprehension of the experiential contents I am currently aware of. I am not making any claim about the external world at all, but merely about the contents of my own mind. Since nothing that I assert transcends consciousness as such, there is in this case a happy coincidence between content and object; they are in fact one and the same thing, i.e., a certain ordered sequence of *qualia* occurring in consciousness that intends a putative state-of-affairs in the external world. Considered in themselves, those contents are nothing more than subjective, mind-dependent mental events whose reality is exhausted by my awareness of them; they have neither hidden aspects nor any features constituting them independently of my consciousness awareness. All the facts about those contents are what Thomas Nagel calls *subjective* facts,[27] since they are true only of my unique and private stream of consciousness. Since there is in this case no distinction between appearance and reality since both content and object possess merely intramental existence as contents/objects of conscious awareness, there is no room either for error or for demon-deception so long as I clearly and distinctly perceive those contents/objects. The absolute certainty with which I grasp those subjective facts under those circumstances cannot be undermined or gainsaid by any skeptical hypothesis.

Subjective facts are not the only sorts of facts about which I can have certainty, however. As Descartes argues, there are certain objective facts of which we can become apprised in introspection. For example, the certainty with which I grasp certain subjective facts, such as *that I am appeared to redly* or *that I doubt the senses as a source of knowledge* makes me aware on reflection that there is such a thing as subjectivity itself, i.e., my apprehension of my own experiential contents as events occurring in consciousness, hence as modifications of consciousness, likewise involves

---

27. See Thomas Nagel, "What is it like to be a Bat?" in *Mortal Questions*, 170–75.

awareness of myself as conscious, however implicit or inchoate this awareness may be in ordinary circumstances. By the same token, my awareness of myself as conscious, a fact expressible in the proposition "I think," involves a general awareness of consciousness as an ongoing mental process or activity, i.e., *conscious awareness*, itself a modification of a more general process or activity, i.e., structured process or activity or *being*, of which mental activity is only one potential variety. By the same token, in being aware of consciousness as structured activity, I am thus made aware of activity-as-such, or *existence*. Thus, in being aware of myself as conscious I am also aware of myself as existent, though again, only implicitly or inchoately so until I engage in a certain line of philosophical reflection: I think, therefore I am.

I shall be at great pains in subsequent chapters to fill in the details of the foregoing account. For now I want to explain in what sense the facts expressed by the propositions "I think" and "I exist" are objective, as opposed to subjective, facts about myself. In the case of subjective facts, as we just saw, the propositions expressing those facts do no more than describe features of my experiential contents, hence are completely dependent on my awareness of them for their existence. However, in the case of "I think" and "I exist," the facts expressed by those propositions are in no way constituted by or dependent upon my reflective, self-conscious awareness of them. To the contrary, I can be conscious and exist without being reflectively aware of either of those facts, as is proved by the fact that, although (as Descartes points out) I can renew my awareness of these facts at will, I am only intermittently aware that I think and that I exist by means of reflective self-consciousness. As such, both my being conscious and my existing are constituted independently of the reflective, self-conscious act of introspection by means of which I am able to apprehend my own consciousness and existence *as such*. In being aware of these facts, then, I am aware of facts which, while given to me in and through consciousness and are essentially about myself, nevertheless transcend consciousness *as such* and succeed in telling me something about the way reality is in itself. In knowing myself in these aspects in this way I thereby know something about reality as well. The propositions "I think" and "I exist" are not merely true about the way things *appear* or *seem* to me to be; they are categorically true or true *simpliciter*, i.e., in the way that any objective truth about reality would be. Indeed, these facts could not appear or seem to me to be so unless they were so independently of the subjective facts by means of which I apprehend them.

This in no way undermines the certainty with which I apprehend the facts that I think and exist on those occasions in which I am reflectively aware of those facts by means of an act of introspection. Obviously, it would not be possible for me to reflectively apprehend either my consciousness and/or my existence at any moment unless I both was conscious and existed at that time. The fact that I am not continuously conscious in a self-reflective way of these facts through the whole term of my life is not due to any limitation in principle on my powers of apprehension, but rather on the exigencies of everyday life and my lack of "mental energy" sufficient to keep up the required level of concentration needed to for this project, for which in any case there seems to be no practical motive or gain. Nothing with regard to my stream of consciousness and its contents, including the existence of that stream of consciousness and of myself as the conscious subject in which that stream of consciousness occurs, lies in principle beyond the examination of introspection, even though it may be impossible as a practical matter for me to exhaustively inspect every aspect of my mental life at every moment of my existence as a conscious subject. There will always be foreground and background, center and periphery in my *intentional field of consciousness*, i.e., the stream of consciousness and its contents as apprehended diachronically at a particular point in time, despite the fact that, given our power of introspection, it is in principle up to us what will be central and peripheral, in the foreground and the background at any particular time.

Descartes, then, is fully justified in concluding that he is absolutely and objectively certain of the facts that he thinks and he exists whenever he contemplates the propositions expressing those facts and that not even God could deceive him about these propositions, since the very possibility of such deception would require that Descartes both be conscious and exist at the time he was deceived. Thus, in accordance with Augustine's *Si fallor, sum* argument, Descartes can refute the skeptic by noting that if I am mistaken, I am both conscious and exist, even if I believe that I am conscious and exist on the basis of a fallacious argument, since this scenario cannot be so much as formulated without making these assumptions. As such, the certainty with which I grasp my own consciousness and existence trumps the deceiving God and Evil Genius hypotheses with regard to the propositions expressing the facts that I am conscious and exist. These are things I know, in the full and proper, internalist/Platonist sense of justified, true belief and represent knowledge of which, as Augustine puts it, "no Greek can dispossess me."

Intrinsic vs. Extrinsic Certainty

So far, we have recognized two general classes of propositions, those whose certainty is trumped by the Evil Genius hypothesis, no matter how clearly and distinctly we perceive them and those which, when clearly and distinctly perceived, trump both the deceiving God and Evil Genius hypotheses. We now need to look more closely into how this all works in each of these cases and to consider other cases, such as those involving putatively self-evident truths such as *2+3=5*, *every square has four sides* and the validity of *modus ponens*.

To begin with, we need to note that, while clear and distinct perception/conception is a necessary condition for the certainty of anything that we apprehend by means of it, it is not the source of that certainty. Rather, it is the experiential content apprehended in clear and distinct perception/conception that is the source of the certainty with which that apprehension is accompanied. Thus, it is the experiential content of my clear and distinct perception *that I am appeared to redly*, i.e., the red *quale* immediately present to consciousness in such a way that I cannot be mistaken or deceived with regard to it, that grounds my certainty of that subjective fact. Further, it is only because of this that I can know that I am not *in fact* deceived with regard my state of mind at the time I report that I am appeared to redly. The mere general truth that I cannot be deceived with regard to the immediate experiential contents of my own consciousness does not, by itself, justify my certainty that I am appeared to redly at some particular time; only the experiential content of my perceptual field at that time can accomplish this.

The same holds of my certainty with regard to the facts expressed by the propositions "I think" and "I exist." It is only because I grasp (however intermittently) my own stream of consciousness and my own existence *as such* that I can apprehend these facts with certainty. Were this not so, I would not be able to "trump" the foregoing skeptical hypotheses in this context. From the mere realization that not even an omnipotent God can deceive me about whether or not I am conscious or exist *if* I am conscious or exist, it does not follow that I am conscious or exist; all that follows from this is that these two states of affairs, i.e., my actually contemplating my own stream of consciousness or my own existence and my being deceived about whether I am conscious or exist are incompatible with one another.[28]

---

28. *Pace* Janet Broughton's interpretation of the method of doubt as involving "dependence arguments" a similar point applies. All her dependence arguments take the form of hypothetical syllogisms, from which it at most follows that *if* I exist, then I cannot be mistaken in so thinking. But to make the categorical affirmation that I exist, I need to

The Deceiver Hypothesis

I know that I am not in fact deceived in this manner only through my prior reflective, self-conscious, clear and distinct apprehension of myself as both conscious and existent. My certainty with regard to these facts is logically prior to, and hence must be independent of, my realization that this apprehension is "demon-proof," i.e., that error or deception is impossible in this context. Only in this case can I "trump" the Evil Genius hypothesis. *Cogito, ergo Sum* precedes rather than depends on *Si Fallor, Sum*.

It appears necessary, then, to distinguish two kinds of certainty, each of which is implicated in my apprehension of facts such as that I am appeared to redly, I am conscious and I exist. The first of these, what we might call *intrinsic certainty*, is the certainty resulting from the clear and distinct perception/conception of an experiential content in those circumstances in which that content is *indubitable* for me because it is inconceivable that this proposition be false, where the appropriate standard for inconceivability is inconceivability in the conception. This is a common feature of mathematical and logical truths, such as 2+2=4 or $\sim(P\&\sim P)$, and some other stock examples (There are no square circles, Nothing can be both red all over and green all over at the same time.) The second of these, *extrinsic certainty*, is possessed by a subset of those propositions that are intrinsically certain that possess the additional property that their contents "trump" the deceiving God hypothesis (here taken as a convenient surrogate for the whole class of skeptical scenarios) by virtue of the character of that content itself. For example, the identity of the experiential content of my perceptual state with its intentional object in the case of "I am appeared to redly" rules out the possibility of demon-deception in that case. Similarly, since I cannot be aware of the contents of my own stream of consciousness without being conscious and existent, my immediate awareness of any experiential content whatsoever presupposes that I am both conscious and actually existent. Finally, given the propositional content of the claim "If I am deceived, I exist," it follows that I cannot be wrong in affirming this proposition, since the supposition that an omnipotent God is deceiving me about the truth of this proposition entails the truth of its antecedent, which, in turn, cannot be true in this particular case unless the consequent

---

have at least one categorical premise, e.g. "I think" in order to derive this further conclusion. But that is precisely what Descartes' claims to have proven. As such, I think we need to conclude that there is more to the *Cogito* than Broughton's dependence strategy. On Augustine's *si fallor, sum* argument, see the classic article "Si Fallor, Sum" by Gareth Matthews in Hilary Armstrong, ed., *Augustine: A Collection of Critical Essays*, 151–67, which inspired my comments here.

is as well, since I must exist in order to be deceived. By hypothesis, then, this is one thing about which the Evil Genius cannot deceive me.

More formally, we can say that a proposition is extrinsically certain for me whenever it is either a) such that its content is identical with its object (e.g., I am appeared to redly), b) such that the actual presence to consciousness of that content is impossible unless that content is veridical (e.g., I think, I exist), or c) such that my clear and distinct apprehension/understanding of that content is sufficient to provide incorrigible evidence for the truth of the proposition expressing that content (e.g., a proposition such as "If I am deceived by the Evil Genius, I exist"). Let us call any proposition of this sort *incorrigibly certain* for me.

It is clear, then, that my clear and distinct perception/conception of certain experiential contents carries with it both intrinsic and extrinsic certainty, what we might call *absolute* or *fully objective* certainty due to its being incorrigibly certain for me. However, there is no obvious necessity in the claim that intrinsic certainty must always be accompanied by extrinsic certainty. It seems not only conceivable that an experiential content might possess intrinsic but not extrinsic certainty but to be actually the case. Consider the following propositions: *2+3=5, Every square has four sides* and *If P then Q, P, therefore Q*. It is hard to imagine any mental contents that possess a higher degree of intrinsic certainty than those that inform us of the truth of these claims. The truth of these propositions appears to be self-evident, inasmuch as we know that they are true as soon as we understand them and their denials are not even coherently conceivable. Even so, there is no aspect of their content which directly bears on the possibility of the deceiving God hypothesis; in particular, there is nothing about these contents that provides any *positive* ground for excluding the possibility of demon-deception or other extrinsic sources of error as we saw were present in the cases we considered previously.

At the same time, however, we note that the deceiving God/Evil Genius hypotheses do not function with regard to these mental contents in the same way they do those that lack intrinsic certainty. For example, an ordinary perceptual content that intends some extramental state-of-affairs, such as would constitute the fact expressible by the proposition "I am typing at the present moment" lacks intrinsic certainty because the experiential content which inclines me to affirm that proposition is distinct from its object in such a way that the content in question could be occurring in consciousness without the existence of the state-of-affairs which is its putative cause. Indeed, it is precisely here that God or the Evil Genius could be exercising his nefarious powers of deception. In such case, the lack of intrinsic certainty residing in the experiential content provides the grist for a deceiving God/Evil Genius scenario providing a *positive ground* for doubting the proposition in question. In the case of a proposition such as 2+3=5, however, the deceiving God hypothesis represents only a *negative ground* for doubt insofar as that hypothesis is not contradicted by the experiential content of the mental act by means of which I clearly and distinctly conceive that proposition. That an omnipotent God is deceiving me about the truth of this apparently self-evident proposition is literally inconceivable for me; nevertheless, this does not amount to a positive ground for excluding such a possibility, since this involves *only* inconceivability in the conception, *not* in what is being conceived.

As such, the foregoing seems sufficient to produce the state of cognitive dissonance described by Descartes in his account of the epistemic plight of the atheist. On the one hand, the atheist cannot doubt the truth of a claim like 2+3=5 given the positive evidence provided by his apprehension; on the other, the possibility of a deceiving God continues to provide a ground for doubting this proposition, albeit a merely negative one. Of course, unless one were able to apprehend the intrinsic certainty of those mental contents that possess it independently of consideration of the deceiving God hypothesis, then the envisaged case would not be possible any more than it could be the case that the intrinsic certainty of other experiential contents could make available the resources needed to "trump" the deceiving God hypothesis in other cases. Since both of these are clearly the case, however, it is likewise clear that we can clearly and distinctly perceive the intrinsic certainty of those experiential contents that possess intrinsic certainty independently of whether or not they are extrinsically certain as well. What Descartes proposes to do, then, is provide a way out of this state of cognitive dissonance, one which will be available to the theist but not the atheist.

Descartes' Way Out

Descartes proposes to eliminate the vestigial challenge of the deceiving God and Evil Genius hypotheses by demonstrating the actual non-existence of these beings. He does this by proving the existence of a veracious God whose benevolence and love of truth logically excludes the logical possibilities envisaged in these hypotheses. This proof will have to proceed from claims that are knowable with intrinsic certainty linked together in some fashion that is certainty-preserving and capable of endowing that certainty on the claim that God, conceived of as a perfect being, exists thus rendering it extrinsically certain as well, since as Descartes claims, it cannot both be the case that a perfect being exists and that it be the case that this being is a deceiver or that an Evil Genius exists. This proof-process will have to obey the strictures of Descartes' method as outlined in the *Discourse*. First, the steps in the proof-process will have to be simple enough and the links between them small enough that we can clearly and distinctly perceive/conceive them, thus apprehending them with intrinsic certainty. Secondly, these steps and their links will need to be organized in such a way that there are systematic connections leading from one to another in an orderly and compelling fashion. Finally, the entire series of steps and their links must be examined, rehearsed and made so familiar that the entire proof-process can become the experiential content of a single mental act clearly and distinctly perceiving that process as a whole, in a single glance as it were, thereby grasping it with extrinsic certainty.

Although the propositions "God exists and is not a deceiver" is hardly extrinsically certain as it stands, it is at least possible that the foregoing process, if successful, could reveal the intrinsic certainty of the fact expressible by means of that proposition and the incompatibility of its truth with the claim that the Evil Genius does. In that case, "God exists" would possess extrinsic certainty as well, since its clear implication would provide a ground for ruling out the possibility of demon-deception, through ruling out the skeptical scenarios that would give rise to that possibility. Such a claim would therefore possess absolute certainty for us. Just as a valid and sound deductive proof is capable of displaying or revealing the apodictic truth of its conclusion, which may neither have been obvious nor even intuitive to us before, the proof-process outlined above bids fair, if successful, to reveal the extrinsic certainty of the existence of God despite the fact that this is neither intuitive nor obvious to mere casual contemplation or the natural attitude informed by pre-reflective experience. We can only discover whether or not this is so by making the attempt.

However, the proof will not take the form of a deductive argument proceeding from self-evident truths grasped by rational intuition *via* the rules of logic (grasped by the same faculty) to the conclusion that God exists, for this is precisely the kind of proof procedure that Descartes has suggested a deceiving God might be capable of deceiving us about. Instead, the proof as I will reconstruct it consists of the immediate, introspective apprehension of a series of ontologically dependent facts related by what I will call the EOG (existent to ontological ground) relation, terminating in the apprehension of the fact that God exists as both my *per se* and exemplary cause. The words used to articulate this proof are merely intended to make explicit and to clearly display what we are already implicitly and inchoately aware of in introspection, i.e., to allow us to clearly and distinctly apprehend these facts, their relations to one another and the implications of these facts for the epistemological project initiated by Descartes. The method employed will be that of directed meditation, similar to that used by Descartes himself in his work of that name, but carried out in a much more careful, detailed and radical fashion than Descartes himself attempted it. The hope is that we may cover the same ground as he did and arrive with him at the place he intended us to find and to do so without circularity or circumlocution.

Where Do We Go from Here?

I conclude, then, that there is circularity neither in the strategy employed in Descartes' Meditations to establish the existence of God nor in the proof-process used by him to establish God's existence. The next step, then, will be to turn to the question of whether God's existence can in fact be established in the fashion that Descartes thought it could. The rest of this book will be devoted to the discussion of this question and to supplying a positive answer to it. Although the proof-process I will follow is inspired to some extent by Descartes' own arguments, I will follow Austin Farrer in attempting to show that a sustained, introspective meditation on the contents of consciousness ultimately results in an intuitive apprehension of God, mediated by my own creaturely existence and nature. In other words, there is a special, attenuated sense in which we are all implicitly and inchoately aware of God's existence and nature in and through the self-conscious appropriation in thought of our own existence and nature. That is to say, we are able, by degrees, to make that implicit and inchoate awareness of God, there from the beginning, into an explicit intellectual apprehension of God. In still other words, our own existence and nature, functioning as the *imago Dei* in us, serves as the foundation for an *itineram mentis ad Deum* culminating in a non-mystical or intellectual intuition of God as a perfect being. In this sense, and in this sense only, the thesis of this book is that *we see God* with eye of our mind and in so knowing Him we acquire the foundation for knowing everything else. Is this too good to be true or too much to hope for? I invite the reader to come along and see for him- or herself.

3

Skepticism and the *Cogito*

BY THE end of the first *Meditation*, Descartes has persuaded himself that all of his former opinions have been called into question, including his belief in an external world. In the second *Meditation*, Descartes rouses himself to see if he can salvage anything from the world-wreck his methodological doubt has precipitated. It is not long, however, before he is able to report that he has arrived at a belief that is beyond question and a likely candidate for the foundational bit of knowledge which will serve as the Archimedean point for a refutation of skepticism. People who know nothing else about philosophy know that Descartes said *Cogito ergo sum* and most of them would erroneously attribute this claim to the body of his *Meditations*. As has been pointed out, however, the *Cogito* is hardly Descartes' unique discovery or even something not widely accepted. It is, in fact, a commonplace admitted even by philosophers whose methods and teachings are quite foreign to those of Descartes.[1] This ought not to surprise us; Descartes is not attempting to foist some odd or unconventional foundation for knowledge upon us; instead, he wants to appeal to something which will be admitted by all. The significance of the *Cogito* in Descartes and its impact on philosophy is a consequence of how he uses this shopworn insight as the foundation for a new way of doing philosophy, one which he pioneered without bringing it to fruition. In this chapter, I propose to explain what I mean by this.

First of all, I will explore the role of the *Cogito* in the refutation of skepticism. Here I will focus not on Descartes, but on the discussion of self-knowledge in Augustine of Hippo, one of the primary philosophical influences on Descartes.[2] Reversing the order of the last chapter, here I

---

1. See, e.g., the selections by Jean de Silhon in Ariew, Cottingham and Sorrell, eds., *Descartes' Meditations: Background Source Materials*, Cambridge, Cambridge University Press, 1998, 177–200; see especially 199–200.

2. On the influence of Augustine during Descartes' time and on Descartes himself, see Stephen Menn, *Descartes and Augustine*, 3–70. For a comparative study that emphasizes both similarities and differences between the views of Augustine and Descartes, see Gareth

will argue that Augustine's *Si Fallor, Sum* argument provides all that is required in order to refute the global skeptic and indicate the introspective foundation for human knowledge. When I turn to Descartes' *Cogito*, I will treat it positively as the entrée into a realm of knowledge revealed to us by introspection, a new realm of knowledge not heretofore explored by philosophers, and, in particular, ignored by Descartes' Scholastic predecessors. I shall suggest that Descartes' discovery of interiority as an object of theoretical inquiry is his most signal achievement in philosophy and that far from being the beginning of the end where philosophy is concerned deserves greater attention and holds greater promise than Descartes' critics are willing to credit. Although Descartes certainly miscarried in his attempts to arrive at the principles of a new philosophy, this does not show that there is anything necessarily wrong with his starting point. To the contrary, I suggest that we need to return to Descartes' discovery and try to do a better job of it than he did. How this may be done will the subject of the remaining chapters of this book.

Augustine's Refutation of Skepticism

It has often been noted that Augustine's *Confessions* is the first true autobiography in the modern sense, because unlike other classical "histories" and "lives" of notable individuals it is the first such document which takes us inside the mind and heart of its author. It is not surprising in one sense that this should be so, since Augustine's *Confessions* is intended above all to be the record of Augustine's conversion and cannot be told without taking us deep into the mental and emotional development of Augustine from his early childhood until the time he finally and irrevocably embraces the Christian religion at the age of 32. Since the *Confessions* is the story of Augustine's—or rather of his soul's—journey to God, it is a classic early exercise in the *itineram mentis* tradition. At the same time, however, it is also Socratic and Platonic as well, since it is both the search for adequate self-knowledge in accordance with the Delphic admonition and involves a turning away from the senses and the quotidian realm in order to seek for that truth within. Indeed, Augustine credits reading the works of the neo-Platonists as a crucial first step in turning away from a life of sybaritic luxury and the pursuit of worldly success and toward genuine fulfillment in the religious life.

For Augustine, Christianity is the true philosophy, which makes sense given that he understands philosophy in the way that post-Aristotelian

---

Matthews, *Thought's Ego*, Ithaca, NY, Cornell University Press, 1992.

Hellenistic philosophers do, as the search, not for theoretical knowledge for its own sake, but instead in the essentially religious sense in which philosophy is the search for happiness through the possession of a wisdom capable of securing our happiness—or at least our equilibrium—in an uncertain and threatening world.[3] On this view, the study of philosophy is a practical, goal-oriented activity and the test of a philosophy resides in its ability to deliver true and lasting happiness to its devotees. As such, we do not find Augustine doing philosophy for its own sake; nevertheless, in developing his version of the *itineram mentis* tradition, of which Descartes is a variant, we find him considering a number of philosophical problems and doing a good deal of creditable philosophical work. One issue that exercised the early Augustine was skepticism and the nature of knowledge. In fact, he devoted his only purely philosophical work, the *Contra Academicos* of 387 CE, to the discussion of this topic. To begin with, then, let us review Augustine's understanding of what skepticism is and how it best ought to be refuted.

Augustine Against the Skeptics

Augustine's primary source for the teachings of the Skeptics is Cicero's *Academica*, a dialogue in which Cicero and his interlocutors discuss the pros and cons of skepticism. In turn, Cicero embraces the non-dogmatic skepticism of Philo of Larissa, founder of the so-called Fourth Academy.[4] The distinctive teachings of this school, as opposed to the older version of Skepticism developed by the Academy under Arcesilaus and Carneades, were the rejection of dogmatic skepticism and the adoption of a probabilistic theory of rational belief. According to Philo, the earlier skeptics embraced the self-refuting position that nothing can be known, which must be false if proposed to be true, thus making the skeptical position incoherent. It is better that the skeptic should make the more moderate claim that so far as we are aware there is nothing beyond doubt, dispute and the possibility of error and so believe accordingly. However, according to Philo, this admission is consistent with the idea that some beliefs are

---

3. Menn, *Descartes and Augustine*, 73–4 and 130–33 emphasizes the point that Augustine sees his conversion to Christianity as the culmination of his search for wisdom. On the attitude of post-Aristotelian Hellenistic philosophers to the search for wisdom, see Giovanni Reale, *The Systems of the Hellenistic Age*, 5–15. Concerning the attitude and contributions of Augustine and other Christian thinkers to philosophy, see Christopher Stead, *Philosophy in Christian Antiquity*, 80–93.

4. My main sources for the teachings of Philo and Antiochus are Giovanni Reale, *The Systems of the Hellenistic Age*, 347–65 and John Dillon, *The Middle Platonists*, 52–69.

more probable or have a greater degree of verisimilitude than others. Unlike Carneades, who treated probability or verisimilitude as simply a matter of the force and vivacity of presentations, Philo treats verisimilitude as an objective property of presentations, an innovation required in response to his student Antiochus's major criticism of Carneades' position. Carneades had denied, as part of his critique of Stoicism, that we could distinguish *cataleptic* (veridical) from *acataleptic* (non-veridical) presentations due to the lack of a certain criterion for distinguishing these two classes of presentations. Antiochus had countered that Carneades' argument, depending as it does on the claim that there are false presentations, collapses as soon as we recognize this fact. After all, if there is no certain criterion for distinguishing true from false presentations, then we cannot know that there are any false presentations and skepticism cannot even get off the ground. In other words, in order for me to be able to judge that there is no certain mark differentiating true from false presentations, I need to be able to compare examples of each kind in order to establish this. Philo's position represents a retreat from ontological to merely epistemological skepticism in that he no longer challenges the claim that there is such a distinction but only the claim that we are in possession of it. Nevertheless, some propositions have more probable truth or verisimilitude than others and thus are more reasonable to believe than others.

Cicero, a student of Philo's and a fellow-student of Antiochus', feels called upon in the *Academica* to embrace and defend his master's position; Augustine, however, though a Ciceronian in rhetoric and writing style sides with Antiochus against the mitigated skepticism of Philo. Having retreated from the dogmatic skepticism of Carneades, which denies that there is any such thing as truth and treats probability as merely a phenomenological feature of presentations, Philo has been forced to give an objective reference to the notion of truth, hence to the notions of probable truth and verisimilitude ("truth-likeness"). Augustine's point in *Contra Academicos* (using perhaps an argument of Antiochus himself) is that this admission is fatal, since we can now no longer "read off" the probability of propositions simply from how they appear to us—their apparent or intrinsic plausibility. Since Philo has made truth an objective standard, the possibility of applying the terms "probable truth" or "verisimilitude" to propositions requires that we actually possess knowledge of the truth in order to make sense of these attributions. Philo's epistemological skepticism, then, turns out to be as untenable as the dogmatic skepticism of Carneades, though for different reasons. Either Philo admits that we have knowledge of the objective truth, in which case he must abandon skepticism, or he no longer has any non-arbitrary basis for making assignments of probability, verisimilitude or likeliness to be true, which seems to be required if skepticism is to be a viable philosophy of life capable of leading us to happiness.[5]

Having refuted skepticism on its own terms, Augustine turns to the task of positive epistemology, maintaining that there are, in fact, truths that we know for certain and of which no trickery of the Greeks can dispossess us. Again, Augustine challenges the skeptical strategy as it was known to him, which is to call into question any knowledge-claim by suggesting that one might be mistaken about that claim and demanding some sort of proof or evidence for it, which in turn leads to the classic dilemma concerning epistemic justification. Augustine proposes to short-circuit this strategy by exhibiting a series of examples of types of beliefs that are grasped by me indubitably and incorrigibly and thus immune from the demand for further justification. In the case of three such examples, namely, his knowledge of his own existence, life and love/desire, Augustine claims to have found propositions that withstand the very possibility of doubt on the ground that such a possibility presupposes the falsity of what is being entertained. Let us now turn to Augustine's discussion of his positive epistemology.

Augustine: Things We Know

In Book Three of the *Contra Academicos*, Augustine presents examples of things we know with certainty as a direct disproof of the claims of the skeptics to the effect that there is no knowledge.[6] He distinguishes three classes of such objects. First, there are *formal truths*, such a mathematical or logical truths, which are knowable *a priori* due to their intrinsic self-evidence; these include propositions such as 2+2=4 and "Either the external world exists or it fails to exist." Augustine's examples, especially of the latter sort, strongly suggest that the self-evidence of these truths is due to their logical form rather than some sort of necessity *a posteriori*, though he does not hesitate to classify the proposition "Either the external world exists or it fails to exist" as a principle of physics. Since these sharp distinctions did not exist in Augustine's time, he can be excused for not having clarified this point. The second class of things we know are the immediate contents of our conscious states, i.e., how things appear to us in, e.g., visual perception. Even if there is no external world, it nevertheless remains that it certainly appears to be the case that there is such a world and this

---

5. Augustine, *Contra Academicos*, translated by Peter King, 5–25.
6. Ibid., 72–78.

is something that I can be certain about. Augustine appears to adopt the "adverbial" theory of such contents, such that my current visual experience of a red patch is best characterized in Chisholmian terms as the state of my *being appeared-to redly*. Since my apprehension of these contents is incorrigible for me, the judgments expressing them are likewise infallible.

The third class of objects of knowledge distinguished by Augustine is the most interesting for our purposes here.[7] Against the skeptic's assertion that I might be mistaken with regard to any and all substantive contingent propositions, Augustine identifies a class of substantive, contingent facts which I immediately and incorrigibly apprehend which includes the facts that *I exist*, that *I am alive* and that *I love/desire*, such that the judgments expressing these facts are themselves indubitable and infallible for me hence known with certainty when affirmed/believed by me. The supposition that I might be mistaken about these propositions and hence that they are doubtful for me is dismissed by Augustine with the phrase *Si fallor, sum*: "If I am mistaken, I exist." According to Augustine, none of the traditional grounds for skepticism can motivate rational doubt in the case of my apprehension of facts of this kind. If I am mistaken, I exist. If I am insane, I exist. If I am dreaming, I exist. If I am being deceived by a god, I exist. So, too, for the claims that I am alive and that I love/desire; I cannot even entertain the possibility that I might be wrong about these facts without having sufficient reason to reject it. As such, concludes Augustine, I do possess some substantive knowledge of which no Greek trickery can dispossess me.

It would appear that Augustine's *Si Fallor, Sum* argument is sufficient to refute the form of skepticism against which it is directed and bears an obvious resemblance to and relevance for the Cartesian *Cogito*. Although Descartes cannot accept Augustine's claim to the effect that we are in possession of formal mathematical and logical truths of the sort proposed as indubitable by Augustine, since these experiential contents are only intrinsically certain for me, hence not demon-proof, it appears that the second and third classes distinguished by Augustine remain as potentially available to Descartes. After all, both classes of examples share in common that they are initially constituted by the immediate apprehension of a non-propositional state of affairs constituting a fact, i.e., something capable of serving

---

7. Augustine actually presents this argument, not in the *Contra Academicos* itself, but in several places, such as *De Libero Arbitrio* 2.3, *De Trinitate* 15.12.21 and *City of God* 11.26; on this see King's edition of the *Contra Academicos*, Appendix Six (158–61) and Appendix Eight (162–3) and Thomas Williams, ed., *On the Free Choice of the Will*, 33. This latter is the passage referred to by Arnauld in the fourth *Objections*. For more on this, see Matthews, *Thought's Ego*, 29–38.

as the truth-conditions for a proposition and grasped in such a way that it can be compared with the judgment expressing or articulating that state-of-affairs by means of propositional content which is, in turn, linguistically accessible. For example, if I am currently appeared-to redly, my judgment to this effect, as expressed in the simple English sentence "I am appeared-to redly" expresses my apprehension of a non-linguistic state-of-affairs or fact. Likewise, if I am aware of my own existence, judge myself to exist and express these judgments in a simple English sentence like "I exist," something similar and just as certain is going on. I shall subsequently argue that this is the case, but in so doing I am not suggesting that Descartes' *Cogito* is a mere retread of Augustine's *Si Fallor, Sum* response to skepticism.[8] To the contrary, Descartes is engaged in something more, i.e., providing a positive account of how we acquire knowledge of our own existence through the introspective investigation of the structures of consciousness. After briefly considering the account given by Descartes and his clarifications of his view in response to objections, I shall attempt in the next chapter to outline the account of introspective knowledge presupposed by Descartes' account and fill in some of the details required to make this account adequate to the tasks of contemporary epistemology.

---

8. As Arnauld obliquely suggests in the fourth *Objections*—see *CSM*, 139. In reply, Descartes simply thanks Arnauld (in a backhanded way) for having invoked the authority of St. Augustine on his behalf. He gives no indication of being aware of or having consciously borrowed from Augustine on this point. Descartes was not a scholar and seems to have been rather proud of this fact; he bragged, for example to William Cavendish, Marquess of Newcastle, that the only algebra book that he had ever read was the textbook by Clavius used at La Fleche. In a 1640 letter to Colvius (no relation to Clavius), Descartes implies that he never read or heard of Augustine's *si fallor, sum* argument until Colvius mentioned the matter to him in an earlier letter; on the likelihood of this, see Gareth Matthews, *Thought's Ego*, 12–15. Descartes was notoriously jealous of his originality and vehemently denied that there were any external influences on his thought—not even Galileo has taught him anything! Further, Descartes rejects all reliance on the authority of experts, maintaining that we can only know we ourselves have independently discovered and verified—see, once again, Matthews, *Thought's Ego*, 125–40. Whatever we may think of this, it remains likely that Descartes' Augustinianism more likely reflects the intellectual milieu of his time rather than any close acquaintance with Augustine's own texts. In contrast to the Scholastics, Descartes is one of the first truly modern philosophers in the sense that he both rejects tradition and puts implicit trust in his own cognitive faculties to construct original theories from his own resources superior to any conceived of in the past. Our tendency to treat those who lived in the past as inferior in knowledge and reliability to ourselves is, I think, in large part a reflection of Descartes' attitude, a complete reversal of the pre-Modern view that attributes greater wisdom to the ancients than to our contemporaries.

The *Cogito* as Positive Knowledge of Fact

Having doubted everything that is dubitable, Descartes turns in the second *Meditation* to the task of reconstructing human knowledge beginning from what appears to be only thinnest possible foundation, i.e., his own existence. In fact, in investigating this claim by Descartes we will find an account of our cognitive powers which is remarkably complex and sophisticated implicitly contained in his seemingly simple reflections in the *Meditations*, one which, had he developed and articulated it, would have greatly enhanced the plausibility of many of the views which have only slight attraction for contemporary philosophers. Before doing this, however, let us briefly consider what Descartes does say.

Descartes begins the second *Meditation* by recording his amazement at the results of the first without weakening his resolve to doubt all, including the existence of his own body, the external world and even God insofar as He is conceived as the author of Descartes' own thoughts. Even so, he finds it difficult to persuade himself that he himself might not exist. Even if he is able to persuade himself that nothing is certain, it remains that he is convinced of something and knows this fact, something which is possible only on the supposition that he exists.[9] In a like manner, even for it to be possible for him to doubt his own existence requires that he exist in order to do the doubting, thus undermining any grounds for doubt he might possess through the contemplation of that fact.[10] Even the supposition that there is an Evil Genius who bends all his powers to deceiving Descartes will not undermine his conviction of this fact, since the possibility that he is deceived by the Demon presupposes that he exists, and hence that he is not deceived in any way in so thinking.[11] Indeed, says Descartes, whenever I so much as contemplate the notion of my own existence, or indeed am aware of anything at all, I am by the same token aware of the fact that I exist, or at least, can be aware of this whenever I chose to consider it. Therefore, says Descartes, "I must finally conclude that this proposition 'I am, I exist' is necessarily true whenever it is put forward by me or conceived in my mind."[12]

We immediately note a singular difference between Augustine and Descartes with regard to the status of the claim that I exist. For Augustine, my knowledge of my own existence is taken to be immediate, as though

---

9. See *CSM*, Vol. II., 16–17.

10. Descartes, *Principle of Philosophy*, Sec. 7 in *CSM*, Vol. I, 194–5. See also *The Search for Truth* in *CSM*, Vol. II, 409–10.

11. See *CSM*, Vol. II, 17.

12. See *CSM*, Vol. II, loc. cit.

the fact of my existence were apprehended as such, in complete isolation from all other facts. For Descartes, however, my apprehension of my own existence is not immediate, but mediated by my prior apprehension of myself as thinking.[13] Indeed, it appears that for Descartes the closest I can come to apprehending my own existence directly is by contemplating that fact in thought; even in that case, my awareness of my own existence is precisely such as to be a thought in Descartes' sense, i.e., a content of consciousness.[14] My awareness of my own existence, then, is never direct or immediate for Descartes; instead, it is always mediated by thought, or conscious awareness, even when it is the fact of my own existence of which I am aware. Further, as Descartes himself points out, the fact that I exist is implicated in any and every thought I have no less than the specific thought that I exist—in the French translation of the Meditations Descartes adds the phrase "or thought of anything at all" to the sentence "No, if I convinced myself as something then I certainly existed."[15] It is not some particular thought or thought-content by means of which I become aware of or apprehend my own existence; rather, *it is my apprehension of the fact of my thinking itself which serves as the ground for my apprehension of my own existence.*

None of Descartes' critics are willing to challenge the soundness of the *Cogito* or the truth of the insight it reveals. Presumably none of us are willing to do so either. Nevertheless, the *Cogito* is not entirely unproblematic as Descartes depicts it. After all, what exactly is the relation between

13. Broughton, op cit. 109–17 argues that Descartes does not derive his existence from the fact that he thinks but instead from the impossibility of his doubting that fact. I maintain, to the contrary, that it follows from this "dependence argument" that I exist only if I know that I doubt and thus can affirm a proposition to that effect. Given that doubting is a mental act and thus a mode of thought, I know that I exist only by first knowing that I think this particular thought: "I doubt that I exist." Thus, my knowledge of my own existence is not immediate, but mediated by self-conscious awareness of myself qua thinker: *cogito, ergo sum.*

14. As is well known, Descartes does not restrict the term "thought" merely to acts of the intellectual contemplation of propositional contents, but extends it include every aspect of conscious awareness and every mental content, including passion, feeling and sense-perception. See, for example, the definition of "thought" given in *Principles of Philosophy*, Sec. 9 in *CSM*, Vol. 1, 195. It is to be noted here that all of the terms used to describe various kinds of thought are *verbs* naming *activities* that represent modes of awareness of or operations over mental contents—I am a *thinking* thing, not merely something that *has* (or merely *suffers*) thoughts. Unfortunately, even Descartes himself often slips into characterizing the mind as a kind of substratum in which thoughts "inhere" much as real accidents are taken to do in Aristotelian substances according to the Scholastics. This contributes to the confusion surrounding Descartes' position here.

15. See *CSM*, Vol. II., 16–17 and footnote.

the fact of my thinking and the fact of my existence? The most natural suggestion is that the relation is somehow *inferential*; the fact of my thinking somehow provides proof, evidence or justification for the *proposition* which I express by the English sentence "I exist," or, given that it is difficult to imagine how a proposition could be directly justified by anything non-propositional,[16] for some proposition from which the proposition "I exist" can be inferred by a valid deductive argument. Descartes encourages us to think in this way by using inferentialist language (such as "conclude," "proposition" and "necessarily true" in the *Cogito* passage) and the formula *Cogito ergo Sum* in the *Principles of Philosophy*, Sec. 7 where he even calls it an inference in the French edition of that work.[17] Descartes reinforces this idea in his response to the fifth *Objections* in answer to Gassendi's query as to why Descartes does not infer his existence from the fact that he is walking just as easily as from the fact that he thinks. Descartes responds, not by denying that there the *Cogito* is an inference, but by denying that the premise "I walk" is known with certainty, since I could simply be dreaming that I walk.[18] Descartes does appear to think that one can infer one's own existence from the fact that one is thinking.[19]

The difficulty, of course, is that the inference from "I think" to "I exist" is not formally valid, since its logical form is P /∴ Q. This is not a valid pattern of inference, as a simple truth-table will show. Despite appearances, Descartes denies that I infer "I think" from "I exist," if what we mean by this is by means of formal logic (which, for Descartes, is essentially syllogistic inference):

---

16. For one version of this concern, see Laurence BonJour's contribution to Laurence BonJour and Ernest Sosa, *Epistemic Justification*, London, Blackwell Publishing, 2003, 17–20. See especially the references in fn. 16 on page 19.

17. See *CSM*, Vol. I, 195 and footnote 1.

18. See *CSM*, 229.

19. Commentators have been in general agreement, contrary to what will be argued here, that the *cogito* is intended to express an inference and is thus somehow to be represented by a valid deductive argument. The difficulties with this sort of view were perhaps first driven home by Jaako Hintikka in his classic paper "Cogito ergo sum: Inference or Performance?" reprinted in Doney, *Descartes: A Collection of Critical Essays*, 108–39. While Anthony Kenny, Bernard Williams and Margaret Wilson all express dissatisfaction with Hintikka's performative interpretation of the *cogito*, none of them resist the idea that the *Cogito* is an inference expressible as an argument. For a more recent reconstruction along the same lines, see Husain Sarkar, *Descartes' Cogito*, Cambridge, Cambridge University Press, 2002. No one, of course, denies that the cogito can be expressed as an argument; the question is whether this argument expresses an act of inference. It is this latter that I intend to deny (or at any rate show to be dispensable) in what follows.

> Whenever someone says "I am thinking, therefore I am or I exist," he does not deduce existence from thought by means of a syllogism, but recognizes it as something self-evident by a simple intuition of the mind. This is clear from the fact that if he were deducing it by means of a syllogism, he would have to have had previous knowledge of the major premises "Everything that thinks is, or exists"; yet in fact he learns it from experiencing in his own case that it is impossible that he should think without existing.[20]

He then immediately adds that "It is the nature of our mind to construct general propositions on the basis of our knowledge of particular ones."[21] Whatever Descartes means when he calls the movement in thought from "I think" to "I exist" an inference, he is not talking about a formal deductive inference. Nevertheless, he wants to insist that this movement of thought is both somehow "self-evident" and confers some sort of "necessity" on its "conclusion," using all these terms in ways that cannot be cashed out in formal logical terms.

In a sense, this is all to the good, since at this point in the discussion the principles of formal logic lay just as much under a cloud as any of the other products of rational intuition. In *Principles of Philosophy*, Sec. 5,(20) Descartes gives arguments for doubting even mathematical demonstrations parallel to those he gave against the senses, presenting both a version of the argument from error and the Evil Genius argument. Descartes can hardly have exempted the principles of formal logic from this general ban, given that these are the very principles used in the sort of mathematical demonstrations most well-known to Descartes, i.e., geometrical demonstrations of the sort to be met with in Euclid. Even had he wanted to exempt these principles from the skeptical net he would not have had any non-arbitrary means of doing so, since the same arguments which call mathematical demonstration into question would surely call formal logical demonstrations into question as well. Descartes would be in a very tough spot indeed if the *Cogito* were intelligible to us only if the principles of formal logic could be trusted.

---

20. *CSM*, Vol. II, 100. This is from Descartes' *Replies* to the second set of *Objections* collected by Mersenne.

21. See *CSM*, loc. cit. Descartes' argument here recalls a sophism of Sextus Empiricus against the validity of *modus ponens*. If P /∴ Q is invalid, then Q does not in fact follow from P. On the other hand, if we make the argument formally valid by adding "If P, then Q," the resulting argument is unsound, since "If P, then Q" cannot be true unless P follows from Q by itself; thus, no one is ever justified in accepting the conclusion of an argument with that form.

At the same time, it might be thought that Descartes is still in a very tough spot as things stand, since he is forced to claim that he can know, from the fact that he is thinking, that he exists in such a way as to grasp that fact with self-evidence sufficient to confer extrinsic certainty upon the proposition "I exist" whenever he considers or entertains it and, more than this, to make that necessity available to me in reflection at every waking moment. Once again, the claim seems plausible on the face of it and readily commends itself to us on the basis of the considerations Descartes has offered on its behalf. The difficulty, however, arises when we begin to raise technical, philosophical questions about exactly what is going on here. What sort of "simple intuition of the mind" is Descartes talking about here? How does it work, and, in particular, how does it confer justification amounting to knowledge, let alone self-evident truth, on the claim that I exist? What is the relation between what I apprehend by means of this simple intuition and the propositional content of my justified true belief that I exist, and so on? These are not easy questions to answer, and to take them up will require that we leave Descartes and take up questions and issues which were not current in his time and about which he could not have had any carefully formulated views. At the same time, however, I believe the results will be compatible with the views that Descartes was formulating and thus would have been useful to him had he known about them by way of clarifying and defending the views he explicitly held. To these topics I now turn.

4

Thinking

As Descartes himself notes in his *Replies* to the sixth *Objections*, I cannot know that the fact that my thinking implies my existence unless I know what thinking and existence are.[1] Thus, in order to explore the connection between "I think" and "I exist" in the *Cogito*, it behooves us to begin by attempting to clarify what thinking and existing are. At the same time, in saying this, Descartes does not imply that we can have or form explicit notions of "thinking" and "existing" prior to our meditative investigation of thinking and existing as we experience them. As such, there is no sense in which I must possess fully articulate conceptual knowledge of these realities prior to my recognition of the *Cogito*; rather, "it is quite sufficient that we should know [them] by that inner awareness which regularly precedes reflective awareness."[2] Thus, there is a kind of inchoate or implicit knowledge of what thinking is and what existing is that precedes the *Cogito* and is sufficient for us to recognize its truth and certainty independently of its full articulation. Certainly, even Descartes' critics felt confident enough of this to affirm the truth of the *Cogito* despite the lack of any such analysis. It remains, however, that the task of explaining the relation between thinking and existing and thus explaining *how* it is that the *Cogito* is possible for us is a task which requires that we reflect on thinking and existing in such a way as to raise our inner awareness from the merely implicit and inchoate state it ordinarily possesses to as much explicitness as is necessary to resolve the issues facing us here. In so doing, we will be performing the sort of meditation of which Descartes' early work is an example, although in this case it will be a kind of meditation on the very process/method of meditation itself. In accordance with Descartes' own procedure, we shall begin with what it most evident and accessible to us, i.e., thought, and proceed to examine its main elements as relevant to our investigation here. In particular, we will investigate four

---

1. See *CSM*, Vol. II, 285.
2. Ibid., See also the rest of the paragraph to the end.

significant aspects of thought as Descartes defines it: *conscious awareness, introspection, apprehension* and *judgment*. In clarifying each of these we will at the same time uncover the relation between thinking and existing upon which the *Cogito* relies. However, since this will require more space than one chapter can reasonably provide, I will carry this discussion on into the next chapter where it will be completed.

Conscious Awareness: An Example[3]

Let us begin our investigation of thinking, as Descartes understands the term, with the most accessible sort of case, i.e., simple perceptual experience as enjoyed by a rational, self-conscious personal subject of the sort that I know myself to be. Let us suppose that my current perceptual experience is of a cup of coffee sitting on the table before me. There are, I claim, four main distinguishable elements of my current perceptual experience:

1. The (putative) *intentional object* of my current perceptual experience: i.e., the (putative) cup of coffee on the table.

2. The *intentional content* of my current perceptual experience: my being-appeared-to as if there were a cup of coffee on the table.

3. The mental act or state containing that content, in this case my perceptual act of *seeing* (etc.) the cup of coffee on the table.

4. That mental act or state as something done by or suffered by *me*, i.e., a reflective, self-conscious rational subject.

Of these, the first, conceived of as a phenomenon, i.e., something (putatively) extramental related to consciousness as present in and to it, is the natural focus of our occurrent thought and action, including speech. The other three are intramental features of and not normally the focus (or present in the foreground) of conscious awareness, belonging instead to the background/periphery of conscious awareness. Let us consider each of these in turn.

It is an obvious fact of everyday life that we naturally interpret sense-experience as the experience of an external world of persisting material objects in which we live and move and have our being. This "natural standpoint" (as Husserl calls it) is ubiquitously reflected in our spontaneous beliefs, desires, and arguably in ordinary language as well. In one sense, the

---

3. I have discussed consciousness in general in great detail elsewhere, most notably in Chapter I of my book on the Trinity, as yet unpublished. What I say here presupposes that account but does not completely recapitulate it.

prevalence of the natural standpoint in our pre-philosophical experience is perfectly understandable; as Descartes puts it, our creator (whether God or nature) has given us the senses not for the purpose of attaining theoretical knowledge of the nature of things, but rather for the sake of our survival by informing us of dangers and opportunities in the environment in which we find ourselves.[4] It is thus most urgent that we interpret our experience in such a way that the intentional object rather than the intentional content be the natural focus of conscious awareness as such. Although I have no space to argue this here, my contention is that the natural standpoint is not the result of any sort of inference or the construction of any sort of hypothesis intended to account for any of the pervasive features of sense-experience. Instead, the intentionality by means of which we naturally interpret the intentional contents of perceptual acts as external objects related to consciousness is part of that content itself; the intentional contents *present themselves* as external objects in the process of being perceived by us and thus "efface themselves" in favor of their putative originals. As such, to call the natural standpoint an *interpretation* of our experience is no way to suggest that it is somehow mediated by the application of concepts, categories or theoretical constructs intended to make our pre-interpretive experience intelligible or meaningful for us. To the contrary, in interpreting our experience in accordance with the natural standpoint we are simply *taking experience at face value*, i.e., acquiescing (as it were) in the assumption that the way things appear is the way they are.

As I argued earlier, neither we nor Descartes would have had any reason to do otherwise had not the New Science and Galilean physicalism come along. For it seems clear enough that these views entail representational realism, and with it the position that it is only the intentional content of perceptual experience of which we are immediately aware, not the intentional object as such. The intentional content *presents* itself as the extramental external object existing in relation to consciousness, i.e., as Kantian *phenomenon* present in and to consciousness by means of the perceptual act. As the Scholastics put it, the intentional object is what is known in the perceptual act, whereas the intentional content is that by means of which it is known.[5] The intentional content is thus at the focus

---

4. *CSM*, Vol. II, 57–8.

5. I have elsewhere explained how this intentionality is possible by reference to the neo-Scholastic version of Critical Realism according to which the intentional content of the perceptual act by means of which I apprehend the intentional object is the intentional object itself existing formally in the mind such that the mind becomes what it knows through the formal identity of subject and object in the knowing act.

of attention in the center of conscious awareness yet not precisely as intentional content; instead, it is there as the intentional object present in and to consciousness. This seems unproblematic so long as there is no reason to suspect that the intentional object considered (as Kant would have it) *noumenally*, as it exists in itself independently of consciousness is different, or at least very different, from the way it appears to consciousness. The new scientific outlook, by drawing a strong distinction between what Kant would call phenomenon and noumenon, i.e., between they way things appear and the way they really exist in themselves, forced philosophers to recognize a strong distinction between the intentional object of conscious experience and the intentional content by means of which we (putatively) experience it and, in so doing, generated the problem of the external world and the crisis of early modern epistemology. No longer is the intentional content thought of as the externally existing intentional object present in and to consciousness; it is now conceived of a set of "ideas" or "sense-data" existing in the mind as the product of external physical stimulation and at best *representing* the object to us in some way. The New Science thus motivates philosophy to turn its attention away from the intentional object of everyday sense-experience toward the intentional content *as such* or *qua* intentional content. This occurs when we, as reflective, self-consciously rational subjects turn our attention away from the intentional object in order to concentrate on the intentional content as such, bringing what is normally in the background of consciousness into the forefront in order to examine its properties and characteristics. When this occurs, there is for the first time the possibility of the recognition of *introspection* as a distinct cognitive faculty which reveals to us the nature of conscious awareness itself.

Introspection, then, is our next topic. However, before proceeding to a discussion of the faculty of introspection itself it is important to clear up a pervasive misconception concerning the introspective turn itself whose consequences for epistemology have been historically disastrous. When we introspect, we turn our attention from the intentional object to the intentional content as such, focusing on (hence bringing into the foreground of consciousness) its intrinsic properties and qualities. In so doing, however, it is signally important that we do not alter that content in any way in the interest of "abstracting" the intentional content from the intentional object in order to thereby grasp it in itself. In particular, the notion of the phenomenological *epoche* by means of which I "bracket the intentionality" of the content in order to isolate its character as intramental content is a great mistake, as is the error of Berkeley, Hartley, Hume, phenomenalists, and "sense-data" theorists who attempt to reduce the perceptual field to a "parti-colored plane" of (at best) externally related, randomly juxtaposed sense-qualities. If, as I strongly suspect and think we have no reason to doubt, intentionality is itself a part of what I have been calling intentional content *as experienced*, to "bracket" intentionality or flatten that content into a collection of "sense-data" is in fact to *falsify* that content as experienced, a procedure which completely undermines the goal of grasping the content *as such* by means of introspection. It is this mistaken methodological assumption, more than anything else, which starts us down the road to idealism and skepticism.[6] Thus, if as I have suggested, introspection involves nothing more than a shift in attention away from the intentional object to the intentional content by means of which we putatively apprehend that object and its properties and features, then introspection does not require any sort of methodological abstraction or *epoche* in order to accomplish its end and is quite consistent with a robust and unwavering conviction concerning the extramental existence of the intentional objects to which the intentionality of that content directs our thought. To the extent that introspection involves abstraction, it is *non-precisive* abstraction, which abstracts not by removing or paring down, but instead by simply concentrating on different features of what is experienced than those to which our attention habitually gravitates.[7] The only *epoche* that I here recognize as binding on me is the Cartesian one arising from the considerations of the first *Meditation*. It is for this reason that I have all along supplied the term *putatively* when referring to the intentional object as something existing extramentally and yet present to consciousness in and by means of the intentional content of perceptual experience. But this is perhaps to get ahead of the game; let us look more closely at the notion of introspection itself and its credentials as a cognitive faculty.

---

6. It is, however, quite congenial to Galilean physicalism. Nevertheless, I have argued elsewhere that the epistemological problems generated by Galilean physicalism are so severe as to undermine the very possibility of natural science along its lines, at least as realistically construed, and as such undermines any motivation we might have to adopt it. If I am right about this, unadulterated Galilean physicalism is untenable and needs to be modified if it is to constitute a genuine account of the ontology of modern physics.

7. On the distinction between precisive and non-precisive abstraction and its epistemological significance, see Joseph Owens, C. Ss. R., *An Elementary Christian Metaphysics*, 63, 132–3 and Owens, *Cognition*, 145–52. The tradition of British Empiricism, beginning with Hobbes, knows only precisive abstraction and quickly concludes (*contra* Locke) that abstract ideas of concrete natures are impossible.

Introspection

Introspection, I have said, involves a shift in attention from one element of our conscious experience to another resulting in a situation in which something previously in the background of consciousness comes to occupy the center stage in my conscious awareness. Although my consciousness is naturally and almost exclusively directed outward toward what, from the natural standpoint, we naturally and pre-philosophically regard as the external world, an occasional surprise can sometimes deflect our attention out of its habitual course. For example, a new pair of glasses which sharpen my vision and enhance my appreciation of colors may cause me to notice, appreciate and savor the very act of seeing itself, as opposed to what is seen (the intentional object of the act) or that by means of which we see it (the intentional content of the act). In a similar manner, a social *faux pas* resulting in my embarrassing myself before the whole company and earning their united disapproval may well result in my feeling both mortified and (as we say) extremely self-conscious such that the focus of my attention comes to be on *myself as subject*.[8] So too, then, does the New Science result in the bifurcation of self and world which leads philosophers from the time of Descartes down to the present to focus on intentional content rather than on the intentional object where the investigation of conscious experience is concerned.

What we only occasionally do as a consequence of surprise we can also do voluntarily as philosophers seeking to understand the nature of conscious experience. In this case, we use introspection as a means for investigating conscious experience as such in order to identify its basic features and essential properties. There is even a branch of philosophy initiated by Kant known as *phenomenology* which attempts to do this systematically. Of course, not all philosophers are convinced either of the propriety or the possibility of such an approach to the investigation of conscious experience. Some of these objections and doubts can refuted or laid to rest *pro ambulo* simply by doing what they say cannot be done; others are clearly motivated by preconceived ideas about what a "scientific" psychology has to be which rules out appeals to conscious experience as either irrelevant, unverifiable or about something non-existent. Such views are easily refuted on the basis of evidence available to anyone, philosopher and non-philosopher alike, provided by everyday experience

---

8. Indeed, the experience of strong emotion nearly always brings the self to the center of one's conscious awareness and provides the most direct access to the self as that which undergoes or suffers its assaults. On this point, see Martha Nussbaum, *Upheavals of Thought*, New York, Oxford University Press, 2004, especially chapter one.

of ourselves as conscious subjects. However, there is one misconception about the philosophical employment of introspection which needs to be laid to rest at the outset. Although introspection is a mental act, in the sense that it is the activity of a conscious subject, it is not a mental act in the technical sense in which that term is often used to refer to an operation over mental content involving a propositional attitude (such as doubting or believing) or specification in terms of its object (like seeing or hearing). Introspection is not a "second-order" reflective act which takes other mental acts as its contents, thereby making the pre-conscious conscious or the merely conscious reflectively so, thereby generating the problem of the "transcendence of the ego." For rational, self-conscious subjects such as ourselves, the reflective grasp of our conscious states is par for the course, i.e., a global feature of our mode of being conscious; no special mental act is required in order to constitute it.[9] At the same time, however, neither does the act of introspection produce or require some new or independent intentional content to specify it as the sort of act it is; indeed, introspection would not even be possible if this were the case, since the very purpose of introspection is to apprehend the contents of consciousness as such. When I introspect, then, there is no change in the content of what I am attending to, only in the way I am *perspectivally related* to that content. Thus, instead of "thinking past" the content by acquiescing to the content in its function as the presentation in and to consciousness of the intentional object, I instead willfully and voluntarily shift my attention to the content itself by focusing on the features and characteristics it possesses solely by virtue of its intramental existence, i.e., *as* pure appearance rather than *as* what appears. However, since this is non-precisive abstraction involving merely a change in perspective rather than a "thinking away" of the other features of the content not relevant to our consideration of it as pure appearance, we remain peripherally aware of those features, which cease to occupy the foreground of consciousness and move instead to the background.[10]

In the case of most of our cognitive faculties, e.g., ordinary perceptual experience, the intentional object (i.e., what we think about: say, an extramentally existing material thing like a chair) and the intentional con-

---

9. As, e.g., BonJour argues in BonJour and Sosa, *Epistemic Justification*, 61–8.

10. This, I believe, explains the priority of such expressions as "I am appeared to X-ly" or "It appears to me that I am seeing an X." Such expressions are clearly parasitic for their meaning on expressions such as "perceiving X-ly" and "seeing an X," as proponents of phenomenalism have discovered to their chagrin. It makes no sense to speak of appearance without at the same time making reference to what appears. However, if what these expressions portend is simply a willful act of introspection which focuses on an intentional content as appearance, rather than as the presentation of what appears, they seem perfectly in order.

tent (i.e., the intramentally constituted presentation of that object) are at least potentially divergent, as the first *Meditation* shows by reference to the Evil Genius and the New Science enforces by means of its commitment to Galilean physicalism. Where the act of introspection is concerned, however, the *object*—the "what is thought about"—and the *content* of that act coincide in such a way as to be numerically identical, i.e., *one and the same thing* or at least *coincident* in my awareness whenever I contemplate them. The numerical identity of content and object will obtain whenever my awareness of the object is exhaustive of its reality (as in awareness of *qualia*); the coincidence of content and object will occur whenever it terminates in a direct apprehension of that object without being exhaustive of the reality of what I apprehend (as in my awareness of my own consciousness or my own existence.) In the first case, the object of awareness will be subjective contents and constitute subjective facts expressible in propositions describing my mental state. In the second case, the objects of my awareness will be constituted independently of my reflective, self-conscious awareness of them, hence as objectively real or actual independently of my occurrent awareness of them. The propositions expressing this sort of awareness, then, will describe objective facts about myself.

Regardless, whenever content and object are identical or coincident in the way just described, the deliverances of introspection are both potentially incorrigible for us and actually so in many cases. Because object and content are identical/coincident, I apprehend the object simply through being consciously aware of the content; there is thus no possibility of error or slippage between the two (e.g., misrepresentation of one by the other) *provided that I clearly and distinct perceive that content*. Since in this case the content is simply a *mode of awareness*, the object with which it identical is thereby known by me simply through conscious awareness itself. The only way in which I can be unsure or doubtful about it is if my state of awareness is vague or confused and this, in turn, is an internal feature of my state of awareness itself, though I may not be well-placed in all circumstances (when drunk, for example) to recognize this. In the ordinary case, however, there is simply no imaginable reason for doubt about my apprehension of my own mental state which is not refutable simply on the basis of that apprehension itself appreciated from the first-person point of view.

This makes the faculty of introspection unique among the other cognitive faculties, because all of these other faculties, such as perception, rational intuition, memory, etc., admit of some sort of distinction between their intentional objects and the intentional contents by means of which those objects are apprehended. This is where the possibilities of error or the deceptive interference by the Evil Genius gain their epistemic foothold, thereby motivating skeptical doubt. In the case of introspection, however, the identity/coincidence of object and content, of that-of-which-we-are-aware with our awareness of it, rules out the possibilities of error or Demon-deception and confers incorrigibility on whatever we clearly and distinctly perceive using that faculty. Introspection is thus (to use George Mavrodes' phrase) "Cartesian-safe" with regard to its deliverances, in which we can rest confidently in their objective certainty.[11] For our purposes here, however, we will concentrate simply on introspection as "deception-proof," which implies that, as Descartes asserts at the beginning of the third *Meditation*, that whatever I clearly and distinctly perceive using that faculty is true and certain for me.[12]

One might well question the epistemological significance of this. Most classical epistemologists were willing to grant us, at least in paradigm cases, both privileged access to and absolute certainty about the contents of our own mental states without the need for the elaborate sort of analysis I have been presenting here. The difficulty, however, remains that despite this concession exponents of introspection have not been able to make any significant headway in solving the outstanding problems of epistemology, such as the problem of the external world. One could hardly be accused of precipitate judgment in concluding that the introspective turn leads to an epistemological dead end. I will endeavor to show the reader that this is not so and that the problems of epistemology can in fact be solved in just the way that Descartes attempted to solve them. However, to do this requires that I introduce some further ideas, beginning with an explication of a term I have been using rather freely up to now, i.e., *apprehension*. This will make the connection between thinking and knowing somewhat clearer and point the way to the connection between thinking and existing.

Apprehension[13]

Apprehension is not so much a cognitive faculty as a (putative) kind of knowing characteristic of a number of our cognitive faculties, including (I shall argue) introspection. Apprehension (*gnosis, intellectus, ver-*

---

11. See George Mavrodes, "Real vs. Deceptive Mystical Experiences," in Stephen Katz, ed., *Mysticism and Philosophical Analysis*, 247.

12. *CSM*, Vol. II, 24.

13. As I use the term apprehension it functions as a technical term within my own epistemological theory, although I believe its use is continuous with that of the mainstream tradition in epistemology.

stand) involves direct, intuitive, pre-conceptual knowledge of reality; it is sometimes referred to as understanding or knowledge by acquaintance.[14] Apprehension, as a form of direct or intuitive knowledge, is often contrasted with indirect, non-intuitive or *discursive* knowledge (*episteme, ratio, vernunft*) such as that provided by inference or by reasoning from hypotheses. However, it is more difficult to distinguish them than it at first appears. The fundamental difference between them is that an act of apprehension, no matter of what sort, whether mediate or immediate, propositional or non-propositional, partial or complete, always terminates in a literal grasp of or confrontation of the subject with the object apprehended, which itself therefore becomes in some sense the content of that act. In this sense, apprehension never transcends our experience of the object and thus grasps it only to the extent that it can be present in and to consciousness, though that object itself may well transcend consciousness in its concrete, actual existence as *noumenon*. Inference, by contrast, whether it concerns deductive relations between propositions or causal relations between events, always concerns something (usually a state-of-affairs) that transcends whatever we are experiencing at the time we make the inference, at least in the minimal sense that it concerns some state-of-affairs which is constituted independently of our consciousness of it. To put it another way, an act of apprehension terminates in its intentional object (i.e., what it is about) through awareness of it, whereas inference terminates in a *description* of an intentional object which is not, at that time at any rate, an object of awareness. It is thus rightly called knowledge by description.[15]

By becoming the content of an act of apprehension, the intentional object becomes related to my conscious awareness. In and of itself, the object remains unchanged by being related to conscious awareness in this way. At the same time, however, in relation to the sort of reflective, self-conscious awareness possessed by human beings the intentional content becomes *factual content* or *data* due to its intentionality. To note this is to do no more than to note that, in becoming acquainted with something I

---

14. The distinction between knowledge by acquaintance and knowledge by description is Russell's—see *Problems of Philosophy*, 25–32. However, it should not be assumed that I draw the line between what counts as knowledge of either sort where Russell drew it; quite the contrary, I maintain that we apprehend (hence know by acquaintance) many things that Russell believed that we know only by description, such as the external world.

15. In my epistemological writings, I have chosen to contrast apprehension with comprehension, another sort of indirect knowledge in which one attempts to apprehend reality not directly but instead by means of hypotheses and other theoretical constructs. This is an intermediate case between apprehension on the one hand and inference on the other, which I do not further discuss here.

acquire information about it, information capable of being propositionally articulated and linguistically expressed. A *fact*, then, is simply an element of the intentional content of an act of apprehension regarded or viewed as providing *information* about the intentional object apprehended in that act. The content itself as such (i.e., as considered in relation to the intentional object) is very often non-propositional; however, in relation to the reflective, self-conscious awareness of beings such as ourselves, that very same content becomes information, something which by nature is capable of being articulated propositionally and expressed in natural language.[16] By the same token, that factual content or information is also capable of serving as the *ontological ground* for the truth of those propositions, the statements expressing them, and the beliefs which take those propositions as their contents i.e., that to which they correspond and in virtue of which they are true. This is because what I have been calling the fact, which is information in relation to reflective rational self-consciousness, is at the same time the intentional content of an act which apprehends the intentional object without affecting or altering it in its nature. Indeed, it is only due to this that the content can function as information in the first place. It thus provides that to which the propositional content, once articulated, corresponds, at the same time satisfying its truth-conditions and, in so doing, making it a potential object of propositional knowledge.

Most of our cognitive faculties are faculties of apprehension, inasmuch as they purport to reveal to us realities existing external to conscious awareness and constituted independently of it. This is includes sense-perception, rational intuition (by means of which we grasp self-evident truths *a priori*), memory, and the "inductive habit" as described by Hume.[17] However, given that we are not able at present to accept the deliverances of these faculties as veridical given the strictures of Descartes' first *Meditation*, we shall continue to suspend judgment with regard to them, except where the faculty of introspection is concerned. Here we have no cause for any such hesitation, since, as we saw above, in the case of introspection, the *identity/coincidence of the object of the act with its content* eliminates any possibility of systematic error or deception in the operation of that faculty. To the contrary, so long as I am careful to insure that I clearly and distinctly perceive the contents

---

16. Apprehension and inference are not hermetically sealed from one another, however. To the contrary, every occurrent, first-order substantive inference is itself an intellectual process occurring in consciousness, hence itself a temporally extended object of apprehension.

17. For the significance of this, see below. But not all—on my view, propositions themselves are also objects of apprehension as well as inferences, theories and explanations, all of which are arguably intrinsically propositional in nature.

of conscious awareness, the results are Cartesian-safe and, as such, deception-proof as well. Therefore, whatever information I derive from acts of introspection will be incorrigible for me and, as such, the propositional and linguistic expressions of that information will be known by me with epistemic certainty. In order to explore this consequence further, however, we need to consider the largely neglected topic of judgment.

Judgment

Judgment, as I use it, is a technical term most closely associated with the account given in medieval theory of cognition.[18] By judgment I refer to a (largely automatic) mental operation by which the information acquired through apprehension is articulated as propositional content suitable for linguistic expression. On my view, judgment so described is a spontaneous operation of the mind and produces the propositional contents which become the content of mental acts of belief, doubt, hope, wishing, etc., in short, the full range of what contemporary philosophers of language call propositional attitudes. Judgment, in articulating this propositional content from information acquired through apprehension is not itself a mental act or a propositional attitude. However, due to its being grist for the mill of our cognitive habits of belief-formation, judgment is always accompanied by an inclination to believe in which we very often acquiesce. Nevertheless, this inclination does not necessitate and our tendencies to form spontaneous beliefs can be curbed, disciplined and, in philosophical contexts at least, declined. Let us look more closely into all of this.

So far we have focused almost exclusively on the perceptual act as the paradigm case of conscious awareness. However, perception is only the beginning of our cognitive life. In the perceptual act, we encounter the intentional object as (putatively) externally existent particular thing. However, by reflection on one or more particulars of the same kind revealed in perception, the mind automatically performs an act of precisive abstraction resulting in a general *concept* expressible by means of a *general term* in ordinary language, capable in principle of referring indifferently to many particulars and potentially the object of definition.[19] Once we pos-

18. On judgment as understood by Thomas, here fairly typical of Medieval scholastic psychology, see Etienne Gilson, *The Christian Philosophy of St. Thomas Aquinas*, 40–1; John F. Wippel, *The Metaphysical Thought of Thomas Aquinas*, 24–30 and Robert Pasnau, *Theories of Cognition in the Later Middle Ages*, 216–19. This is not the sense in which the term was used by Descartes and the early modern philosophers; see below.

19. This, of course, is the work of the fabled Agent Intellect of medieval cognition theory, an idea that has its roots in Aristotle. As for the origin and the natural history of

sess such concepts, it is possible for us to use them in *existential judgments*, which bid us affirm the existence both individuals of a type and of the type itself as well. Thus, when I see or hear about a giraffe, I subsequently form the abstract concept of a giraffe; this makes it possible for me to form and entertain the judgment that "this giraffe exists" and as well that "Giraffes exist"—both of which are subsequently translated in the predicate calculus as (∃x) Gx—"There exists an x such that x is a giraffe." The medievals refer to the mental operation by means of which general terms are formed and existential judgments thereby made possible as the first operation of the intellect; the mechanics of this operation are regarded as pre-conscious and automatic and as such non-introspectible.

The second operation of the intellect, likewise pre-conscious, automatic and not capable of being introspected is synthesis, by means of which terms serving as the names things and properties are brought together in order to form *synthetic propositions* expressible in categorical statements. Of course, from the moment we have concepts we are at least potentially in possession of statements, since the semantic content of concepts can be expressed in what Leibniz and Kant call *analytic statements*, in which the predicate term simply repeats part or all of the meaning of the subject term. Genuine synthetic statements, however, simply express those propositional contents which result when, in response to experience, the intellect synthesizes concepts not analytically related in meaning to form propositions such as *this ball is red* or *Giraffes are tall*. Again, these propositional contents are not yet the objects of belief or knowledge, being merely the propositional articulation of the non-propositional contents of acts of apprehension resulting from the operation of judgment. Such propositions become beliefs only when they are *affirmed as true* by the intellect, something which occurs semi-automatically in most cases due to the force of habit but which is at least potentially the object of deliberation and free choice.

In regard to the apprehension of our inner states supplied by introspection, the incorrigibility of the contents of the act of apprehension insures that the propositional contents expressing those contents will likewise be certain for me hence to be affirmed as true. Thus, if the focus of my current act of perceptual awareness is a giraffe, corresponding to that awareness is the fact, evident to me as a self-conscious rational subject,

---

language, the nature of language acquisition, and so on, neither I nor anyone else, so far as I am aware, has anything plausible to say about this topic, though it will be clear that my view implies that, in some sense, thought precedes language and that language exists as a medium for thought rather than as something in its own right. I regard this latter view as ultimately self-refuting.

that it appears to me that there is a giraffe before me now. The operation of judgment thus yields the propositional content "It appears to me that I am now seeing a Giraffe." Given that I clearly and distinctly perceive the non-propositional content, the proposition articulating that content is likewise epistemically certain for me, hence is rightly classed as one of my justified true beliefs.

However, it might be thought that I have opened the door for the possibility of error or demon-deception by introducing these additional, pre-conscious mechanisms by means of which the non-propositional contents are articulated conceptually and propositionally in such a way as to be expressible in language. Couldn't these mechanisms be flawed in some way or subject to interference on the part of the demon so that there is some sort of slippage between what we apprehend pre-conceptually and non-propositionally and the conceptual and propositional contents produced by the first and second operations of the intellect? The possibility cannot be ruled out *a priori*; however, it can be *discounted* or disconfirmed by the use of introspection itself, given that the products of apprehension and the propositional contents corresponding to them are both internal to conscious awareness and thus potentially comparable by means of introspection itself.

Since the propositional content produced by the operation of judgment simply articulates that non-propositional content, it has an essentially *descriptive* relation to it, and thus, will be structurally isomorphic to it as well.[20] Thus, by shifting our attention from one to the other we will be able to judge whether the second corresponds to the first by an act of introspective apprehension which detects that structural isomorphism (or lack of it). In the case just mentioned, for example, both the non-propositional content of my perceptual act and the propositional content generated by judgment are located within my consciousness at the same time. Thus, I can compare my visual perception of a Giraffe with the judgment "It appears that I am now seeing a Giraffe" in order to see that the second corresponds to the first by accurately expressing the information contained in that perceptual act as descriptive of a particular state-of-affairs, i.e., the current content of my visual field. Thus, given that introspection is a Cartesian-safe cognitive faculty when I clearly and distinctly perceive the contents of my own states/acts of sensation and judgment, it will not be possible for undetectable error or demon-interference to undermine our confidence in the propositional articulation of the information acquired

---

20. This expression is BonJour's; see his contribution to BonJour and Sosa, *Epistemic Justification*, 70–76. In making this reference, I make no claim that I am adopting BonJour's view or that he would approve of the position I have presented in the text.

through the introspective apprehension of the contents of our inner states of judgment, since such error or interference could in principle be detected and thus eliminated through the sort of internal comparison I have just been describing. Further, since this is an act of comparison between two contents simultaneously constituted in consciousness, both of which are available to introspection at the same time, there is no need to postulate any further act encompassing these two acts that itself in turn needs to be articulated in judgment, generating a further act of comparison, and so on. Introspection, though a cognitive faculty, is (as I noted above) constituted by a power to shift our attention within the intentional field of consciousness from one element to the other, rather than either to receive a certain sort of content (as in a mental state like visual perception) or to operate over mental contents received or generated by other cognitive faculties (as in a mental act such as belief or doubt). Thus, just as content and object, awareness and what I am aware of are identical/coincident in introspection generally, so too in this case; the fact that the propositional content produced by judgment corresponds to the non-propositional content it articulates is identical to my introspective awareness of that fact. This closes the circle without any hint of circularity.

Even if the skeptic were to attempt to generate a regress here, he would find it unavailing. First of all, given that my introspective awareness of the fact here in question, i.e., of the correspondence of the propositional to the non-propositional content produced by judgment, is internal to consciousness, it counts as direct apprehension of a sort analogous to that involving non-propositional contents; the fact that in this case it involves propositional content as well does not alter that fact. Therefore, neither does it taint the incorrigibility which attaches to that state. As such, there is no need to articulate that content as a special judgment in order for me to have perfect confidence that that fact obtains. Thus, even if such a judgment were to be generated, there would be no problem that would recur, since my apprehension of the fact in question does not rely on judgment but merely on introspection alone; this is sufficient, then, to guarantee the certainty of my propositional knowledge of my own mental states. By the same token, any attempt to generate an infinite regress here, the possibility of error or deception could be met by a further use of introspection comparing the previous one to the judgment articulating it, thereby ruling out the envisaged possibilities. Thus, the skeptic can never trump me, since I can always perform another act of comparison of precisely the same sort, and possessing the same substantive content, as the one before. We can keep it up until the skeptic either gives up and goes away or we reach the practical limit of the generation of "levels of reflective awareness" in a single pair of minds.

This does not prevent it from being the case, of course, that the articulation of my apprehension will necessarily be comprehensive or incapable of being deepened, improved or supplemented by further inquiry, in which case my initial, superficial characterization of that apprehension, though all right as far as it goes, may well be superseded by a more detailed, sophisticated and nuanced articulation of what is thereby apprehended. In such case, the previous conception of that cause will be deepened, corrected and superseded by another; yet the earlier conceptions are not simply dismissed as false, useless or irrelevant. To the contrary, they become incorporated into the conception that supersedes them as a partial apprehension of what that conception articulates more fully; they are thus *aufgehoben* in Hegel's sense, "cancelled yet preserved" in the articulation which supersedes them. In principle, there is no intrinsic limit to how deep and detailed our apprehension of anything of which we are consciously aware can go or become. Much of what I will be doing here is an attempt to provide a deeper explication of what Descartes can plausibly be thought to have discovered.

I conclude, therefore, that we can grasp the truth of judgments concerning our own mental states and the other facts about ourselves apprehensible by introspection with incorrigible certainty and that this thus constitutes genuine knowledge. One might question, however, the epistemic significance of this. After all, such knowledge seems to remain wholly within my consciousness and thus contribute little, if anything, toward the solution of any important epistemological problem, such as the problem of the external world. However, if Descartes is right, there are at least two substantive facts that I can know by means of introspection which are not merely subjective facts about our own conscious contents, namely, that I think and that I exist. In order to grasp the significance of this, let us return once again to the phenomenon of thinking as conscious awareness.

Self-Awareness

So far in this chapter we have been concerned more or less exclusively with the elements of consciousness as revealed to us by introspection. We saw that the primary focus of consciousness in everyday life is not consciousness itself but instead the putatively external world and its denizens as presented to us in consciousness by intentional contents purporting to be *phenomena*, i.e., those externally existing things as related to consciousness. By means of introspection, however, those intentional contents can themselves become the focus of consciousness and, since in this case object and content are identical, we can grasp these contents in such a way that they are incorrigible for us when we perceive them clearly and distinctly. As such, the possibility of error or deception with regard to these contents is eliminated.

By means of judgment, these non-propositional contents become *facts* in relation to the propositional, linguistically expressible contents that articulate those contents as we experience them. Since we are capable of introspectively comparing those non-propositional contents with the propositional contents produced by judgment which purport to articulate them and thereby detect any slippage or failure of fit, we are in a position to confirm, with incorrigible certainty, those propositional contents which fully and correctly articulate our non-propositional experience. These propositional contents, in turn, become knowledge (i.e., justified true belief) when affirmed by those who entertain them and possess objective epistemic certainty: they are "Cartesian-safe."

In addition to intentional contents and cognitive powers such as introspection and judgment, we must also recognize various kinds of mental *states* and *acts*, such as seeing, belief and so on, since we have made constant reference to these in the foregoing. The distinction between these two is far from hard and fast; it reflects the varying degrees to which we are likely to see our minds as either passive or active with regard to our mental contents. Mental states are so-called because they are specified by the contents which are seen as actualizing them. Thus, the presence of visual *qualia* is sufficient to determine that my current mental state is one of *seeing* or visual perception, the presence of auditory *qualia* of hearing, feelings of pain as being in pain, fear of being afraid, representation of past events of memory, imaginary events experienced as presently occurring of dreaming and so on. Each of these mental capacities is a potentiality for a distinct class of conscious experiences, actualized and determined by contents received as imposed or impressed on us by an outside source or cause. Again, since these states can be "read off" from their contents, we rarely advert to them as such; however, the disciplined use of introspection on the part of the phenomenologist can make even these states objects for us by a kind of non-precisive abstract which focuses on the state itself as such in preference to the content that actualizes it.

Mental acts, however, are *self-actualizing* insofar as they involve voluntary *operations* over mental contents that we experience as initiated by ourselves rather than specified by an object existing independently of consciousness. As we have seen, the propositional contents produced by judgment are potentially the object of numerous propositional attitudes: belief, disbelief, doubt, hoping, wishing and so on. They can also be the object of desire and aversion, deliberation and choice. These contents by themselves cannot specify or determine which of these mental elements attach to them; indeed, the content of an act of belief or doubt can be qualitatively identical so far as their content goes in either of two persons or in a single person at different times. In at least some of these cases some of the time, e.g., with regard to the exercise of the cognitive power of introspection, deliberation, belief and doubt, we experience these as under our voluntary control. Further, we experience ourselves as possessing the power to resist our inclinations, such as desires to believe or doubt, to acquire or avoid various objects of desire and aversion as well as to suppress our passions.

Reflection on the difference between mental states and acts, on the contrast between introspection and judgment considered as cognitive powers and on our ability to resist our passions, desires and inclinations leads us to recognize ourselves as self-conscious, rational subjects, as the "I" in the formula "I think." This self, ego or I is grasped by us, not as a content of consciousness, but rather as the subject who enjoys conscious experience and as the agent exercising and directing our conscious lives by means of voluntary mental operations. This subject is thereby revealed to us in the very exercise of our power of introspection itself, which in turn is inconceivable apart from the existence of that subject. Certainly, as we have seen, there is a natural focus and foreground of consciousness with mental contents ranged in degrees or levels of distance from that center of focus, determined presumably by various conscious and non-conscious factors. When we introspect, however, we willfully and voluntarily direct our attention away from those contents as naturally constituted in consciousness in order to change the focus of awareness and alter the foreground and background of our field of awareness, something that we experience as requiring a certain *effort*. We are thus aware of *our selves* as the agents affecting this change in our conscious experience. By the same token, we are led to recognize that this mental operation is only possible on the supposition that this self, ego or I is always present in and to consciousness as the subject of those contents, since unless this were so, it would not be able to exercise these operations voluntarily as it is in fact experienced to do. The ego, I or self is thus revealed as the subject of conscious awareness, as the Kantian "I that accompanies all my representations" as always present in and to every element of occurrent consciousness and itself an element of consciousness only in the exercise of its agency, i.e., by means of what it affects there. Although I cannot argue for this claim here, I take it that this is an act of an immaterial agent and I do not believe that it will be discovered to be correlated with any brain-process.

It is precisely this feature that is typically denied to animals according to traditional accounts of animal consciousness. Animals, we are told, are *conscious but not self-conscious*.[21] To say this is to say that animals enjoy mental states but are incapable of any mental acts and possess no agency with regard to the elements of their mental lives. Animals possess mental states such as sensation, feeling, desire, and passion but the arrangement of these mental states with regard to their centrality in consciousness as the focus of awareness is wholly determined by the internal and external conditions that produce the contents of their consciousness. Lacking the status of conscious subjects, animals have no power of introspection, to deliberate or to form beliefs. Rather, their desires and inclinations directly cause their behavior in accordance with instinct and acquired habit. For this reason, animals appear to lack all cognitive powers; as such, animal behavior is much simpler and more stereotyped than human behavior. Since animals have sensation and thus are capable of experiencing pleasure and pain both on the level of sensation and in terms of satisfaction and frustration of desire, animals have some claim on us with regard to their treatment; however, they are not persons and do not have rights.

Whether or not one accepts the foregoing account of animal consciousness, I offer it here only to contrast it with the account of self-awareness as it revealed to us introspectively in our own case. With the investigation of self-awareness, however, we have reached the end of our investigation of the elements of consciousness insofar as it is revealed to us in conscious experience by the power of introspection. It is now time to return to the main topic of this chapter, i.e., what is thinking?

---

21. See, for example, the standard neo-Thomist account of this matter, defended by James B. Reichmann, S. J., in his *Evolution, Animal 'Rights' and the Environment*, 81–108. Reichmann does not specifically address the question of animal consciousness, any more than does Aquinas, for whom consciousness does not even exist as a theoretical concept. For Aquinas' views on animal intelligence, see Robert Pasnau, *Thomas Aquinas on Human Nature*, Cambridge, 209–14, 270–2 as well as the other scattered references listed in the index. I believe that what I say about animal consciousness is compatible with what Reichmann and Pasnau say about this matter although neither of them regards consciousness as having any genuine philosophical interest. At any rate, my view is certainly closer to theirs than to Descartes own, according to which animals altogether lack souls and consciousness and are merely organic analogues of machines, a view which strikes me as utterly implausible outside of the context of Galilean physicalism.

Awareness-as-Activity

What, then, is consciousness, thought or thinking and what is its relation to the various elements of consciousness (intentional objects as phenomena, introspectively apprehended intentional contents, the propositional contents of judgment, mental states and acts and self-awareness as revealed in mental agency) that our excursion into informal phenomenology has revealed to us? It seems to me that what is ubiquitous and common to all forms of consciousness, whether animal or human, clear and distinct or vague and confused, is *awareness* and every element of consciousness, from sense-data to self-awareness is a mode of awareness. Awareness, then, is the "stuff," as it were, of consciousness or its "matter" in the Aristotelian sense in which this word means that which receives form or the Lockean substratum which the aforementioned modify or affect. By contrast, the various elements of consciousness are forms or modes of this common non-physical stuff, matter or substratum. However, this common "matter" or substratum is hardly conceivable as a mere inert thing or pre-existing material in which the elements of consciousness inhere as a kind of external addition, the way that, in the past, the perceptible surface qualities of bodies were thought to exist in relation to substances according to the scholastic theory of real accidents. Even less is it plausible to suppose, as do Hartley and Hume, that the elements of consciousness are psychological atoms capable of existing without anyone being aware of them or that are themselves aware or proto-aware in their own right.

Instead, conscious awareness, i.e., that which is common to all conscious episodes, which admits of contrary determinations and serves as the principle of unity across time in our mental lives, seems most plausibly conceived of as an *activity* both in the sense that it is something real or actual (as opposed to merely possible or potential) and that it is an ongoing process subject to coming-to-be, passing-away and change by alteration. Of course, the term "conscious awareness" is to some extent pleonastic, since there is no contrasting notion of "non-conscious awareness"; all awareness is conscious by definition. Rather, the point of the phrase is to contrast the activity of consciousness with its forms or modes which come and go in dizzying succession without thereby compromising the unity of consciousness itself. At the same time, just as we never find any of the elements of consciousness existing except as a form or mode of conscious awareness, we never find conscious awareness existing without some particular mode or form, at least in ordinary, non-mystical experience. Nevertheless, conscious awareness retains a certain ontological priority over its modes or forms inasmuch as it is able to exist independently of each and every one of them taken individually, whereas forms or modes of consciousness lack this sort of independence. No mode or form of consciousness is capable of existing independently of the conscious awareness of which it is an element or modification.

In the second *Meditation*, Descartes immediately turns from the *Cogito* to the question "What am I?" Descartes famously arrives at the view that he is a *res cogitans* or thinking thing, a claim which he later interprets in the sixth *Meditation* as the thesis that his essence is to think or be conscious. This, in turn, appears to entail the claim that Descartes is *nothing but* a consciousness, i.e., the total collection consisting of Descartes' conscious awareness and its modes, which becomes the basis for his argument for the immateriality and immortality of the soul. However, our survey of consciousness and its elements, awareness and its modes, strongly suggests that the matter is more complicated than Descartes' easy-going Platonism would seem to suggest. The presence in consciousness of structured *qualia*, abstract concepts and the propositional contents produced by judgment strongly suggests that there are powers and capacities present in the subject of consciousness whose operations are pre- or non-conscious and executed independently of our wills while being essential to the constitution of experience as we are immediately aware of it. Since these products are themselves immaterial, it is natural to assume that the operations producing them are immaterial as well. But, regardless of whether or not this is so, there evidently appears to be more to the subject of consciousness, i.e., the-what-it-is-that-*I*-am, than just conscious awareness and its modes. Thus, even though insofar as I (*qua* conscious subject) am a *res cogitans*, it does not follow that the thing which is currently a *res cogitans* is so necessarily or in such a way that consciousness is inseparable from it, regardless of whether or not it is an immaterial substance.

Given the foregoing phenomenological analysis, the most we can conclude is that conscious awareness is an immaterial activity or process occurring in that which is a conscious subject and in virtue of which that thing, whatever it is, enjoys both conscious awareness and its modes. However, the powers and capacities by means of which conscious awareness acquires its various modes belong to the subject of consciousness independently of the presence of conscious awareness, although the subject of that awareness has no scope for the operation of those capacities without the presence of conscious awareness to receive them. Where the non-voluntary operations of the conscious subject require no more than the presence *in* that subject of conscious awareness, the voluntary operations involve something more, i.e., presence *to* consciousness on the part of that subject by means of which it becomes conscious *as subject within the intentional field of consciousness itself* and thus able to execute voluntary operations with regard to the elements of consciousness produced by the non-voluntary operations requiring only the presence of consciousness in the subject of the sort we share with the beasts. More than this we cannot say here; indeed, perhaps we have already said more than what we can justify by reference to the phenomenological data we have presented so far. Let me bring this chapter to a close by explaining how I understand the function of Cartesian meditation within the context of thought and thinking as I have characterized them here.

Meditation[22]

Having characterized what thinking is, and thus clarifying the "I think" portion of the *Cogito*, it remains that we characterize what *existing* or *being* is in order to clarify the "I exist" portion of the *Cogito*. However, before doing this I want to focus on the question of how *I think* and *I exist* are connected to one another. Although it may appear that this question is out of order here, I think that the way they are in fact connected makes this the appropriate place to broach this topic rather than at the end of the next chapter.

Since the time of Locke, philosophers have generally recognized only two kinds of relations: logical and causal. Logical relations, such as implication, hold between propositions and are expressible as inferences in which the truth of the first proposition or set of propositions is seen as entailing the truth of some further proposition. Causal relations, on the other hand, are relations between events or states-of-affairs, such that one event, or set or antecedent conditions, *brings about* or *produces* some subsequent event or state-of-affairs existing independently of it. Although Aristotle recognized four causes, or four causal factors in the constitution of objects, since the rise of the New Science only one sort of cause, the efficient cause as interpreted in accordance with modern mechanics, has been recognized as a genuine cause. Causes of this sort precede their effects in time such that the cause has usually ceased to operate by the time its effect comes into existence and requires no on-going relation between cause

---

22. For more on the role of meditation in Descartes and its possible roots in Ignatius of Loyola's spiritual exercises, see Gary Hatfield, "The Senses and the Fleshless Eye" in Amelie Rorty, *Essays on Descartes' Meditations*, 45–79; this is summarized in Hatfield's *Descartes and the Meditations*, 45.

and effect. As Hume puts it, "cause and effect are distinct existences," i.e., only externally related to one another.

Now it seems clear enough that the relation between "I think" and "I exist" cannot be any merely logical relation. In the first place, *thinking* and *existing* are states of things, not propositions and it seems hardly likely that the relation between them is going to be expressible as a logical relation. As we have already noted, we cannot successfully infer "I exist" from "I think" by means of any immediate inference, nor can we affirm the truth of the generalization "Whatever thinks, exists" prior to having grasped a necessary connection between these two states. Nor does it seems to be the case that there is a non-trivial conceptual connection between our notions of thinking and existing which justifies such an inference, so that "whatever thinks, exists" is somehow analytic. Neither, however, does it appear that this connection is a causal one in the sense that we ordinarily use that term in philosophy since the time of Locke. In the first place, it sounds completely odd to say that existing is the cause of thinking, in the sense that it produces it or brings it about. Nor does it appear to be the case that thinking, considered as an "effect," is a "distinct existence" in relation to existing conceived of a "cause," since this would make thinking something other than or existing beyond existence, something which is difficult to even conceive, let alone comprehend and affirm.

Although it seems obvious that thinking and existing are related to one another and indeed in some sense necessarily so, that necessity does not seem to be expressible either as logical or as causal necessity as these are understood by modern philosophers. The only alternative, then, is that there must be some further sort of relation, a metaphysical one, between thinking and existing which is straightforwardly reducible neither to logical nor mechanical causal ones. Such a relation will be like a causal relation, in that it obtains between contingent things or states-of-affairs and involves the *ontological dependence* of one thing or state-of-affairs one on another, but unlike it in that it is neither a productive relation between things or states-of-affairs nor such as to constitute them in such a way as to be merely externally related to one another. Such a relation will be like a logical relation in that it is capable of being apprehended with complete certainty simply through self-conscious reflection on one's own nature as revealed in consciousness, thus neither requiring nor even admitting external confirmation by sense-experience or experiment. At the same time, this apprehension will be the grasp of an objective, substantive fact which reveals more than simply a phenomenological fact about consciousness or a relation between abstract objects, but instead an ontological truth.[23]

How then to characterize this relation? For lack of a better term, I will call this relation that of something *existent* (i.e., anything real or actual, of whatever sort, whether or not it exists extramentally) to its *ontological ground*. This relation I conceive of as a one-way dependence relation between that existent something and on some other thing or principle whose operation is continuous, immanent necessary for to the being of that existent something such that the cessation of that operation has as a consequence the ceasing to be of that which depends upon it. The relation is therefore one of *continuous dependence of the existent something* on whatever constitutes its ontological ground. Conceived of in this way, the operation of an existent something's ontological ground is ingredient in it, though since ubiquitous as a consequence of being coterminous with the whole span of that something's existence in time, easy to overlook unless one is specifically looking for it. I make no assumption here that there is an ontological ground for every existent, only that it clearly obtains in certain cases in which this can be shown to be the case; in particular, I shall claim that this relation holds between thinking and existing.[24]

One example of this sort of relation (let's call it the EOG relation) would be the relation between substance and accident in understood in traditional Aristotelian metaphysics. According to this theory—sometimes called the theory of *real accidents*—accidents *inhere* in substances in such a way that they are ontologically dependent in their individual existences on the substances in which they inhere without being intrinsic to or merely modes of those substances.[25] As such, these accidents are merely externally

---

23. For a general discussion of the concept of a metaphysical, as opposed to a logical or efficient causal, relation, see Farrer, *Finite and Infinite*, 16–25.

24. This relation as I describe it here appears to be cognate to the modal distinction recognized by some of the later Scholastics; see, for example, the account given in Suarez, *On the Various Kinds of Distinction*, translated by Cyril Vollert, S.J., 27–32.

25. Descartes, of course, rejected the doctrine of real accidents along with Aristotelian form/matter analysis and substantial forms, leading him into trouble with ecclesiastical authorities over the Eucharist; he maintains that every substance has a dominant attribute identical with its essence and that all other inherent properties of that substance are mere aspectual *modes* of that attribute. On the scholastic view, real attributes are really distinct from the substances in which they inhere; for Descartes, what the Scholastics call real attributes are only modally distinct from the substances in which they inhere, this latter being understood as Suarez defines it. On this point see, e.g. Rozemond, *Descartes' Dualism*, 3–12; for the modal distinction, consult Suarez, *On the Various Kinds of Distinction*, 27–32. I do not introduce the theory of real accidents in order to endorse it, but only to illustrate the EOG relation, a metaphysical relation of continuous and intrinsic dependence of a

related to the substances in which they inhere in such a way that a gain or loss of such accidents need not involve any substantial change in the objects whose accidents they are. Since these accidents are only externally related to the substances in which they inhere, they are separable from them without any intrinsic change to the substance which gains or loses them; it is precisely for this reason that such changes are possible without affecting the identity of the substance which undergoes that change. Thus, if I take a white chair and paint it red, I have not altered the chair considered in itself in any intrinsic way although I have changed its surface color-quality; a new color-quality exists on the surface of the chair but it remains the same chair both before and after. However, that color-property clearly does require for its own existence that the chair continues to exist; if I destroy the latter I destroy the former as well, despite the fact that considered in itself it is only externally related to that chair. As such, the chair's color is necessarily dependent on and, in that sense, internally related to the chair with regard to its existence. The relation of the inherence of a real accident in a substance, then, is an example of the EOG relation. Considered as an existent something, a real accident as inherent is in (or on) a substance without being a proper part of it, so in that sense is only externally related to it. At the same time, however, not being a substance, i.e., something existing capable of existing in its own right, the existence of that real accident becomes internally related to that of the substance in which it inheres due to that very fact. The real accident then, through its inherence in a substance, becomes continuously and intrinsically dependent on that substance for its existence.

Another, similar distinction is the medieval one between causation *per se* and *per accidens*.[26] A *per accidens* cause or causal series is a series of what we would now call "efficient causes," like one billiard ball striking another. Both billiard balls exist independently of each other and are merely externally related; the first ball causes the second to move by striking it, but having acted to change the state of the second ball ceases to have anything to do with it: the second ball continues to move without the cooperation of the first as though by its own power. Efficient causes of this sort do not constitute the only sort of *per accidens* causes, however; Aquinas' own example of a *per accidens* cause is generation, by means of

---

something existent on its ontological ground which is neither a logical or an efficient causal relation, nor obviously reducible to these. Neither do I assume that existential dependence is the only possible instance of this relation, though I shall not stop to consider other sorts of examples here.

26. The best account of this distinction is to be found in Patterson Brown, "Infinite Causal Regression," in Anthony Kenny, ed., *Aquinas: A Collection of Critical Essays*, 215–36.

which the parent brings the child into existence but is not necessary for the continued existence of the child who is begotten. By contrast, a *per se* cause is one which exists simultaneously with its effect and is necessary not simply for its initial coming into being, but also for its continued existence for the entire term of its existence. As so conceived, the operation of the *per se* cause is *ingredient* in the effect, i.e., the operation of the cause continues to "affect the effect" of which it is the cause for as long as that effect occurs. Aquinas' standard example of a *per se* causal relationship is that of heating; heating begins when (e.g.) a kettle is placed in proximity to a source of heat such as a fire, continues for as long as it is being heated and ceases as soon as that heat source is removed and is replaced by its contrary, cooling. The relation between a *per se* cause and its effect would be another illustration of the EOG relation as I have characterized it.

Supposing that such a relation between thinking and existing did exist, how could we detect and confirm this fact? To this I answer: by means of introspective meditation, just as Descartes does. By this I mean a directed program of introspective investigation which reveals the ontological dependence of thinking on existing (which, due to its ubiquity, is not obvious to us but is nevertheless something of which we are implicitly and inchoately aware) and makes it explicit in such a way that we can grasp it clearly and distinctly. It thus employs the one deception-proof cognitive faculty left to us by Descartes in order to bring the fact of our existing into the center or focus of conscious awareness by introspective reflection on the fact of our thinking. This process of meditation is neither the tracing of a series of logical implications usefully modeled by an inference (although, for exposition's sake, it can be modeled as such after the fact), nor the construction of an explanatory theory which arrives at an efficient cause, nor even an *a priori* investigation of the transcendentally necessary conditions for the possibility of thought. The process here is most closely analogous to sense-perception, except that the perception in this case is internal and intellectual rather than external and sensible, while at the same time, being the product of introspection, Cartesian-safe and thus knowable with certainty. What happens as a result of this process of meditation is that we come to realize explicitly, clearly and distinctly something that we were implicitly or inchoately aware of all along but had overlooked or failed to see; when this occurs, we subsequently articulate that fact through judgment and affirm it in belief as certainly true, by means of which it becomes knowledge for us. The best possible illustration of this is simply by proceeding to the topic of explicating our apprehension of existing by means of thinking. However, there is one more preliminary I wish to discuss first.

Innate Ideas

Perhaps no idea is more famously (or notoriously) associated with Descartes than the doctrine of innate ideas, which since Locke's discussion of it in the *Essay* has been characterized as the view that certain of our ideas, e.g., those of the self and God are inborn in us, implanted in us by our Creator in such a way that we have occurrent knowledge of those ideas prior to and independently of experience. Ever since Locke's critique of Descartes' theory, it has been regarded as one of the weakest and least plausible teachings of the *Meditations*. Unfortunately, Descartes gives us little reason to suspect that Locke's characterization of his view is a caricature. For example, he insists against Gassendi in the *Replies* to the fifth *Objections* that not only would someone who was born deaf and blind possess the innate ideas of self and God, but that he would comprehend them all the more clearly due to his not being distracted by the senses.[27] This is unfortunate, since as Descartes actually *defines* innate ideas, he is not necessarily committed to any of the claims that are usually regarded as making his doctrine implausible.

Descartes tells us that innate ideas are those which we acquire simply by the contemplation of our own nature, through the sort of guided process of introspective reflection that Descartes himself employs in his *Meditations*. On this account, it makes perfect sense that some of our ideas are innate, i.e., born with us in the sense that they can be acquired simply by the introspective investigation of our own nature, with no questions begged or implausible appeals to past lives or direct divine endowment. In particular, it is easy to see how the ideas of thought, being and truth could be innate since, as we have seen, we easily discover these notions by considering the nature of our own thought processes. As I shall subsequently argue, the idea of God is also plausibly thought—indeed *discovered* by us—to be an innate idea in this sense. However, even in the case of the ideas for which this is a plausible account, Descartes makes no real attempt to show how these ideas are in fact derived introspectively by means of meditation. To the contrary, eager to make things a little easier for himself by making all apparently self-evident/*a priori* truths innate, Descartes generally uses a putatively innate idea (such as that of God) as the starting point for meditation, rather than illustrating its status as an innate idea

---

27. See *CSM*, Vol. II, 258.

(regardless of its empirical origin in consciousness) by showing how it can be acquired by introspective reflection on our nature. In what follows, I propose to do this for two of the central notions employed by Descartes' in the *Meditations* project of finding the foundations of knowledge: being and God. In the next chapter I will discuss being and existence.

5

Being

COGITO, ERGO sum—*I think, therefore I am.* The foregoing, as everyone knows, expresses what Descartes takes to be the fundamental, deception-proof insight revealed to us by the form of introspective reflection he calls meditation. In discussions of Descartes, it is natural for us to concentrate on the "I think" portion of the *Cogito*, if only because Descartes is the first one to focus on consciousness itself as philosophically significant and to employ introspection as a cognitive faculty without altogether recognizing it as independent of and even more fundamental than either sense-perception or rational intuition. At the same time, hardly anyone takes any trouble over the "I exist" portion of the *Cogito* other than to ask how it is that it can be justified by appeal to the "I think." Even this is, to some extent, a merely academic question since there is no one, I believe, who is not persuaded that the *Cogito* is true and something that we know with incorrigible certainty. However, that no one should concern him- or herself with what it means to say or affirm that I exist is somewhat perplexing. The terms "being," "a being," "existence," and "existent" are among the most abstract and difficult to characterize terms in natural language; although ubiquitously presupposed in every inclination, judgment, and action—including every speech-act—we are struck dumb when we attempt to deal with them and seemingly unable to articulate these notions without sounding portentous and paradoxical. At least partly for this reason, many philosophers have wished to dispense with these notions altogether and the branch of philosophy—metaphysics understood as the science of being-*qua*-being—that studies those notions, as well.[1] By the same token,

---

1. For a classic statement of the "case" against being, see Sidney Hook, *The Quest for Being*; see especially the title essay, 143–71 and 'Scientific Knowledge and Philosophical "Knowledge"', 209–28. I shall not take the time to consider these essays in the text; attentive readers will be able to detect the inadequacies of his criticisms and the self-refuting character of his position from the positive account I shall present here. For a more sophisticated critique of the Thomistic account of being, which I (following Farrer) am presenting here, see Anthony Kenny, *Aquinas*, 33–60 and Kenny's *Aquinas on Being*, Oxford, Oxford University Press, 2002. Although I cannot discuss the matter here, I humbly submit that I

the "friends of being" and of metaphysics as a science often play into the hands of their opponents by emphasizing the difficulties in understanding these notions.[2] Still, to explicate the *Cogito* fully, it is unavoidable that we consider these notions in order to apprehend what it is to say, in such a way as to be able to affirm, that I exist.

The Two Senses of 'Exists' in Ordinary Language

As I noted in the last chapter, the most common use of the term 'exists' is in existential judgments, in which I affirm or deny the existence of some object of thought or perception. In this case, the use of 'exists' derives from its relation to the subject who uses it to *posit* (as Kant would say) something as real, actual, or objective or to refuse to posit it as such. In this sense of the term, I use "exist" in order to affirm that giraffes exist, deny that unicorns do, and frame the question as to whether or not God exists, i.e., I posit the existence of giraffes, refuse to posit the existence of unicorns, and wonder as to whether or not I ought to posit the existence of God. In this sense of 'exists,' the word is univocal in meaning in that it applies in the same way, relative to an act of existential judgment, in every context in which it appears. Thus, when I was discussing the EOG relation in the last chapter, whenever I used the word "existent" I meant it precisely in this sense, merely as something posited as real. There can be no doubt that this is the primary use of the term 'exists'; the question which arises, however, is whether, as Kant and many modern philosophers seem to think, this the only legitimate use of that term.

A moment's reflection ought to be sufficient to dispel this suggestion. Surely, only an extreme relativist or subjective idealist would suppose that

---

have avoided the pitfalls pointed out in these works.

2. Consider, for example, Jacques Maritain, *Existence and the Existent*, Joseph Owens, *An Interpretation of Existence*, and his *An Elementary Christian Metaphysics*. In these works, we are told that we have no concept of being, that being is not related to beings as a genus to a species, that being is analogous and, as such, indefinable, that being adds nothing to our knowledge of things, and that it is grasped through an ineffable operation of judgment which somehow dispenses with the need to take the problem of the external world seriously. There is a sense in which all of these claims are true, but to begin one's discussion of the matter with these disheartening assertions simply undermines any hope of communicating one's point of view. Even someone sympathetic to traditional metaphysics can be forgiven for doubting that there can be a science devoted to such an object, let alone such as to be the supreme philosophical science. In what follows, however, I will attempt to motivate the traditional account of being without emphasizing the radical near-incomprehensibility of that notion and thereby "gild the philosophic pill."

our acts of positing are sufficient by themselves to constitute the existence of what is posited; indeed, such a supposition is incoherent.[3] It is simply part of the logic of ordinary, everyday existential judgments that they are intended to be objective and factual, reflecting rather than creating the way things are. Saying "X exists" is not like saying, "I promise," i.e., a speech-act that creates a fact merely by being uttered. When we posit something in ordinary existential judgment, we do so precisely as real or actual hence as something objective and independent of my act of positing in whatever respects it is that I am positing that thing by means of that judgment. In whatever way I conceive of what it is that I posit in existential judgment, whether as an idea, a property, a perceptual object, or a theoretical entity, in positing it I am attributing a status to it that my judgment reflects but does not itself constitute. In other words, existential judgment, just like perceptual judgment, has an *object*, i.e., the *fact* of existence it articulates and which provides the truth-conditions for that judgment. A true existential judgment, whether affirmative or negative, is one which posits or refuses to posit, in accordance with the fact of the matter concerning the existence or non-existence of the object of the judgment. For the same reason, a false existential judgment is one that fails to reflect the existential facts by either positing something non-existent or refusing that status to something that exists. The existential facts, then, are normative for existential judgment, not constituted by them.[4]

This leads us to realize that the very logic of ordinary existential judgment requires that we recognize a second sense of the term 'exists' which has a substantive meaning independently of our acts of positing and which, in fact, judgments expressing those acts of positing presuppose as normative for their truth. The objective, non-linguistic, and non-mind-dependent *fact* of existence is something constituted independently of our acts of positing, the object of those acts of positing and normative for them. We cannot attempt, then, to limit the meaning of 'exists' simply

---

3. Immanuel Kant, *Critique of Pure Reason*, translated by N. K. Smith; in Plantinga, *The Ontological Argument*, 57–64.

4. Indeed, regardless of what some philosophers (and even physicists) say, I know of no one who affirms this palpably self-refuting position. Most philosophers, whether continental or analytic, who affirm views such as "ontological relativism" or the "social construction of reality" do so on epistemological or linguistic grounds, rather than through commitment to some sort of idealist notion that the finite mind literally creates (*ex nihilo?*) the world. The conclusions of these philosophers reflect more on the inadequacy of the presuppositions of their worldviews than on our ordinary beliefs and practices. For a critique of relativist and constructivist accounts of reality, see Paul Boghossian, *Fear of Knowledge*, Oxford, Oxford University Press, 2006.

to its use in relation to acts of positing; those judgments themselves only make sense on the supposition that 'exists' has a substantive meaning in relation to the object of that judgment. Still, one might resist the notion that reference to the fact of existence requires that we recognize *existence* as an objective, non-linguistic feature of those things to which it is attributed in existential judgments.

To see the motivation for doing so, consider once again Kant's hackneyed example of the hundred real vs. the hundred imaginary dollars.[5] It is obvious that there is a great deal of difference between an imaginary and a real hundred dollars, which becomes painfully clear when the pragmatic aspects of one's own finances are in view—as Kant himself points out. For one thing, I can spend or save or lose a hundred real dollars but cannot do any of these things with a hundred imaginary ones; at most, I can imagine doing these things. It is natural, then, to suppose that there must be some difference between the two by means of which one is real and the other not (or at least not in the same sense). If we examine the matter, however, we will find, just as Kant did, that there is no conceptual difference between the imaginary hundred dollars and the real hundred dollars such that this can be isolated in thought. Surely, the concept of a real hundred dollars does not differ from that of an imaginary hundred dollars insofar as essence, nature or definition goes; neither is the difference between them merely that the real hundred dollars possesses or has superadded to it some additional attribute or property that the other hundred dollars lacks. Presumably, non-existent things lack actual, non-relational properties; to conceive of a non-existent essence as possessing actual properties and lacking only one additional property—existence—in order to be instantiated in fact is a metaphysical fantasy. The difference between a real and a merely imaginary hundred dollars does not seem to consist in anything we can easily identify with any sort of ordinary difference of which we are typically aware.

By the same token, however, it is precisely for this reason that, just as we cannot successfully cash out the notion of existence in terms of acts of positing, neither can we cash out the notion of existence in terms of conceptual differences between real or actually existing things on the one hand and merely possible, potential, or imaginary things on the other. For no such differences are readily available; nor is this notion "cashable" by reference to the fact that the imaginary and the real hundred dollars are differently related to my mind or in terms of the differences in linguistic practice with regard to each reflected in ordinary language. For these are

---

5. Immanuel Kant, *Critique of Pure Reason* A599/B627; in Plantinga, 60.

not, after all, self-explanatory and, to the contrary, appear to be parasitic upon antecedent differences between the intentional objects to which the mind is so related or to which those practices are directed precisely as those differences are constituted in the objects themselves independently of thought or language. In the end, it seems that we are ineluctably led to recognize and affirm the presence in the objects of affirmative existential judgment a distinct and unique *entitative principle, existence*, which is presupposed by those judgments and the linguistic practices surrounding them but not expressible in the language of things or properties.[6] Of course, at this point, to refer to this principle as *existence* is simply to baptize our ignorance; to the extent that all we can say so far is that things exist through the presence in them of existence is hardly informative. Thus far, however, it has only been my intention to motivate the view that the word 'exists' has a substantive meaning and that this meaning is to be explained by some principle internal to the intentional objects of existential judgment on the basis of the "linguistic facts" revealed in ordinary language. There is, in fact, more to be said, but to say it requires that we approach the matter from a slightly different angle.

Existence and Quantification Theory

Another challenge to the traditional metaphysical account of existence arises from modern logic, in particular, quantification theory, which years ago was often presented as a means of exposing and eliminating the "confusions" which give rise to the tendency to "hypostasize" existence and non-existence. Oftentimes, when we express existential judgments, we use locutions in which some form of the 'is' of existence appears in and replaces the predicate: "I am," "The Grand Canyon still exists," "There are tigers but no unicorns," and so on. According to some philosophers, locutions of this sort lead us to think of existence as something real and the word 'existence' as substantively meaningful, as perhaps the name for a special kind of property that things possess. Modern quantification theory, at least in the hands of some of it proponents, supposedly puts paid to this sort of thinking. As understood in modern logic, existence is not a

---

6. The term "principle" here is a technical term that refers to the most fundamental, basic or "radical" (from *radix*, "root") elements of a thing. As such, it is a wider notion than (though inclusive of) that of "cause." All causes are principles, but not all principles are causes. Existence and essence, for example, are principles by constitution while being inseparable from the whole they constitute; privations can also be principles in this sense. See the discussion of this notion in Alfred Freddoso's introduction to his translation of Suarez's metaphysical disputations 20–22, published as *On Creation and Concurrence*, xxv–xxvi.

predicate, hence not the name of a property. Instead, it is interpreted as a logical function expressible by a pair of operators known as quantifiers which allow us to reinterpret the misleading surface grammar of existential statements giving rise to the confusions leading to the formulation of the questions that become the subject matter of metaphysics conceived of as the science of being. How do we accomplish this?

Take a sentence like "Tigers exist." Although it appears to be attributing a property, i.e., "existence," to some class of individuals ("tigers") this is merely an artifact of the surface grammar, a mistaken impression which proper logical analysis dispels. The sentence "Tigers exist" can be *translated*, using the apparatus of modern logic, in such a way that any apparent reference to existence disappears, as follows: '$(\exists x)\,Tx$', read as "There exists something which is a Tiger." On this reading, reference is now made only to some unspecified individual something (represented by the 'x') and to that thing's being a tiger, which now occupies the predicate place in the sentence as translated. The notion of existence is now simply treated as part of the quantifier and thus merely a logical function in principle replaceable by 'some' and the predicative function of the sentence shown to involve only reference to ordinary properties.

Quantification theory also shows how we can interpret references to imaginary objects and negative existentials without the embarrassment of "quantifying" over nothingness, non-being, and non-existent things. In the case of imaginary beings, for example, we can interpret them as universal statements about everything, so that a statement like "Old King Cole was a merry old soul" becomes (on one possible reading) $(\forall x)\,((x = o) \supset (Mx))$ which is read, "For all x, if x is identical to Old King Cole, then x is a merry old soul." In this case, reference is made only to actually existing things, in fact, to all existing things, and it is simply asserted that if anything is Old King Cole, then that person is a merry old soul, which in no way implies that Old King Cole exists. In a like manner, we need not see a statement denying existence (e.g., "There are no unicorns") as attributing the property of non-existence to some subject or class of subjects in which that property inheres but instead as simply denying some ordinary property or set of properties of whatever happens to exist. For example, statements of this sort can be read either as statements about everything, e.g. $(\forall x)\sim Ux$ ("For all X, it is not the case that X is a unicorn") or as denying that any existing individual possesses or instantiates the property or set of properties denied, e.g., $\sim(\exists x)Ux$ ("It is not the case that there exists an x such that x is a unicorn"). Once again, we refer only to actually existing entities and their properties. These solutions are not completely successful even on their own terms; however, they work well enough to persuade many philosophers that we have eliminated the need to investigate "existence" or "being" as such.

In fact, however, this quantificational analysis does not eliminate reference to existence from our judgments; it merely disguises it. While quantification may be a logical function, existence is not. When Quine says "to be is to be the value of a bound variable in a quantified expression" what he says is literally false, though not perhaps false in the sense he intended it. Quantifying is no more capable than positing of constituting something as existent. Our willingness to quantify over a particular class of entities may be a measure of our "ontological commitment" to that class of entities but is surely irrelevant to whether or not the judgment expressing that commitment is true or false. In turn, that has everything to do with whether or not those entities *actually exist* in the ordinary sense that treats existence as constituted independently of existential judgment, positing, or "quantifying over" as an expression of ontological commitment.[7] If the foregoing is correct, there is no prospect of eliminating or superseding metaphysics i.e., metaphysics as the science of being-*qua*-being. Be that as it may, we are happily past the time in which anyone would claim that philosophy does (or can do) no more than isolate the logical forms of sentences or construct the world using the categories and techniques of mathematical logic.[8]

However, one thing that we can take away from the quantificational analysis of existential judgment is that it is not existence *by itself* that we apprehend but existence as an entitative principle in and of things and their properties. It is things and their properties, not existence, which primarily exist. While existence is an entitative principle in things, and necessary for them to be real or actual, it is not itself a thing or a kind of thing; neither does it wholly constitute things and their properties, at least as we are normally aware of them. There must then be more to these things than just existence *as such*. If existence is that entitative principle in things that realizes or actualizes them, it seems that there must also be in them some other entitative principle that is present as that which gets actualized

---

7. Of course, ordinary existential judgments are no more Cartesian-safe than are ordinary perceptual judgments, being subject both to error and to demon-skepticism. Thus, the oft-repeated claims (they are no more than this) of neo-Thomists like Maritain and Owens that we directly and thereby unproblematically apprehend the existence of external things cannot be sustained. Despite this, I have refrained in this context from qualifying all my claims with "putatively," etc. as this becomes tiresome after a while. I trust that the reader will be able to supply the necessary qualification for him-or herself.

8. For a parallel account of the analysis of existence pioneered by Kant and canonized in modern logic, see Robert Adams, *Leibniz: Determinist, Theist, Idealist*, 159–60.

or realized and in so doing results in the actualization or realization of the thing itself. The traditional name for this other entitative principle is *essence*; it is to this principle we now turn.

Existence and Essence

According to Aristotle, the two most fundamental questions we can ask about anything are first, "Is it?" (i.e., "Does it exist?") and second, "What is it?" The first question concerns the existence of the thing, the second its essence. For our purposes here, I shall use the term *essence* to refer to that entitative principle by means of which any existing thing is what it is in such a way as to be distinct from other things. This formula is clumsy and abstract, but intended to provide an overall account of essence as an entitative principle rather than simply as the notion of essence functions in Aristotle's account of substance. Let me briefly attempt to clarify it to some extent.

First of all, things do not differ with regard to their existence, at least insofar as the term functions in the first sense distinguished above; this is precisely why it is that we can use the term 'exists' univocally of every object of existential judgment, including God.[9] At the same time, however, there is no more obvious fact than that things differ from one another. This fact, then, must be due to some entitative principle other than existence and essence presents itself as the natural candidate for this role. Essence, then, is the principle of difference among things such that things are different by instantiating different essences or natures.[10]

---

9. Of course, I shall subsequently argue that this is not the case, despite appearances; in the case of God, existence realizes itself and is, in fact, a thing in its own right possessing the nature or essence which is simply the expression of existence when not arbitrarily constrained by essence conceived of as a distinct entitative principle such as we find it in finite beings. What I say here, however, does hold for finite beings such as ourselves and the external objects revealed to us in perception.

10. In saying this, I in no way mean to suggest that existence is a universal or a kind of undifferentiated substratum (like prime matter) out of which individuals emerge. Existence is individual in each existing thing, though not through itself; rather, it is so due to realizing distinct and different essences. Further, as will emerge below, in using the term 'existence' as I do in referring to the entitative principle that actualizes or realizes essence, I distinguish it from being. Thus, while it may be true that there are modes of being and that "being is said in many ways," it does not follow that there are modes of existence or that existence is said in many ways. Only in the case of God do existence as entitative principle and being as operation coincide; in such case, then, it is perfectly acceptable to speak of God as a necessary being or of God's necessary existence.

Secondly, essence is the principle of intelligibility in things, the object of conceptualization and definition. Thus, whatever we can think or say about a thing *as a thing* is in some way related to its essence, including the fact that it exists. Of course, it is obvious that this is so with regard to any of the substantive, conceptualizable aspects of things to which discrete property names can apply; each of these things is related, either directly or indirectly, to that essence. But more than this, to the extent that we can conceptualize existence at all, we can do so only relationally *as that which actualizes or realizes essence* and hence in relation to essence. Since existence can be conceptualized only in relation to essence, it can be apprehended only mediately and thus conceptualized and defined only *functionally* rather than lexically. How this is possible, I shall attempt to explain later in this chapter. For now, I simply wish to concentrate on the relation between existence and essence.

I have already said that, to the extent that existence is conceivable or conceptualizable by us *as such*, we can do so only in relation to essence as that entitative principle which it realizes or actualizes. However, it is perhaps possible by analogy to acquire a positive, if only partial, notion of existence. We can do this by conceiving of existence as *activity*, not some specific kind of activity to which other activities arise through something being superadded but instead as *activity-as-such*, as the activity common to all things no matter how diverse by means of which they are real or actual as opposed to merely possible or potential. This, as we shall see, is precisely what activity-as-such is when conceived of in relation to being-as-operation, i.e. the inherent principle in every being that realizes or actualizes essence and thus is the same in every being. On this view, essence is (as it were)[11] *mode* of activity, the principle in things that diversifies them as individuals with distinct natures. Each thing, then, is both activity and yet a specific mode of activity as well, existence realizing and actualizing a particular essence. The product of this union of

11. I say "as it were" because this is a stretched or extended use of the notion of "mode." Existence is not a substance or a kind of stuff capable of successively instantiating different essences; the relation of existence to essence is therefore not a case of substance and accident. Nor is it a case of matter/form composition. Like both of these cases, the relation between the first and second in each case is an external rather than an internal one (at least in the case of finite being.) Unlike them, however, the first member of the pair (i.e., existence) is not something in its own right apart from essence capable of receiving or switching essences. To use Suarez's terminology, they are only conceptually, not modally distinct; nevertheless, against Suarez I would maintain that this is a case of a conceptual distinction *a parte rei*, i.e. with a foundation in the thing and not merely relative to the finite intellect's powers of precisive abstraction. Concerning this, see James F. Ross's introduction to his translation of Suarez's disputation VI, *On Formal and Universal Unity*, 10–13.

existence as activity and essence as mode of activity is *being*, i.e., *essence actualized or realized by existence-as-activity*. Because essence can by grasped conceptually and is the object of definition, it is often thought that the notion of essence is more or less completely captured by thinking of it as that collection of properties that are inseparable from the concept of that being and which cannot be lost by any being without its ceasing to be or be what it is. There is nothing wrong with this notion of essence as far as it goes. However, it is neither exhaustive of the notion of essence nor even metaphysically fundamental. The way to understand the notion of essence in its most profound sense is to reflect on the foregoing formula, according to which essence is that which is realized or actualized by existence, hence more positively as the *structural principle of the act of existence* by means of which any thing is constituted as a being. In this sense, essence is more fundamental than and the entitative principle of all that thing's properties whether we class them as essential or accidental. On this account, essence becomes one of two entitative principles of being, each of which is equally necessary for the constitution of concrete being along with all its properties. I will subsequently defend the thesis that, despite their inseparability in fact in concrete finite being, these two principles not are sufficient by themselves to account for the substantial unity of those beings, but this will have to wait for now.

Existence and Being

If existence is *activity*, being is *act*: as Farrer puts it: *esse* is not *percipi*, *esse* is *operari*. 'Being' is a verbal noun, like 'running,' which in ordinary contexts refers to concrete activity, activity really or actually occurring. 'Being,' then, captures activity as realized or actualized as some concrete thing, for which the term *operation* can be used to distinguish that which is both *act*ivity and *act*ual. Beings, then, are individual somethings or instances of being. Since each being has an essence and is actualized or realized precisely insofar as that essence is actualized or realized by existence, operation takes the form of a *structured activity*. Being, then, is more than just existence, i.e., activity-as-such. Activity-as-such is merely an entitative principle in beings, that through which essence is actualized or realized; it is only the thing as actualized or realized that is, exists, or has being. As such, being carries with it ineluctable reference both to essence (i.e., that which, being realized by existence, structures it and becomes its so to speak *mode*) and to existence as act, i.e., the concrete actualization or realization of essence.

Just as existence conceived of abstractly as the activity which realizes essence fails to capture the whole connotation of the notion of being, so too does essence as the principle of intelligibility conceivable independently of existence. It is to be emphasized that essence, conceived in this way, is regarded as something merely possible or potential, existing only as an object of thought. In no way does essence "pre-exist" its actuality or reality as being in and as a particular being, which is the way in which it is present to us in consciousness as the intentional object of external or internal perception. In sense-experience, external objects present themselves to us as real, actual, and concrete, in short, as beings, concrete structured activities or operations—essence actualized or realized. Things are thus presented to us as *beings*, hence as instances of being. As such, being, i.e., concretely realized or actualized essence, is the metaphysical ground for the *fact* of existence, which in turn serves as the truth-condition for ordinary existential judgments. Thus, in apprehending being we apprehend at the same time essence and existence, the twin entitative principles of being, as mutually related to and inseparable from one another, as the two fundamental elements of operation: activity and that which structures activity as its mode. Nevertheless, we are subsequently capable of distinguishing these two principles in thought through an act of non-precisive abstraction that focuses on each of them separately by making each in turn the central object of attention. When we apply this form of abstraction to essence, we apprehend it conceptually as potentially or possibly existent in a concept capable of definition and apprehend it concretely as that potentially or possibly existent thing which has received actuality or been realized in fact by existence-as-activity. In this case, we are made aware of the second entitative principle in that thing by means of which we are aware of it as more than simply possible, potential, or exhaustible by a concept. This something more, which we apprehend not directly but only in relation to essence as that which realizes it is *existence*, the proper object of existential judgment.

We can judge something as existent solely through the fact that it is presented to us as a being. In this sense, the apprehension of being, i.e., concrete essence as actualized or realized as structured activity, precedes the apprehension of existence (activity-as-such, the function of which is to realize or actualize essence), which is the proper object of existential judgment. In apprehending something as a being, one is directly aware of it as concretely realized essence, hence as related to that entitative principle in that thing that actualizes or realizes its essence, i.e., what I have been calling existence. One's act of apprehension thus genuinely terminates in a grasp or awareness of existence: not in, and, or of itself but only as mediated by its relation to essence. The apprehension of existence is thus *direct* in one sense, insofar as it is the genuine terminus of an act of intuitive understanding/knowledge, but *indirect* in another sense, because mediated in such a way as to be inseparable from the concomitant awareness of that which mediates it. For all that, there is no reason for resisting the claim that existence, at least as characterized above, can be clearly and distinctly perceived.

Back to the *Cogito*: From I Think to I Exist[12]

Descartes claims that he apprehends his own existence with infallible certainty due to his incorrigible introspective awareness of the contents of his own mental life, i.e., from the fact that he thinks. In being aware of the ever-changing contents of consciousness, Descartes is thereby made aware of the *fact* of consciousness itself, which he expresses in the famous Cogito as the "I think." In turn, as we have seen, the fact of consciousness is constituted by the activity of *awareness* of which all specific forms of awareness are *modes*. Thus, when Descartes asserts the "I think," he at one and the same time indicates all of his individual thoughts (states of consciousness), his thinking of those thoughts (the activity of awareness), and the relation between them (mode to activity.) The activity of awareness, then, stands to the whole collection of individual thoughts as that fundamental activity of which each of them is a variation or mode. It is what gets altered or changed in such a way as to instantiate each of these different modes of awareness, whether this be of intentional objects, intentional contents, its own states and acts, or self-conscious awareness as such. This "awareness of awareness as such" is not a special kind of awareness beyond awareness but again simply an exercise of our introspective power of non-precisive abstraction, which allows us to distinguish, in every conscious episode, between what we are conscious of in the broad sense, the *content* of consciousness (whether or not this is what I earlier called intentional content) and our consciousness of it. This is something that we can easily do without requiring that we be able to identify some element or aspect of the content itself as our "awareness of awareness." Indeed, such a supposition is evidently impossible, since it would reduce awareness to one of its own modes. Rather, for beings such as ourselves,

---

12. Having rejected the idea that the *cogito* is an argument, I have thereby embraced the notion that the *cogito* is some sort of immediate intuition. For an exposition of this view and its difficulties, see Peter Markie, "The Cogito and Its Importance" in John Cottingham, ed., *The Cambridge Companion to Descartes*, 140–173. I hope I have resolved these problems in what I have said here.

who possess the power of introspection, "awareness of awareness" is a built-in feature of awareness itself and lacked only by those creatures (such as the lower animals) that lack the ability to shift their attention in such a way as to make consciousness its own object and thereby recognize themselves as conscious beings. Such beings (which, of course, include all of us on occasion) are conscious and aware of the contents of their own consciousness but only as they are related to the intentional objects those contents make present to them in consciousness. Lacking the power of introspection, they are unable to shift their attention away from the intentional object to the intentional content and thus consider those contents as such, i.e., in their relation to consciousness, which is precisely to consider them as we are aware of them as contents of consciousness. It is therefore sufficient for, and indeed constitutive of, "awareness of awareness" that one recognizes the contents of consciousness as something of which we are aware and yet something other than an intentional object presented to us in consciousness. It is thereby also sufficient for our apprehending ourselves as consciously aware and thus for possessing the notions of thought, awareness, and consciousness as well.

Given that through introspection I am able to grasp and articulate the distinction between thought and thinking, i.e., between mode and activity in consciousness, I am also enabled to grasp myself as self-conscious subject, i.e., as the being who both experiences the contents of consciousness and exercises agency with regard to them. Animals are conscious subjects as well, but being completely passive in their mental lives and without the power of introspection are unable to become aware of that fact. By means of introspection, we are able to recognize the contents of consciousness as modes of awareness-as-activity, hence of awareness as the ontological subject of those modes, i.e., as what possess them or that in which they "inhere." This, in turn, is the awareness of the conscious subject that I am, since it is precisely in and as awareness that consciousness instantiates or exemplifies its various modes; I cannot be aware of modes of consciousness *as such* through introspective awareness without being a conscious subject by that very fact. Thus, it is strictly speaking impossible for one to be introspectively aware of conscious awareness and its modes without being at least implicitly aware of one's self as a self-conscious subject. This is further enforced by the fact that we experience our selves as exercising agency with respect to the contents of consciousness, most primitively in the voluntary exercise of the power of introspection itself as well as in mental acts of belief, doubt, positive disbelief, and other propositional attitudes. In being explicitly aware of thought and thinking I am also thereby ineluctably (though, most of the time, only inchoately) aware of these thoughts as *my* thoughts and that thinking as *my* thinking. Further, this can be so even if I only occasionally advert to that fact in the course of everyday life. Awareness of thought and thinking, then, inevitably carries with it the Cartesian *I think*.

In each of these cases, then, we discover an instance of the EOG relation characterized in the previous chapter. Since subjective mental contents (*qualia*, etc.) are modes of awareness, they are ontologically dependent for their occurrence on awareness-as-such, which becomes an individual stream of consciousness (considered synchronically) or an intentional field of consciousness (considered diachronically or at a moment) through the inherence of some particular set of such modes; thus, in being aware of those contents I am at the same time aware of awareness itself as the ontological ground without which they cannot occur, hence as present or occurring along with them. I thus apprehend the objective fact that I am conscious. In the same way, since I am reflectively aware of this fact as incorrigibly certain for me, I am at the same time aware of myself as a conscious subject, since such awareness is possible only for a being capable of reflective, self-conscious awareness, hence ontologically dependent upon it. Thus, I cannot explicitly apprehend the fact that I am conscious without at the same time being aware of the conscious subject exercising the introspective power by means of which that fact is apprehended.

Now, what about the *I exist* in relation to the *I think*? As far as I can see, the tie between them appears to be as follows. In the way just explained self-awareness is, at least in part, simply a consequence of explicit awareness of awareness. Awareness of awareness is nothing more than awareness of *awareness as distinguished from its modes*. This, in turn, takes the form of an awareness of *awareness-as-activity*, i.e., as that which receives those modes and changes over time with regard to them while remaining the same, much as a radio wave can change its amplitude and frequency without thereby ceasing to be one and the same thing. Introspective awareness, then, is awareness of *activity*; activity, however, is precisely what we have identified with existence under the notion of *activity-as-such*. In thus being aware of awareness-as-activity, we are thereby at one and the same time aware of that awareness as something existent, and one of the modes of existence when conceived of as activity-as-such. Just as, e.g., a perceptual experience of a red ball is a mode of conscious awareness (one aspect of which is awareness-as-activity), so too is awareness of awareness (one of the modes of existence-as-activity) also awareness of existence (activity-as-such). We can express this series of nested acts of awareness, each of which is implicit in the one before it and revealed by a further exercise of the power of introspection using the traditional device of analogy of proportion, as follows:

content of awareness (e.g., a red ball) STANDS TO awareness-as-activity
AS
awareness-as-activity STANDS TO existence (=activity-as-such).

To say this is to say that the same relation that holds between content and activity in the case of conscious awareness also holds between conscious awareness and existence, i.e., each is a mode of the other. Thus, given that awareness-as-activity figures as one of the terms in both proportions, whatever instantiates the first also instantiates the second. Thus, awareness of anything at all, which involves awareness-as-activity, likewise involves existence, of which awareness-as-activity is one of its modes. By the same token, awareness of anything is likewise implicitly and inchoately awareness of existence, which awareness is itself mediated by awareness of awareness.

Existence, then, is the ontological ground of awareness-as-activity and the relation between them one of activity to mode. Just in the same way, awareness-as-activity is the ontological ground of the mental contents constituting its modes. Further, since introspective awareness of awareness reveals to me that awareness in my case constitutes a self-conscious subject, in being aware of thought and thinking I am aware of myself as thinking, i.e., as that which thinks. I can express this using the locution *I think* just in case I am aware of myself not simply as abstract thought or a dissociated act of thinking but instead as the subject of thought and thinking. Finally, then, in being aware of myself as a conscious subject I am at the same time aware of my existence as the existence not merely of thought or thinking but rather of myself as self-conscious subject, which I can express using the locution *I exist*. These too, then, are instances of the EOG relation.

As we have already seen, however, existence is only one of the entitative principles implicated in the notion of being and that as such it is not capable of standing alone. Instead, being is more than merely existence, i.e., activity-as-such. To the contrary, being is *operation*, i.e., structured activity as real or actual, a notion which makes ineluctable reference both the essence (as that which structures existence) and to the actualization or realization of essence by existence as *fait accompli*. Thus, in being aware of my own existence, I am also aware of myself as being, or rather, as *a being* or *thing*. Therefore, in being introspectively aware of anything as thought, I am at the same time aware of my thinking and thus of awareness as such and thus of my own existing as the ontological ground of awareness as

Being

such and so of myself as a being or thing, which thus involves another instance of the metaphysical EOG relation considered earlier. Given this, I am also aware of myself as a thing which thinks and so of myself as a *thinking thing*.[13]

Again, although we do not have to explicitly represent all of this to ourselves in order to grasp this sufficiently to recognize its truth it is useful to do so in this context in order to illustrate the fact that we do, in fact, clearly and distinctly perceive/conceive our own existence rather than infer it or postulate it as some sort of explanatory hypothesis. Further, we note that we accomplish all of this from within the perspective provided by introspection. Since, as we have seen, the clear and distinct products of the employment of this power (which, insofar as it is a source of knowledge doubles as a cognitive faculty in its own right) are incorrigible for us, each of the foregoing claims partakes of the certainty that belongs by right to products of that employment. Having achieved these results, then, we must now endeavor to extend them, as does Descartes, to the case of our knowledge of God.

---

13. One must be cautious here, however. In my opinion, Descartes is too quick in identifying my essence with thought in the further sense of occurrent consciousness. As I have argued elsewhere, while thought may be essential to personhood, persons are not substances in their own right although certain substances, i.e., rational souls, become persons by becoming the self-conscious subjects of the intentional field of consciousness associated with and at least partially produced by it. In the case of God and the Angels, who are not merely spiritual substances but naturally disembodied spirits, consciousness is intrinsic to and inseparable from them. However, in the case of the human soul, which is dependent in operation on the body with which it is associated, only the capacity for consciousness is intrinsic and occurrent consciousness only intermittent. As such, since only self-conscious subjects are persons, neither are souls intrinsically persons though they can become persons and are so whenever the intentional field of consciousness produced by that soul in cooperation with the body has a perspective on its own contents, i.e., becomes a self-conscious subject. Since animal souls lack the capacity for self-conscious awareness, animals are not capable of being self-conscious subject and thus are not, and cannot become, persons.

6

How Can God Be Apprehended?

Having used Descartes' introspectively based meditative method to reach knowledge of one's self as a thinking thing, it remains to conclude the second half of Descartes' project by showing how we apprehend God through the apprehension of our own existence. However, the notion that God can be apprehended, i.e., that an act of intuitive understanding can terminate in an awareness of an infinite, necessary being seems both impious and impossible at first glance. One can apprehend oneself by apprehending one's own mental states and it is not surprising that this should be the case. It may even be the case, as I hope to argue elsewhere, that we are able to apprehend external objects through sense perception although at this point we are not yet able to affirm this possibility. However, given the way that God is described by classical theists, the apprehension of God seems initially at least out of the question.

In the third *Meditation*, Descartes begins his discussion of God's existence by simply reporting that he finds himself in possession of a clear and distinct idea of God as a perfect being and proceeds to prove that this idea has a genuine referent.[1] His presentation of his intuitive grasp of this idea treats it as an original and underived feature of his mental life, one which he has apparently simply stumbled across in the course of taking an informal inventory of the contents of consciousness. This idea of God is apparently a sort of inner representation of God, somewhat as Descartes and other early modern philosophers sometimes treat the ideas which represent external objects to us as something like mental pictures existing in the mind that are caused by those objects. Descartes immediately begins to cast about for a plausible cause for the presence of that idea in his consciousness, a strategy captured in the first of the two third *Meditation* "proofs" for God's existence from the objective reality of that idea to the reality of God as the only possible cause of that idea.

---

1. See *CSM*, Vol. II, 28.

It is at this point that Descartes' project begins to derail. Prior to this, Descartes' critics have made only minor objections to his project and have acquiesced in most of his claims, including the *Cogito*. Indeed, they have not even seen anything genuinely novel in Descartes' project. Where the third *Meditation* is concerned, however, Descartes meets with significant resistance on the part of his critics, much of it directed at a claim that Descartes feels entitled to take for granted, i.e., that he in fact possesses a clear and distinct idea of God. In a certain sense, of course, Descartes cannot be wrong in claiming this if he is, in fact, introspectively aware of this clear and distinct idea. However, Descartes' critics present arguments to the effect that he could not, in fact, possess any such idea and that therefore his project of proving God's existence from that idea is stillborn. Descartes, for his part, can do no better than simply protest that he does too have this idea and is able to make no more than merely negative rebuttals to the claim that he does not.

Further, while Descartes continues to use the language of the meditative method it becomes increasingly difficult to sustain the conceit that we are relying even largely, let alone exclusively, on the power of introspection. Most of Descartes' contemporaries and most scholars since his time have taken for granted that Descartes is offering proofs or arguments for God's existence in the third *Meditation* similar to, say, the five ways of St. Thomas. The only difference is that instead of starting from some feature of the external world, such as that some things are in motion, Descartes' arguments begin from facts about myself derived from introspection such as that I have an idea of God or that I exist. God's relation to these facts is still regarded as a merely external, efficient-causal relation in principle no different from that between external objects and the ideas they cause us to have through merely mechanical influence on our sense-organs and, as such, justifiable only inferentially. The difficulty, of course, is that, having called our powers of rational intuition into question, Descartes can no longer depend on inference as a source of certain knowledge, since this is precisely the sort of cognitive process that an Evil Genius could systematically interfere with in order to deceive us.

It is not enough in this context that Descartes be able to infer God's existence from what is certain for him through introspection. God himself must be introspectible in some sense in order for us to have demon-proof evidence for His existence. Descartes undoubtedly believed that he was protecting the divine transcendence by substituting occurrent awareness of God with an innate idea of God implanted in us like a painter's signature on his work.² Nevertheless, and regardless of what Descartes' intentions were, I think we need to explore the possibility that our idea of God is the consequence of an apprehension of God, rather than merely innate in the sense of implanted by God through some purely external causal process.

However, the task of explaining how such an apprehension is possible still remains. Obviously, what is required is an explanation of how we can arrive at an apprehension of God from the fact of our own existence, something requiring that we continue the course of meditation that has carried us this far. However, prior to doing this, I want to consider whether such an apprehension is possible. Of course, the only truly effective proof that such an apprehension is possible can be provided *pro ambulo*, i.e., by showing that it is actually the case. However, I want to begin by considering the objections raised by Descartes' critics against the idea of God, most of which are equally objections against the supposition that God can be apprehended as well.

Do we have an Idea of God?

Descartes' starting point in the third Meditation is the clear and distinct idea of God he claims to possess. Both Hobbes and Gassendi object to this claim, asserting that there can be no idea of God, let alone a clear and distinct idea of Him and that to think such a thing is impious, amounting to the denial of both of God's transcendence and his incomprehensibility. The dispute, however, turns out to be not so much about the idea of God as about the nature of ideas themselves; neither Hobbes nor Gassendi is a logical positivist who is trying to claim that we have no concept of God or that the term God is meaningless in such a way that talk of God is impossible. To the contrary, 'idea' is a technical term in this discussion reflecting different philosophical analyses of what an idea is and what it is to have an idea of something; as a consequence, the combatants tend to talk past each other on this issue. Still, by a review of these criticisms, we can at least attempt to arrive at clearer conception of what it could possibly mean to say that I have an idea of God.

According to Hobbes in the third set of *Objections*, Descartes' view is that to have an idea of something is to have a mental image or picture of it.³ He even quotes a passage from Descartes in which Descartes appears to assert that only mental pictures are properly called ideas, since only these represent external objects. However, says Hobbes, I can have an idea of a bodily being, such as a man, the sky or a chimera, but not of an angel,

---

2. In *CSM*, Vol. II, 35.
3. In *CSM*, Vol. II, 125–6.

since my mental image of an angel (e.g., a naked baby with wings) does not resemble that object. How much less, then, does my mental image of God (e.g., an old, bearded man sitting on a cloud) resemble or represent an infinite and perfect being. Indeed, Hobbes suggests, it is impious to suppose that God could be represented to us in an idea and this is why we are warned by Scripture not to make graven images of God; to do so would be to fall into the heresy of *anthropomorphism*, of regarding God as though he were literally just a superhuman man.

In response to this, Descartes denies that he ever claimed that all ideas are mental images. By 'idea,' he says, he simply means 'whatever it is of which the mind is immediately aware' which includes much more than just mental images. Descartes points out that, even in the passage quoted by Hobbes, he included our awareness of feelings (fear, anger) and our introspective awareness of our own mental acts (affirmation and denial) among the class of ideas, even if not ideas properly so-called since they are non-representational. The suggestion is that the idea of God need not be conceived of as a mental picture of God intended as a literal representation of its object, but perhaps something more like a concept capable of definition. However, Hobbes can be forgiven for supposing that Descartes thought that the idea of God was a mental picture of God. In the very passage that Hobbes quotes, Descartes includes the idea of God among those thoughts that are "as it were images of things" and for which the term 'idea' is "strictly appropriate."[4] If Descartes does not intend to classify the idea of God as a mental image, he owes us a little more of an explanation of what he does intend. It is not hard to agree with Hobbes that Descartes ought to have given a better explanation of this idea of God before he goes on to try to prove his existence.

Gassendi offers other trenchant criticisms of Descartes' account of the idea of God. His first objection is that God would indeed be something insignificant if He could be represented in our intellects by an idea.[5] Gassendi apparently comes out of the tradition of Scholastic psychology described earlier, according to which an idea is the thing itself, existing formally and intentionally in the intellect in such a way that the intellect becomes what it knows by taking on numerically the same form in itself as exists in the object itself as its nature. To have an idea of a thing, then, is to take in and on the form of that thing, which has been transferred from an external object (in which it exists as the thing's essence or nature) to the intellect by means of the causal processes involved in perception.

4. See *CSM*, Vol. II, 25.
5. See *CSM*, Vol. II, 199.

The essence or nature of the thing becomes a *species*, which is then emitted from the object and is carried through the air to the sense organ, where it is taken in and converted into a *sensible species* existing as a state of that organ.[6] Thereafter, it is taken up by the agent intellect and converted into an *intelligible species* at which point it becomes completely immaterial as a state of the passive intellect. The form as intelligible species, then, comes to exist in the intellect as the form of its act of knowing in such a way that it exists simultaneously in the object known as its nature and intentionally in the knowing mind. According to the medievals, then, the intellect becomes identical with what it knows through taking on its form as intelligible species and thus is conformed or connatured to that object which, for Aristotle, is precisely what knowledge consists in.

Of course, the medievals did not have Descartes' notion of idea, and would never have said that we have an idea of God in this sense.[7] Neither does it seem that Descartes would want to claim this. Even if he did, such a solution would not be available to him, since the medieval psychology requires that things possess essences or natures as substantial forms, which Descartes rejects along with the rest of Aristotelian physics and metaphysics. In line with the New Physics, Descartes admits only an efficient causal account of perceptual knowledge according to which ideas are ontologically distinct from and at best merely represent external objects. As we have seen, this rules out any identity between subject and object in the knowing act and creates for us the problem of the external world, i.e., the need to justify *by inference* the belief that an external world exists. This problem is exacerbated by the New Physics to the extent that it rules out any relation of resemblance between ideas and what they putatively represent—something that Berkeley will later make much of in his critique of scientific realism.

Where God is concerned, perhaps this is just as well. After all, if my idea of God is God Himself existing in my intellect, then just as it is the case that my mind in knowing a chair becomes the chair it knows, as least formally and intentionally, so too would my mind become God (albeit only formally and intentionally) in knowing God, and the divine essence

---

6. See *CSM*, Vol. II, 202.

7. Anselm, however, does not stint to draw this consequence. In *Proslogion* II, he asserts that God, insofar as we have a concept of Him, exists in the intellect that conceives of him in accordance with the definition of God. He then goes on to argue in his famous Ontological Argument that it is impossible for us to conceive of God as existing only in this way, since to exist in the intellect alone is less perfect than to exist both in the intellect and reality, which is contrary to the definition of God as the being greater than which none other can be conceived.

would come to exist in my soul as well at least intentionally. However, it is surely the height of impiety (and nonsense) to suppose that my intellect can contain the Divine Essence, let alone *be* that essence, even formally and intentionally. Whatever my idea of God is, it is not the "form" of God (i.e., the divine essence or nature) existing in my soul or intellect. Yet what could this idea possibly be?

Gassendi does not stop here, however; he enforces the foregoing with a further point. The idea of God, says Gassendi, is the idea of an infinite being and we have, by definition, no idea of the infinite since the infinite can never be contained in a finite mind possessing merely finite acts of thought. Therefore, since the notion of infinity is part of the notion of God, neither do we have an idea of God. Few of us nowadays are likely to be as impressed as were Descartes and his contemporaries with this sort of argument. The idea of the infinite need not be an infinite idea (whatever *that* would be), i.e., represented by something existing in the mind which was itself somehow an example of what it represents. Since the pioneering work of Cantor in the nineteenth century, it has become natural for us to think of infinity as a largely mathematical concept, as a functionally specified property of certain generable series of numbers some of which have limits and others of which do not. In Descartes' time, such clarity with regard to the notion of infinity was not available; infinity was a largely metaphysical notion, one tied up with the vague (Descartes calls it the "indefinite") idea of being boundless or unlimited. Clearly, the sense in which God is said to be boundless or unlimited has nothing to do with any sort of spatial extension; divine "immensity" is not infinite size, but spacelessness combined with omnipresence in knowledge and power at every place and time.[8] However, in Descartes' time the spatialization of the notion of infinity seems to be so strongly entrenched that it seemed impossible to conceive of it in any other way.

Even Descartes, however, is able to make some sort of response to Gassendi and others who push the same sort of objection. In the first place, he argues that just because God has many more attributes than we are able to grasp with our intellect this does not rule out the possibility that the limited number of attributes we can confidently attribute to God is sufficient to constitute a clear and distinct idea of that being.[9] Further, it is not necessary in order for me to apprehend a thing that I grasp it *in toto*.

---

8. "Divine Immensity" is Scholastic term; see Ludwig Ott, *Fundamentals of Catholic Doctrine*, Rockford, IL, TAN Books and Publishers, 1974, pp. 37–8 for an account of this notion as traditionally understood.

9. See *CSM*, Vol. II, 32.

I can see the Atlantic Ocean by seeing just that part of it that can be seen from my favorite beach on the Jersey shore. Likewise, as Descartes points out, I can touch a mountain simply by touching just as much of it as I can make contact with using my fingertip and without the need to touch every inch of its surface or encircle it with my arms.[10] Therefore, it is possible for me to apprehend something immense and even to do so clearly and distinctly without attempting to encompass it completely with my limited mind or intellect. The result will be some sort of mental content to which Descartes annexes the term "idea."

However, if my idea of God is neither a mental picture of God nor the Divine Essence existing in my intellect as an intelligible species, what does Descartes take it to be? In answer to this, Descartes responds that the idea of God is an *innate concept* implanted in us by God Himself. As we shall see, unpacking this notion (about which it appears that Descartes himself was none too clear) is a difficult business. The clue to doing so properly is to remember that Descartes *defines* innate ideas as those ideas that we are able to acquire simply by contemplating our own nature, to which I would add through the power of introspection. As we shall see, making sense of this notion requires that we clarify the sense in which this idea is innate and the manner in which it has been implanted in us. I shall maintain that Descartes' view is both more subtle and plausible than has usually been thought, though he himself did not perhaps completely work this out. Before we consider these topics, however, let us consider some alternative accounts of the origin of this idea.

Alternative Accounts of the Origin of the Idea of God

In criticizing Descartes' first proof for God's existence in the third *Meditation*, Gassendi offers a couple of alternate accounts of the origin of the idea of God.[11] First, he says, it is very likely that in fact Descartes originally acquired the concept of God from his parents and other teachers rather than from any sort of meditative reflection on his own nature or simply through having noticed one day that he has an idea of God. To this suggestion it seems to me that Descartes makes a perfectly adequate response by asking "And where did my parents get the idea of God?"[12] Surely, not everyone could have acquired the belief in God from someone

---

10. See *CSMK*, 25; see also *CSM*, Vol. II, 81 where Descartes makes the same point using the example of seeing the ocean.

11. See Gassendi, fifth set of *Objections*, in *CSM*, Vol. II, 205–6.

12. *CSM*, Vol. II, 251–2.

else and even if Descartes did in fact acquire his *occurrent* idea of God from his parents, it does not follow from this that he has no innate idea of God as well. Of course, it is incumbent on Descartes to prove that this is so and he endeavors to do so in the *Meditations*, so we ought to suspend judgment on this argument until we review the evidence.

Gassendi's second suggestion, one that has appeared in other philosophers such as Locke, Hume and Feuerbach as well, is that we form the idea of God from our idea of ourselves by means of a kind of precisive abstraction. I form my idea of God from my idea of myself (or myself as an exemplar of humanity) by a kind of abstraction in which I "think away" my creaturely limitations. The result, then, is the idea of a being that is infinite in the merely negative sense that it lacks those features that belong to me by nature that I perceive as limitations to either my operation or my aspiration. This, then, is my idea of God. Alternately, I form this idea by imagining my own positive powers and abilities increased incrementally until they achieve their intrinsic maximum, thereby arriving at the notion of a being who is the sum of all perfections—the Feuerbachian human ideal writ large whom we project as existent and call "God."

Neither of these proposed explanations of the origin of the idea of God can account for the truth of Descartes' claim to have a clear and distinct idea of God. The first of these, of course, is (as Locke failed to see but Hume and Kant clearly saw) not properly an idea at all, but simply incoherent, an attempt to conceive of something (i.e., myself) without those characteristic limitations which are inseparable from my nature and thus apart from which I cannot be conceived. The second strategy is also stillborn, as Descartes points out.[13] No matter how far I imagine my own powers or abilities extended in thought, wherever I stop the result is always going to be something finite and exceedable; I can no more achieve a clear and distinct concept of infinite being in this way than I can count to infinity by twos. In both cases, the idea of God we arrive at is going to be an indeterminate idea, one without any positive content, like the spatialized concept of infinity itself, not a clear and distinct idea. Perhaps if one already had good reason for believing that there can be no such concept then there might be a reason for investigating the possibility that the concept of God is merely a pseudo-concept. However, to this point, no such reasons have yet emerged and so this cannot simply be assumed.

In fact, Descartes' anticipated both of these objections and his counter to both of them is that in order for us to even conceive of ourselves as finite, limited or imperfect in the first place requires that we already

---

13. *CSM*, Vol. II, 32.

possess a concept of the infinite, unlimited and perfect to serve as the standard against which I implicitly compare myself and find myself wanting.[14] The concepts of finite and infinite are not separable any more than the concepts of left and right or up and down are separable. Possession of one concept requires already the possession of the other because the referents of those concepts are internally related in meaning rather than merely externally so. Thus, to attempt to begin from one such concept and work one's way to the other is a hopeless enterprise. According to Descartes, then, if I can really possess a concept of myself as finite, limited or imperfect this can only be because (as Farrer puts it) "I am aware of the privation of not being the ultimate being." This, in turn, presupposes that I already possess the concept of an infinite, unlimited and perfect being, i.e., the innate idea of God.

Well, perhaps. Descartes has not yet justified the claim that he does in fact possess a clear and distinct idea of God and (as we have seen) there are those who for one reason or another are not going to be willing to grant this merely on his say-so. At the very least, Descartes owes us an account of *how* such a concept can be innately possessed by us, which in turn requires us to consider a question that Descartes never considers but ought to have, i.e., how this innate idea of God is contained within us. In the context of my project here, this turns out to be same question as the question "How it is possible for us to attain to an apprehension of God by means of the introspective method used by Descartes in his *Meditations*?" To this question I now turn.

How the Apprehension of God is Possible

At first glance, the notion that God might be apprehensible through introspection seems both impossible and impious. In the first place, God as classically conceived wholly transcends the created world and thus anything that I might be able to experience, yet my supposed apprehension of God would have to terminate in a direct confrontation between my mind and God as its object. Given divine transcendence, the idea of an apprehension of God seems ruled out in principle. It is for this reason, for example, that I cannot have a concept of God if what I mean by this is the Divine Essence existing in my intellect as an intelligible species, since in that case not only would God be wholly comprehended by me but I would be God Himself, intentionally if not actually. Surely it would the height of

---

14. *CSM*, Vol. II, 31.

impiety to claim anything of this sort, though this has not stopped some mystics from asserting just such claims.

Obviously, the foregoing rules out any sort of direct and unmediated apprehension of God acquired by means of reflection on creatures. However, this does not necessarily rule out the possibility that God be indirectly or mediately apprehended by means some relation God has to his creatures, one that is revealed to us or put on display in virtue of their inner constitution itself. In other words, if creatures present themselves to us precisely as *creatures*, i.e., as the products of divine creative causality and as continuously dependent on God in one or more respects, then in apprehending creatures as such, we thereby apprehend God as that to which they are related as both created and dependent; in knowing the effect as effect we also at the same time conceive and know the cause. In displaying themselves in this way, things function as *images* of God, ontologically distinct from but nevertheless internally related to Him, hence bearing His visage in a manner analogous to that in which a mirror image reflects my own face and makes it possible for me to admire it.[15]

We can make this a bit less metaphorical if we explicate a little more carefully in what sense God is an object of apprehension, i.e., what it means to say that some act of the intellect *terminates* in God as its object while nevertheless remaining indirect or mediated. At first glance, it appears that the notion of "mediated apprehension" is self-contradictory, since the very notion of apprehension involves the notions of immediate confrontation and direct mental grasping; these seem to be plainly inconsistent with the notion of mediation. These metaphors may be misleading here, however. For example, in the Scholastic theory of perception presented above, the form existing in the external thing as its nature becomes, as intelligible species, the form of the intellect in the act of knowing it, thus bringing about the identity of subject and object in the knowing act. It is due to this fact that a set of structured *qualia* existing in consciousness can present itself *as* an external object existing in relation to consciousness, because *this is precisely what it is*: the external thing *itself* existing formally and intentionally in consciousness without thereby compromising its independently-constituted external existence as a thing in its own right. In consequence of this fact, the external thing becomes the intentional object of the perceptual act, at once both an object of apprehension and yet apprehended as transcendent to consciousness itself. This resolves the essential paradox of perception which so troubled Berkeley, i.e., how something existing in

---

15. For further explication of these notions, see Farrer, *The Glass of Vision*, 57–95.

and dependent on the mind can at the same time present itself as existing independently of and transcendent to consciousness.

By the same token, we saw earlier that our apprehension of our own existence is likewise directly the terminus of an act of reflective self-awareness while at the same time inseparable from (hence, to that extent mediated by) our awareness of ourselves as conscious. It is precisely because of this that we were able to introspectively grasp first, the mode of consciousness, then consciousness itself (awareness-as-activity), and then finally each his or her own existence (activity-as-such), in each case discovering the ontological ground of what is first apprehended by us as ingredient in it, hence as capable of being apprehended in turn by an introspective shift in attention.

The forgoing are examples of how it is possible for there to be direct but mediate apprehension. This will not work in precisely the same way for the apprehension of God but suggests a different sort of mediation that bids fair to do the trick. Due to the fact that external things present themselves as external (hence *transcending* consciousness in being and in other respects as well) at the same time that they present themselves as related to it in perception, we can exercise our power of introspection to focus merely on those aspects of what is presented that are seen to be inseparable from the external object *as such* just as much as we can focus on those aspects that are presented as mind-relative and mind-dependent. Whatever these features may be, they will all be related either to the existence or to the essence of that thing. The essence is that which, as Lockean *nominal* essence, will be present to us as the structural principle unifying the perceptible surface qualities of that object while at the same time serving as the source of our everyday concept of that thing. Then, as Lockean *real* essence, that essence will be an inherent, imperceptible structural principle strongly supervening upon that thing's atomic microstructure while serving as the object of scientific theorizing. The thing's existence is the object of spontaneous judgment consequent upon the presentation of the thing in consciousness as *some thing* or *being* in the sense distinguished above other than myself. It is the thing as *being*, i.e., as act or operation, structured activity as realized and actualized through the act of existence, which serves as the image through which God can be apprehended. In order to see how this is so, we need to make a brief detour into some of the familiar claims of theistic metaphysics.

According to the mainstream tradition of Western monotheism, nowadays often called *classical theism*, God is both Creator and Conserver of everything that exists other than Himself. Nothing, not even matter, exists besides God unless God creates it and because of this, the act of creation is itself *ex nihilo* in relation to what is created. Since created things exist solely through God's creative act and no other principle, they likewise lack within themselves any principle by means of which they can sustain themselves in existence apart from God's continuous creation or *conservation* as it is typically called. Thus, *as existent*, created things depend continuously on God's exercise of his creative power with regard to them at every moment in the entire term of their existence. As such, God stands in the EOG relation to every one of his creatures and his continuous exercise of divine creative causality is *ingredient* in them as their *per se* cause of existence.

Thus, the first way in which creatures might function as images of God is as the effects of divine creative causality by in some way revealing or testifying to their EOG relation to God. This, of course, is the basic idea behind the cosmological argument in whatever form it takes, with different versions of the cosmological argument taking off from different ways in which external objects are taken to reveal their dependence on divine creative causality. God is thus originally apprehended as that which stands in the EOG relation to ourselves and the other things we see around us. Of course, given the Cartesian context, we cannot claim that our putative apprehension of external things is veridical, since the Evil Genius could be deceiving us about this. However, there is at least one existent thing, i.e., myself as thinking thing, the existence of which is incorrigible for me and such that the judgment expressing this fact is Cartesian-safe. If an examination of my own existence as such reveals to me the ingredience of an external principle to which I stand in an EOG relation, I will by that token possess the starting point for a full-blown apprehension of God as the *per se* cause of my individual existence, though it may take sustained reflection in order to bring it to full clarity and distinctness.

According to classical theists, it is not existence alone that is received from God in the exercise of divine creative causality; rather, one's whole being, both existence and essence, is received from God. Each individual is an individual belonging to a specific natural kind in virtue of the essence it exemplifies or instantiates and individuals differ either by instantiating different essences or by being different instances or examples of the same essence as grasped by the intellect in precisive abstraction and articulated in a concept expressible by a term or substantive referring expression. Further, insofar as essences are realized or actualized by activity-as-such in an operation extended in stages through time, the beings instantiating them are subject to change, development and becoming. God is also a being, but not a being of the same sort as myself or the other beings of my direct acquaintance. Indeed, it is traditional to say, not that God is *a* being, but rather that *God is Being Itself*, i.e., the being in whom operation or act receives full, complete and perfect expression. God is, so to speak, the *ne plus ultra* of being not exceedable in principle, even by Himself. One aspect of this notion is expressed in the idea that God is *actus purus*, i.e., operation which is completely realized or actualized as a totality and as such lacking both the capacity and/or necessity for change or development. More than this, God is activity-as-such as it realizes itself when not constrained by some arbitrary, as though externally imposed limit or boundary on its self-expression as activity. God, then, does not merely realize or actualize his own peculiar essence to the highest possible degree; rather, He realizes that essence which is uniquely highest and best in the sense that it most perfectly expresses the highest and best mode of existence-as-activity.

Given that God is not just one being among others but rather Being Itself, it remains that all other things created by God, to the extent that they actualize or realize their natures as determined by their essences, are themselves beings and thus each in its own way an expression of being. As such, each is a finite, limited or reduced version of that of which God is the infinite, unlimited and complete expression. Thus, created beings as such (just by *being beings*) participate by imitation in God's being, in that operation of which God is the full, real, and actual expression. They do so not by materially resembling God but rather by each in its own way attempting to do what God actually and totally accomplishes, i.e., express the fullness of activity-as-such to the extent allowed by essence acting as a brake on the aspirations of existence.[16] Every being, then, insofar as it partakes of existence or activity-as-such, strives (as it were) to express the fullness of activity-as-such and so to realize or actualize Being itself in and as its own being. Since every being other than God possesses essence as the limiting principle of its operation, hence of the expression of activity-as-such, every such effort miscarries, falling infinitely short of the goal that animates it. At the same time, however, each in its own way points beyond itself to the perfection of being as possessed by God and in which each of them is synthesized into a single, non-repeatable instance of that essence or nature that fully expresses activity-as-such. This, then, constitutes a sec-

---

16. I do not assume that there is any other teleological principle at work here than simply that involved in the natural tendency of existence (=activity-as-such) to seek its own self-expression. In this context, we no more need think of beings as either implicitly or explicitly goal-directed than we need think this of Schopenhauerian Will. Rather, activity-as-such seeks its own self-realization in the same way that water always seeks and arrives at the lowest place regardless of how circuitous a route it has to take to get there.

ond and different way in which creatures can function as images of God, as reduced or limited examples of what God is as Supreme Being. In each created thing's striving within the limits of its essence to achieve the closest approximation to God that lies within its power to achieve, each gestures dumbly, like a sign, in the direction that supreme perfection which is the Divine Nature or Essence: and, since that unsurpassable nature is the synthesis of all perfections (formally and eminently, as the Schoolmen say) it is infinitely participable by creatures, each of which reflects the divine image in a slightly different way, like the same object reflected by the thousand separate shards of a shattered mirror.[17]

What holds of beings in general will also hold of my being. Thus, by investigating the ways in which my (consciously appropriable) aspiration for the perfection of my own nature, or rather for the full realization of the perfections I perceive to belong to me by nature, is inevitably frustrated by the limitations of that nature and other circumstances, my being thus points beyond that nature and those circumstances to those perfections as fully actualized and realized only in a being freed from my creaturely limitations and whose nature is precisely such as to be the nature which realizes those perfections in fact. In this way, my own nature provides me with the tools and resources for the apprehension of the divine nature or essence insofar as reflection on my limited nature gives me some access, however partial and inadequate, to what it is like to be God. Initially, at least, we can conceive of the divine nature or essence as that nature or essence which actualizes or realizes all of my perfections without suffering from or requiring any of my limitations in order to fully exemplify those perfections in the highest and best way possible in principle.

Much of the foregoing will strike those unfamiliar with this way of thinking about things as strange, arcane, and 'metaphysical' in the worst sense of that word, such that even many who consider themselves sympathetic to metaphysics in general will wish to distance themselves from these views. In the next two chapters of this essay, I will endeavor to lay out both of these paths to the apprehension of God in detail and thereby motivate acceptance of this initially strange and, for many, unattractive way of looking at the world by reference to the second proof of God's existence given by Descartes in the third *Meditation*. We will begin with the way based on existence first, since this will be the most familiar and direct approach and then consider the way based on essence. Let us at long last turn to the Cartesian cosmological argument.

17. See Farrer, loc. cit., especially 86–95.

7

The Cartesian Cosmological Argument[1]

J. L. Austin once said that whenever a philosopher is faced with a distinction, one half of which appears unproblematic and the other of which seems fraught with paradox, the best thing to do is to re-examine the supposedly unproblematic half of the distinction, the idea being that there might be subtleties that we have overlooked. In this chapter, I propose to do precisely that with respect to the notion of a contingent being as this plays a role in the second argument for God's existence in the third *Meditation*. In this argument, Descartes attempts to arrive at the existence of God from the fact of his own existence. Although the text can be interpreted as a formal deductive argument, I will attempt to reconstruct it as an exercise in the application of the introspective/meditative approach to philosophical investigation that I have attributed to Descartes as the source of his knowledge of his own existence. This is advisable if for no other reason than that Descartes has yet to justify the use of deductive reasoning in the investigation of the philosophical issues. In short, what I shall be attempting to display or induce is the apprehension of God as the *per se* cause of my own existence.

With this in mind, let us turn to Descartes' claim to the effect that he can find within himself no principle that explains his own continued existence.[2] Descartes takes it for granted that his continued existence is not at all guaranteed by the fact that he existed in the past and that it therefore requires some sort of cause outside of himself. In his support, we can even enlist the words of David Hume, who said, "There is no absurdity in the

---

1. For a review of the standard, classical critique of the cosmological argument, see Michael Martin, *Atheism: A Philosophical Justification*, 96–124 and J. L. Mackie, *The Miracle of Theism*, 81–101. For a critique of some of these traditional criticisms, see William L. Rowe, *The Cosmological Argument* (second Edition), New York, Fordham University Press, 1998. In what follows, of course, I endeavor to either avoid all these criticisms or answer them *inter alia*. The reader who has familiarized him- or herself with standard examples of this literature will be able judge how successful I have been.

2. See *CSM*, Vol. II, 33–5.

notion of anything's simply ceasing to be in the next instant."[3] It is on considerations such as these that most of us, philosophers and non-philosophers alike, recognize that we are contingent beings, i.e., beings subject to coming-to-be and passing-away, whose existence is logically contingent and dependent for its continuance on numerous factors external to itself. At the same time, most philosophers find this notion of contingent being completely familiar and unproblematic. After all, we ourselves and everything else we directly experience, are contingent in these ways and the universe as a whole bids fair to be so as well, whether or not (as currently seems unlikely to turn out to be the case) it is in fact eternal. Similarly, the notion of a necessary being seems to most philosophers strange and largely incomprehensible. If theism is true, however, precisely the opposite is the case: it is not necessary being, but rather contingent being, that is paradoxical and in need of some sort of account. The first step, then, must be to display what it is about contingent being that makes it unintelligible apart from its completion in relation to necessary being.[4]

To begin with, let us note something about the claim "I exist" that has often been mentioned in passing but not really appreciated in its full significance. On the one hand, I grasp this proposition with incorrigible certainty. On the other, unlike typical examples of *a priori* knowledge, both the proposition "I exist" and the state of affairs that proposition characterizes (i.e., the fact that makes that proposition true) are logically contingent rather than necessary. Unlike "2+3=5" or "Nothing can be both red and green all over at the same time," we cannot claim to know that "I exist" simply from apprehending the meaning of the words that make the statement up. To the contrary, as I have already explained, I know the truth of this proposition by means of my incorrigible introspective grasp of the *fact* of my own existence as revealed to me in my self-conscious awareness of my own mental activity. Nevertheless, this fact is quite clearly contingent. It need not have obtained at all and I can renew my wonder at this fact every moment that I consider it. The contingency of my existence is given along with the fact of my existence at every moment that I advert to it.

The contingency of my existence is not merely a matter of my origin, i.e., of the fact that I might not have existed at all. I am not only contingent with respect to my coming-to-be but also with regard to my passing-

3. See David Hume, *Treatise of Human Nature*, edited by Selby-Bigge and Nidditch, 79.
4. As Farrer puts it (*Finite and Infinite*, 263) we must make it (i.e. finite being) look all wrong somehow, even though we ordinarily suppose that it is all right.

away, in such a way that nothing necessitates or guarantees my existence at any moment that I exist. At any moment that I actually exist, I could in principle cease to exist. It is ubiquitously the case that I am simultaneously both *actually existent* and *potentially non-existent* at every moment at which I can apprehend the fact that I exist, from my initial coming-to-be to my final passing-away. As we shall see, this is a remarkable and puzzling fact as mysterious as it is commonplace and undeniable. Sustained meditative reflection on this fact leads us to apprehend the further fact that contingent existence is ultimately non-self-explanatory. On the one hand, if it were self-explanatory at any moment, then whatever it is that explains the fact of my existence at that moment would exclude my potential non-existence at that moment and make my existence to that extent necessary (and my non-existence impossible) at that time. On the other hand, supposing that I am truly *potentially* non-existent at that time, then there must be a gap between what I contribute to my own existence at that time and the fact of my *actual* existence at that time sufficient to make my non-existence genuinely possible at that time. As such, the difference must be made up by some other principle external to me operating upon me to make me actually exist at that time.

The rejoinder to this will undoubtedly be that contingent existence is *inertial*, such that once something comes into being it simply persists in that state until something else makes it stop.[5] In this case, contingent existence is simply *interruptible* existence and its persistence in any particular case simply explained by the fact that at that moment nothing has acted to interrupt that existence and make that existent cease to be. However, as we shall see, even in order for one's existence to be interruptible in this way requires that contingent being be contingent in a much more radical fashion than this. What we ultimately have to realize is exactly the opposite of what philosophers ordinarily take things to be the case: for contingent being, non-existence is the default position and actual existence needs explanation, whereas for a necessary being existence is the default position and non-existence an impossible supposition.

One way of attempting to induce this insight is to consider what has to be the case for something to be a contingent being, i.e., a being that actually exists but need not do so. Apparently, as we have seen, it must be the case, at one and the same moment, that one and the same thing is both actually existent and yet potentially non-existent. At every moment, then, that a contingent being actually exists it is at that very same time capable of non-existence, i.e., such that it could cease to exist at that very moment

---

5. This was apparently Gassendi's view; see the fifth *Objections*, *CSM*, Vol. II, 209–10.

despite the fact that, e.g., it existed a moment previously. This in turn requires that existence be somehow *separable* from whatever actually exists as a contingent being at every moment of its existence. On the assumption that this potential separability is not somehow miraculous, (as the separability of life from the soul is thought to be by many theologians) there must be some inherent feature of contingent beings themselves that accounts for this fact. For, as the Scholastics say, actuality precedes potentiality, so that the potential separability of existence from any being can only arise from some distinction within contingent beings themselves which makes that separation *really* as opposed to merely logically possible.

Now, given that there is some inherent feature of contingent things in virtue of which they are potentially non-existent at the very same time that they are actually existent, it would appear that the mere actual existence of that thing is never sufficient by itself to account for the fact that the thing exists. If existence is in fact separable from that thing, then accounting for the fact of the existence of that thing will inevitably require reference to something outside of the thing itself as part of the explanation of that fact. To confirm this, however, requires that we look more deeply into the matter.

The Paradox of Contingent Being

Being, as we saw earlier, is *operation*, i.e. structured activity, and has two main entitative principles, existence (activity-as-such) and essence (form or structure). Existence is that which actualizes or realizes essence while essence is that which gives shape, form or structure to the activity of existence. Every being, then, possesses both existence and essence as its fundamental "components." It is time that we looked more closely at the relation between these two.

First of all, then, we must reject the notion that essence and existence are "proto-beings," i.e., independently constituted realities that somehow combine together to become beings. Only beings, i.e., structured activities, actually exist; existence and essence are merely components of being and neither is capable of remaining in being apart from the other. Existence, conceived of as wholly apart from essence, would be a completely indeterminate, structureless, featureless, propertyless something-or-other to which nothing could be attributed and about which nothing could be said, surely an unintelligible fantasticality if ever there was one. Essence without existence is at best an object of thought and without any objective constitution other than that belonging to it as a concept. To picture the essences of things as something existing as a kind of outline waiting to be colored in by existence is surely misleading and unfounded.

The supposition that naturally follows from this is that essence and existence as found in actual beings must be inseparable from one another, since neither is a being in its own right and neither can be except as a component (i.e., one of the entitative principles) of a real or actual being.[6] One way we might put this is to suggest that perhaps essence and existence are *identical* in every real or actual being, in the sense that they are somehow indistinguishable except as aspects of a single, unified entity, i.e., that being itself.[7] On this view, existence and essence can be distinguished only in thought and are only conceptually, not really, distinct. This supposition, however, has an untoward consequence. If existence and essence are identical and together jointly constitute real or actual being, it seems that existence, insofar as it is inseparable from essence, would also be inseparable from the real or actual being they jointly constitute. So, if identity of existence and essence were sufficient for the inseparability of existence from real or actual being, it follows that if essence and existence are identical in any being then existence is inseparable from that being, in which case that being is not contingent but necessary, in the sense that it is incapable of ceasing to exist, either by simply passing away or through the

---

6. This is the view of Suarez; see his *On the Essence of Finite Being as Such* (Metaphysical Disputation XXI), translated by Norman Wells, *passim* but see especially section 12, pages 178–207. Furthermore, the use of "real" and "actual" in this context is strictly speaking pleonastic, hence merely emphatic. In no way am I intending to contrast real or actual being with "irreal" or "non-actual" being. To the contrary, being is *eo ipso* real or actual and there is no other sort of being, though there are modes of real being, such as intentional inexistence as enjoyed by ideas and concepts, the kind of being possessed by properties, by substance as substrate and by contingent and necessary substances.

7. Suarez argues this claim in the foregoing; he presupposes his account of what a real distinction is as developed in his *On the Various Kinds of Distinctions* (Metaphysical Disputation VII), translated by Cyril Vollert, S. J., 16–35. Suarez defines being as actualized essence conceived of as real or actual outside of its causes and maintains that, conceived in this way there can be no real distinction between existence and essence since these are intrinsic to actualized essence inasmuch it cannot be conceived without them. However, Suarez equates actualized essence with being itself so this claim is largely analytic. He does not prove that existence, considered as the first actuality of essence *considered as secondary substance* and thus merely as one component of being, are internally related. As such, he does not undermine the doctrine of the real distinction as I have characterized it here. Dom Mark Pontifex, another critic of the real distinction who begins from a Suarezian account of being, ultimately admits the distinction in a sense equivalent to that intended here and thus takes a view that ultimately is only verbally different from my own. See his contribution to Pontifex and Trethowan, *The Meaning of Existence*, 61–81, especially 76–8.

action of some external cause.[8] Since, *per hypothesi*, existence is inseparable from that being, it is therefore impossible for there to be any cause, either internal or external, capable of making it cease to exist, since it is a necessary condition for the potential non-existence of any thing that existence be separable from it in some manner. So, then, on the supposition that it is not even possibly non-existent, it follows immediately that neither can it ever be actually so; in turn, it follows from this that if there are any contingent beings then it is necessarily the case that there is a real distinction between essence and existence in those beings. The paradox of contingent being, then, is precisely this: conceived *in relation to each other*, essence and existence are as though distinct and independent principles at best externally related to one another; this is a necessary condition for the separability of existence from essence constituting the very contingency of contingent being. Nevertheless, *conceived of in relation to being*, i.e., to concrete existing reality or structured activity, existence and essence are found in the unity of a single thing, inseparable from one another and constituting mere aspects of that being to which they belong; this, in turn, is a necessary condition for the substantial unity required for concrete actuality. However, this is surely not the case where finite being is concerned. To the contrary, such beings are contingent just through the fact that they can cease to exist; this in turn entails that existence is separable from their real or actual being, though of course not in such a way that this real or actual being can continue in its absence. In the case of contingent being, then, essence and existence possess a unity that they are incapable of constituting on their own in relation to each other.

Now, if there are contingent beings in which existence and essence are really distinct, it follows that in all such cases existence and essence are present, as Farrer puts it, *without proper unity*, i.e., without intrinsic cause or principle capable of explaining the presence of the substantial unity without which being, i.e., concrete actuality, is impossible. If existence and

---

8. As far as I am aware, Suarez nowhere faces this objection directly; for his account of how finite beings can cease to be—either by annihilation or corruption, see *On the Essence of Finite Being as Such*, op. cit., 197–9. As far as I can see, what he says there presupposes, rather than provides a means for, the solution of the above objection. For an exposition and critique of Suarez, see Gilson, *Being and Some Philosophers*, 96–107. For as clear a positive account of these matters as one might expect, see Leo Sweeney, S. J., *A Metaphysics of Authentic Existentialism*, 67–189. According to Sweeney, the distinction between essence and existence constitutes a real minor distinction, which appears to correspond to the Scotistic conceptual distinction *ratiocinatatae* or *ex parte rei* discussed below (footnote 13), a distinction that Descartes recognized and accepted; this suggests that he may have been open to the notion of the "real distinction" as understood in this way.

essence were identical in some being and thus intrinsically constituted as one thing in that case, as our natural supposition would have it, then there would be no room to raise any question about what constitutes the unity of existence and essence; since existence and essence would be merely aspects of a single thing, their identity with one another would make any such question moot. However, as we have seen, the identity of existence and essence would make existence inseparable from that being and thus rule out the possibility that it might cease to exist and thus cancel its status as a contingent being insofar as to be contingent requires that a thing be capable of ceasing to exist. Thus, in order for existence to be separable from contingent being requires that essence and existence not be identical, hence that they be really distinct. In that case, then, the question of how it is that existence and essence are able to constitute the unity of a single being becomes both fully legitimate and pressing.

Contingent beings, if such exist, will possess substantial *unity*, i.e., be one thing rather than another and distinct from all other things. Further, as we argued earlier, they will not be resolvable into any distinct parts or elements, e.g., existence-as-activity and essence as form or structure, as though these were more fundamental than and capable of being somehow apart from the whole of which they are parts. At the same time, however, we have just seen that the potential non-existence of a contingent being shows that existence and essence are really distinct in that thing. However, if existence and essence are really distinct, then those two entitative principles are not sufficient by themselves to account for the unity of the being they jointly compose. A contingent being, then, is such a unity but apparently not intrinsically so. These two characteristic features of contingent being considered as such, i.e., substantial unity and potential non-existence, both of which are necessary in order for something to be a contingent being, turn out to be apparently incompatible. To the extent that a contingent being is a being it possesses the unity of a single thing; to the extent that it is contingent, it is not intrinsically so. As such, it appears that we are faced with a paradox: a contingent being is both a unity and not a unity at the same time.[9] To enforce this result, let us consider more

---

9. Clearly, contingent beings are not of all of a piece here. Some contingent beings are composite substances composed of separable parts capable of retaining their individual natures when removed from the complex they compose by being externally related to other separable parts jointly composing it. Here I am speaking only of simple substances. I follow Locke in identifying only three sorts of simple substances: God, the soul and corpuscles (by which I mean the smallest units of matter/energy, whatever these turn out to be). Of these, only the latter

precisely what it means to say that existence and essence are really distinct in contingent being.

We have already rejected the idea that existence and essence are independently constituted principles capable of being apart from the being that contains them. So when we claim that existence and essence are really distinct in contingent things—here contrasting real with merely conceptual distinction in relation to our powers of abstraction—we are not saying that they are separable from one another in fact while remaining in being. Instead, we are claiming that (a) neither is the principle or cause of the other and (b) there is no third thing of which each is an aspect or element capable of explaining their unity in the being they jointly compose. Given the foregoing, we can eliminate alternative (b) straightaway; the only thing of which existence and essence are component parts are the being they jointly constitute and it would be circular to appeal to this being as the source of the unity of existence and essence by means of which that being is itself constituted. At the same time, it is fairly easy to eliminate alternative (a) as well. In contingent being, essence in relation to existence is as something distinct from it and imposed upon it, while existence in relation to essence is as something received by it. However, since essence does not "pre-exist" the being of which it is a component, it is not there either to impose itself or to receive. In a like manner, existence-as-such is unintelligible apart from essence as form or nature and so is there neither to be imposed on nor to be received. The paradox simply worsens the more we explore it.

Of course, the obvious alternative is to suppose that the principle of unity in a contingent being must be something external to that being itself; a source capable of simultaneously constituting existence and essence as being in such a way that essence is imposed on existence and existence is received by essence. Since neither existence nor essence "pre-exists" the being they constitute as real or actual, both must simultaneously come into being as the entitative principles of a being and thus be apportioned to each other by this external principle so that they constitute the unity of a single being. For the same reason, since potential non-existence is a permanent feature of contingent being, the same external principle that constitutes the unity of existence and essence in contingent being must likewise continue to conserve that unity for the entire time that this being remains in existence. This external principle of the unity of existence and essence in contingent being is therefore nothing less than the *per se* or sus-

---

two are contingent beings.

taining cause of my being, what the Medievals call its *causa in esse* (being) as opposed to its *causa in fieri* (becoming). It is not merely something that sustains my act of existence as it realizes essence, or simply imposes essence on existence-as-activity. Rather, it sustains this unity in such a way as to constitute the being of each contingent being while preserving its capacity for potential non-existence. Let us refer to this principle as the *per se* cause of contingent being.

The Nature of the *Per Se* Cause of Contingent Being

If the foregoing analysis is correct, the existence of contingent beings seems to require the existence of an external principle of unity in that being which stands in what I earlier referred to as the EOG relation to that being, or in more familiar language, is its *per se* cause upon which it depends not just for its origin but for its continuous existence, hence which continues to sustain its existence at every moment at which that thing exists. Now, if we apprehend the existence of any contingent being as such, i.e., it becomes evident to us that we in fact apprehend the existence of some being (such as one's own self) which is in fact contingent in the way above described, we then apprehend by that same token a being whose continuous existence depends upon the constant sustaining activity of some principle external to that thing and thus whose operation is immanent in and ingredient in that being. Thus, in apprehending that being as contingent we are at the same time apprehending its *per se* cause as that which acts in such a way as to make up the difference between what a contingent being's act of existence and essence as form or structure contribute to its being and what is needed to constitute the unity of that being as real or actual.

Although I have used the language of causation here, I am not speaking as though this were a case of mere efficient causation, or what the Medievals would have called *per accidens* causation. Since efficient causes precede their effects in time and need not exist or operate at the time we observe the effect, it is appropriate to describe the judgment that posits the cause because of the effect as a case of inductive inference, involving a causal generalization and an observational premise that strongly supports the causal conclusion. In this case, however, it is more appropriate to describe what is happening as apprehension rather than inference. It would be odd to describe my judgment that a paper theater poster plastered to the wall of a building covers that wall as an inference. This is not because I can somehow see the wall through the poster but because I know that the poster will not remain rigid and upright unless there is something in back of it to which it is attached. Theater posters lack the capacity to remain rigid and upright unless they are literally backed up by something else, thus, in seeing such a poster, I am at the same time aware of the rigidity and uprightness of that poster as the consequence of the poster's having been attached to something which backs it up and to which it remains attached for so long as it possesses those properties. As such, I apprehend the wall, not as such, but instead as that which backs up the poster and makes it rigid and holds it upright, as the *per se* cause of those properties of the poster. Since the relation of a *per se* cause to its effect is much more immediate than that of a *per accidens* (efficient) cause to its effect (because its causal action occurs simultaneously with the production of its effect and the effect continues only so long as the cause acts), in being aware of the one it makes sense to say that one is at the same time aware of the other. That is to say, in apprehending the first we also apprehend the second as the *per se* cause of those properties of the first.

Of course, I have not yet motivated the claim that we do, in fact, apprehend any contingent beings: that is where Descartes comes in. However, before returning to the *Meditations*, let us pause to consider briefly what the nature of the *per se* cause of contingent being might be as first or primarily apprehended. We apprehend that *per se* cause as that which constitutes or is the principle of the unity of essence and existence in contingent being. However, in order for this cause or principle to accomplish this task, it seems that such a being could not be contingent, at least not in the same way as the contingent beings it sustains. For, suppose that cause or principle were such that existence and essence were really distinct within it. In that case, either this cause or principle would require some cause or principle external to itself serving as the cause of its unity or that being would not, in fact, consist in the unity of a single being after all. On the assumption that we do in fact apprehend such a cause or principle, the second alternative is ruled out, since that alternative is inconsistent with the actual existence of that cause or principle and thus with our apprehending it. It remains, then, only to consider the first alternative. If we assume that the cause or principle that sustains contingent being is itself contingent in precisely the same way as the beings it sustains and thus requires a sustaining cause or principle in its own right, then the same question will arise with regard to that additional sustaining cause, i.e., is it, in turn, contingent in precisely the same way as that which it sustains? In that case, it too will require a further sustaining cause to guarantee its being about which the same question will arise, and so on. We are clearly off on an infinite regress; is it also an infinite vicious regress as well?

It is. The order of causes or principles we are currently considering is a *per se* series, each member of which exists and operates simultaneously with the effect it produces. However, if none of these causes or principles possesses substantial unity in its own right, it seems impossible that it could be a cause or principle of substantial unity in something else. For, lacking any intrinsic principle of substantial unity each will require an external principle of exactly the same sort to account for its own substantial unity and thus fail to provide an explanation for the case or cases it was invoked to explain. In this case, the analogies to an infinitely long chain holding up a five-pound weight or an infinite stack of books supporting some book two feet off the floor are obviously *apropos*. If none of the books or the links in the chain can hold itself up, neither can it hold up or support any of the other books or links; to extend such a series to infinity is simply to compound the problem infinitely, not solve it by vague appeals to the unique properties of infinite sets.[10]

In thus being aware of the existence of any contingent thing, then, I also apprehend the activity of its *per se* cause ingredient in it as the principle of substantial unity in that thing. Even if this activity is mediated by the secondary operation of other contingent causes, as Aquinas thought,[11] the series must necessarily terminate in some being possessing substantial unity in its own right, by nature, rather than through having received it from some external source. Since the lack of substantial unity in contingent things is a consequence of the real distinction between existence and essence in those things, to have substantial unity by nature means that in such a being existence and essence are not really distinct, but *identical* in a unique sense to be explained in the next chapter. Such a being, often characterized as *the being whose essence is to exist* is also traditionally referred to as *necessary* being, again in a unique sense that while differ-

---

10. For and excellent exposition of this point in the context of the Aquinas's discussion of the first two his Five Ways in the *Summa Theologiae*, see William L. Rowe, *The Cosmological Argument*, 10–39. For further defense of these claims, see Patterson Brown, "Infinite Causal Regression" in Anthony Kenny, ed., *Aquinas*, 222–3 and Norman Kretzmann, "Aquinas's Disguised Cosmological Argument" in Daniel Howard-Snyder and Jeff Jordan, eds. *Faith, Freedom and Rationality*, 185–204. On the uselessness of extending such a series to infinity, see Germain Grisez, *Beyond the New Theism* 64–7 and Norman Geisler, *Philosophy of Religion*, 197–201. For a more general response to the typical criticisms of the cosmological argument based on the possibility of an infinite regress of mutually dependent finite beings, see Rowe, op. cit. 144–7.

11. On this point, see Patterson Brown, loc. cit and Kretzmann op cit. 201–2.

ent from modern notions of logical necessity is not altogether opposed to them.[12] I will be at great pains in the next chapter to lay out exactly what is meant by these mysterious expressions to the extent possible for human reason. For now, by necessary being I mean only to refer to a being in which essence and existence are not distinct but identical and inseparable from one another: such a being possesses necessary being insofar as it is a *non-contingent* being.

Let us return to the main topic and once more address the question whether any contingent beings exist. Thomists argue that the existence of contingent things is an obvious fact of observation revealed in our awareness of external objects. However, within the Cartesian context in which we are operating, we have as yet no reason to suppose that any such objects exist. Further, we have seen that, even if the existence of external objects is somehow apprehended in existential judgment, it is not apprehended in such a way as to provide an epistemic guarantee of the truth of those judgments. We have no choice, then, but to return to Descartes and the status of my own existence, which alone can be apprehended by me with complete epistemic certainty.

I am a Contingent Being

According to Descartes, I do indeed grasp my own existence with epistemic certainty, such that not even the Evil Genius could confuse or deceive me about this fact. Further (and contrary to what the Thomists teach), I do so *directly*, thanks to my power of introspection, in such a way that I am aware of and grasp my existence prior to grasping my essence. I know that I exist, that I am a being, prior to apprehending my nature or essence.[13]

---

12. Why necessary *being*? Answer: Because nothing can be cause or principle of something else without existing, and nothing can simply exist without being something or other, i.e., without possessing an essence or nature. Thus, this *per se* cause of my being is likewise a being, although, as we shall see, not merely one being among others. Rather, this per se cause of my being turns out to be Being Itself—see below *vide supra*.

13. In a letter to an unnamed correspondent written in 1645 or 1646 (*CSM*, 279–81), in which he apologizes for any confusion that might have resulted from its hasty composition, Descartes follows Scotus in maintaining that existence and essence are formally distinct, i.e., conceptually distinct *ratiocinatatae* or *ex parte rei*—founded somehow in the thing itself. He denies that there are any conceptual distinctions *ratiocinantis*, i.e. relative solely to our powers of precisive abstraction, on the ground that every distinction requires a foundation in reality in order to be conceivable. In this he appears to coincide with the opinion of Suarez; see his Disputation 30, *On the Essence of Finite Being*, Translated by Norman Wells, 95. Descartes' reason for saying this is that essence considered in itself is something different from essence considered as existent outside the mind. The first is

Indeed, by this very fact it is arguable that I already grasp the contingency of my own existence; if my existence and my essence were such as to be identical rather than really distinct in my being, then I could not apprehend the one without thereby apprehending the other. However, the fact—as Descartes himself admits—that I can mistakenly believe that I am a body or that my soul is a kind of vapor and other such absurdities demonstrates that existence and essence are not identical in me, but really distinct. Of course, Descartes believes that he can go on to apprehend his own essence introspectively, identifying himself as a being whose essence is to think, i.e., to be conscious. However, Descartes has not succeeded in persuading anyone that one can arrive at knowledge of one's own essence in the fashion he describes in *Meditation* II. Even those most sympathetic to Descartes, such as myself, have to admit that things are more complex in this area than Descartes supposed them to be.[14] In this context, however, the truth of this claim, if accepted as such, simply reinforces the point I am making here. If, in fact, even incorrigible knowledge of my existence does not require or involve an inchoate apprehension of my essence, then existence and essence must be distinct, i.e., non-identical, principles in my being.[15]

---

merely an abstract concept and the other is something posited outside the mind, so that this difference in objective being in the two ideas must have a cause in the thing itself other than essence as such, which is presumably the principle of existence. However, he goes on to say that essence and existence considered in the concrete being itself are not in any way distinct. This also appears to coincide with the view of Suarez; see *On the Essence of Finite Being*, 87–92. However, neither Suarez nor Descartes intend to dispute the doctrine of the real distinction as I, following Farrer, have drawn it here. Indeed, both affirm that only in God is existence the principle of essence; see *CSM*, Vol. II, 47, Suarez, *On the Essence of Finite Being*, 95–6. For more on the various sorts of distinctions drawn by Scholastic philosophers, see Clemenson, *Descartes Theory of Ideas*, 24–30 and 111–12; he concentrates on the Coimbran authors whose textbooks were used in the philosophy courses at La Fleche and which Descartes might therefore have been exposed as a student.

14. Consider, for example, Malcolm's famous critique of the "imaginability" argument (already clearly anticipated by Arnauld and Gassendi) given in "Descartes Proof That His Essence Is Thinking," *Philosophical Review* 74 (1965) 315–38, reprinted in Doney, *Descartes*, 312–37; all scholars today appear to agree that this argument not only fails, but is a logical howler. However, recent Descartes scholarship has convinced me that Descartes is not making the argument attributed to him by Malcolm and does not claim to have shown that the essence of the soul is to think and that soul and body are genuinely distinct until the sixth *Meditation*. I here reserve judgment concerning the soundness of the argument given there, while noting that contemporary scholars appear to have uniformly rejected it.

15. Here I am in broad agreement with Malebranche's critique of Descartes as reconstructed by Tad Schmaltz; see his *Malebranche's Theory of the Soul*, New York, Cambridge University Press, 2003.

Descartes' own account of the matter, however, fails fully to convince due to his failure to isolate precisely what it is in which contingent existence consists. Descartes focuses on persistence (continuous existence through time) *as such* and makes things easier for himself by making the Occasionalist assumption that time consists of a series of discrete moments rather than existing as a continuum.[16] For this reason, he rejects the notion that the actions of his parents in generating him (a classic example of a *per accidens* cause of existence) or his previous existence at earlier times is a sufficient explanation of his existence *now*, i.e., at some later time. Further, he reports (what is surely true) that he detects within himself no principle which operates to guarantee his persistence over time which surely he would if it were there. Despite this, all of these points, however sound, are vulnerable to the "inertial theory of existence" suggested by Gassendi. According to this view, it is conceivable that existence is like motion as conceived of in the New Science, merely a persistent state of whatever exists and only externally related to it, such that once something is brought into existence it simply continues to exist, without any external cause or reason, until something makes it cease to exist. In response to this, Descartes simply dismisses this suggestion on the ground that it attributes to the creature that which can only belong to the creator.[17] This is in fact true, I think, but Descartes does not present any justification for it in the *Replies* to the fifth *Objections*. To justify Descartes' response requires that we go deeper into this matter than he does, and this will have to wait until the next chapter.

However, given what we have established so far, it is clear that the inertial theory of existence will not do. For the Cartesian Cosmological argument as I have sketched it here does not rely on the mere fact of existence, nor of mere persistence, nor the merely logical (i.e., no contradiction involved in my non-existence) or physical (i.e., no necessity in its having been the case that I existed) contingency of my existence. The sort of contingency mentioned here is properly *metaphysical* contingency, i.e., the lack of any intrinsic principle accounting for the substantial unity of existence and essence in my being without which my existence would not be contingent in any of these other senses. Even the "inertial" theory of existence presupposes this, since it admits that existence is separable from essence due to the operation of an external cause, which would not be possible unless the unity of existence and essence were something less than the

---

16. See *CSM*, Vol. II, 33.
17. See *CSM*, Vol. II, 255.

proper unity of identity or inseparability.[18] Since I *do* exist as a substantial unity over a determinate period of time (at least at any moment at which I contemplate that fact), there must be ingredient in my being the operation of some external principle, a *per se* cause of which the fact of my existence is an effect. Thus, in apprehending my own existence as contingent in this way, I am thereby made introspectively aware of my dependence on the continuous, ubiquitous operation of that principle in my being.

It does not follow from this that this "lack of substantial unity" I have been describing is an altogether unique notion peculiar to a particular metaphysical system, i.e., neo-Thomism. To the contrary, that there should be a real distinction between essence and existence is implicated in each of the other sorts of contingency I have just distinguished; the (unrealized) logical and physical possibilities of my non-existence at the present moment are themselves conceivable only on the supposition that existence and essence are really distinct in me. For me to conceive of (as opposed to merely imagining) my non-existence requires precisely that I be able to conceive of my essence as non-exemplified or uninstantiated, hence as completely and thoroughly specifiable apart from my existence and in a manner indifferent to it. Only in such case, then, will it be possible for me to conceive of myself as non-existent, i.e., of my non-existence as a *counterfactually unrealized possibility*. By the same token, the *fact* of my existence requires that some principle other than essence be (as it were) added to existence in order to account for that fact and that the co-presence of these two principles constitute no mere juxtaposition but a genuine unity. It is not existence *as such* but *being*, i.e., the constitution of essence and existence in the unity of a single, self-identical entity of which each is an inseparable,

---

18. Furthermore, it is arguable that there is no such thing as "existential inertia." If existence were merely a persistent state of something, like motion in a body, it would be a merely extrinsic, accidental feature of that thing that it could either have or lack without affecting its actuality; existence, of course, cannot be anything like this. Nor is there any "existential inertia" in the sense of a natural tendency on the part of things to continue to exist once they come into existence. In fact, we have no conception of such a tendency as the cause or explanation of the continued existence of any real or actual being. To the contrary, in every case we find that the continued existence of every observable thing is dependent at every moment that it exists on the copresence of the independently necessary and jointly sufficient conditions that preserve it in being. The removal of any of these conditions will bring about the passing-away or non-existence of whatever depended on them and they are powerless to stay in being in their absence. The concept of "existential inertia" then is quite useless as an alternative to admitting the real distinction; instead, it is completely superfluous and neither necessary for nor even capable of explaining any aspect of the fact of existence for any finite being.

wholly integrated aspect that requires to be explained and to be explained in such a way that it does not compromise the separability of existence from essence necessary for the potential non-existence of that being which is the hallmark of contingency in all the senses distinguished above. Because of this, we are led to realize that, in apprehending ourselves as *beings* (i.e., concrete actualities possessed of substantial unity) and yet at the same time as *contingent* beings (i.e., in which existence and essence are really distinct, hence incapable of constituting that substantial unity by themselves) we are led to recognize the immanent operation of some external cause or principle which constitutes the substantial unity of our being without annulling the separability of existence from essence in that being.[19]

This apprehension can be described as both *direct* (in one sense) while being at the same time *mediated* (in another). My apprehension of the operation of this external *per se* cause or principle is direct insofar as my act of introspection, beginning from my incorrigible grasp of my own existence arrives at and terminates in an apprehension of that cause or principle constituted by my very awareness of my dependence on such a principle and of the fact of my existence as the effect of its immanent operation in my being. However, it is nevertheless mediated insofar as my grasp of this cause or principle is limited to an awareness of how that cause or principle is related to me rather than terminating as such in a phenomenologically

---

19. Could this *per se* cause consist in other contingent beings whose simultaneous causal activity combines to conserve my being? This is a big issue that I cannot fully discuss here and hope to do elsewhere; let me just briefly summarize my reasons for rejecting this possibility. First of all, since each of the members of a set of contingent beings will all require a *per se* cause in its turn, postulating such a set will in turn either require postulating a further cause of each of its members individually or for the entire group as a whole if we simply postulate it as a completed totality of mutually supporting things. In the first case, we are off on an infinite, vicious regress and in the second, we need some cause not a member of the group to account for its actuality; in neither case, then, is the group sufficient to account for my continued existence: the problem is simply deferred, not solved. Nor can this be avoided by making the group into a series infinitely extended into the past. Once again, either we will have to postulate this series as a completed totality, in which case the same problem recurs as in the first case we considered, or we must try to claim that the series is self-explanatory by virtue of the fact that previous members of the series explain each member of the series. However, since such a series need not have existed *at all*, neither need any of its members have done so; so the existence of the series cannot be accounted for in this way. Therefore, none of these suppositions can account for the gap between what I contribute to my own substantial unity and the fact of that unity as the necessary and partially constitutive condition of my being. It remains then that, in apprehending the gap and the fact that the gap is closed, I apprehend the action of a non-contingent being ingredient in my being and acting as the *per se* cause of my substantial unity and thus of my being.

isolable awareness of that cause or principle that characterizes it as it is in itself. In so doing, I arrive at the same time at the concept of this cause or principle as that which constitutes the unity of my being as its *per se* cause through its immanent operation ingredient in my being, or more simply as the *per se* cause of my being. By further reflection, I am led to recognize that this *per se* cause of my being is a being whose own substantial unity is intrinsic rather than constituted by some further external principle or cause external to itself, hence as a being in whom existence and essence are *identical*. Since, in such a being, existence and essence are inseparable, I am likewise led to recognize the non-contingent *per se* cause of my being as a *necessary being* in the traditional sense of that term, a being whose non-existence is impossible in all the relevant senses of impossibility alluded to above. In recognizing these further features of the *per se* cause of my existence, I deepen my introspective apprehension of that being and arrive at last at the recognition of the existence of a necessary being as the transcendental complement of my apprehension of my own existence as something apart from which the fact of my existence is not possible.[20]

Thus the Cartesian Cosmological "argument" (really an extended introspective meditation on the fact of my own existence and its transcendentally necessary conditions as revealed in reflection) arrives at the traditional conclusion that there exists a necessary being on the basis of my actual introspective apprehension of such a being through its immanent operation in my being itself as that by which the fact of my existence is constituted. Is this, as Aquinas suggests, "What all men call God?" Whether this is so or not, it certainly falls short of what Descartes claims for himself, i.e., nothing less than a clear and distinct *idea* or *concept* of God as a perfect being and which he requires in order that his other two arguments for God's existence can get off the ground. Do we have the resources to arrive at such a clear and distinct idea or concept based on our apprehension of God as a necessary being? I claim that we do, and will devote the next chapter of this study to the justification of this claim. Essentially, we shall simply continue on the line of reflection I have initiated in this chapter, deepening our intellectual grasp on the object of apprehension it has revealed.

---

20. Of course, this is going a bit too fast at this point. The next chapter will further explicate all these claims and fill in the *lacunae* in such a way as to further motivate and confirm the truth of these claims.

8

The Concept of God

According to Descartes, we have an idea or concept of God as a being who possesses all perfections. However, as we have seen, this is a claim that his critics, such as Hobbes and Gassendi, are not willing to grant, asserting either that we have no such idea, or that the idea is simply the product of our imagination, which invents this idea by abstracting from our creaturely limitations and designating the result our concept or idea of God. Further, while Locke accepted that this is a genuine idea, Hume, more properly, does not. In assessing Descartes's claim (which constitutes the first premise of his first *Meditation* III argument for God's existence) we need to consider whether we do *in fact* possess such an idea and consider what sort of idea this might be. My strategy will be to begin from the results of the Cartesian Cosmological argument, which arrives at the existence of a non-contingent being, i.e., one in which existence and essence are identical, and by further contemplation of that notion, arrive by degrees at the conception of God as a perfect being.[1] Having shown how meditative reflection on the idea of a necessary being leads to the conception of God as a perfect being, I shall conclude that we do, in fact, possess such an idea. Later in this chapter, I shall then argue, *a la* Descartes, that this idea bids fair to be an innate idea.

In discussing this matter, I shall attempt to explain how it is that it can be the case both that I arrive at the concept of God by reflection on my own Cartesian-safe apprehension of my own existence functioning as the

---

1. I have been inspired in this undertaking by the efforts of Descartes' one-time rival, Jean-Baptiste Morin, whose treatise "That God Exists," in Roger Ariew, John Cottingham and Tom Sorrell, eds., *Descartes' Meditations: Background and Source Materials*, 230–51, takes this approach. On Morin himself, see Daniel Garber, "J. B. Morin and the *Second Objections*" in Ariew and Grene, eds., *Descartes and His Contemporaries*, 63–82. I am hopeful that my presentation rescues the Cartesian conception of God from the criticisms leveled against it by Jean-Luc Marion in his "The Essential Incoherence of Descartes' Definition of Divinity," trans. by Frederick P. Van de Pitte, in Amelie Rorty, ed., *Essays on Descartes' Meditations*, 297–338.

image or likeness of God in me and yet that idea be innate.[2] In this regard, I shall maintain that despite the innateness of the idea of God, it is not evident to us in itself or as such. Instead, it is present in us only inchoately as a ubiquitous feature of the conceptual background of our experience of the world. Thus, while every rational being in some sense possesses this concept and thereby apprehends God by means of it, not everyone does so explicitly or to the same degree. Thus, it is false to say, as Locke does, that the idea of God is not innate because not everyone believes in God, or worships him or conceives of deity in the same way as classical theists like Descartes.[3] Explicit, fully articulate knowledge of God is the achievement of the same sort of introspective meditation that reveals the *Cogito*. Just as every rational being is immediately aware of his or her own existence despite the fact that he or she may never have consciously formulated the *Cogito* to him-or herself, so too is it the case that every rational being is inchoately aware of God (as is revealed, for example, by ordinary language) without explicitly recognizing it. The sort of meditation undertaken here does not create that idea; it simply articulates it and makes it explicit in reflection.

Having established that we do, in fact, possess an idea of God as a perfect being, we will then be in a position to evaluate Descartes' "proof" for the existence of God drawn from the special features of the idea of God. The first step will be to show that, given those special features, the idea of God cannot be the product of sense experience, imagination (which presupposes sense-experience) or mere extrapolation from my concept of "my self." Against the background of an explicit awareness of the concept of God it will be much easier to see the point of Descartes' criticisms of these alternate proposals. We will then be in a position to appreciate Descartes' claim that only God could be the source/cause of that idea and that therefore our mere possession of this concept (which, as it turns out, is inseparable from my concepts of self, being, intellect and will) is sufficient to establish the reality of its object. In so doing, we will complete the project we began in the last chapter, i.e., of showing how an apprehension of God is possible by means of the apprehension of my own existence.[4]

---

2. See *CSM*, Vol. II, 35.
3. Locke, *Treatise of Human Nature*, edited by A. C. Fraser, Vol. I., 95–108.
4. See chapter ten below.

From Non-Contingent Being to Necessary Being

By means of the Cartesian Cosmological argument, we arrive at the existence of a *per se* cause of my existence in whom existence and essence are identical rather than really distinct. However, we as yet apprehend that being only *negatively* as a non-contingent being in which existence and essence are identical only in the sense of not being distinct in such a way as to be separable from one another.[5] In order to improve our apprehension of this being, we need to consider how this identity of existence and essence can be conceived positively. We will begin, again, from reflection on contingent being. In the case of a contingent being, there is a real distinction between essence and existence such that existence and essence are separable from one another. As such, even supposing that being to be real or actual for a period of time, it will be, at every moment that it exists, capable of ceasing to be real or actual as well. By contrast, a non-contingent being of the sort we have apprehended using the Cartesian Cosmological "argument" is one in which essence and existence are identical, i.e., not really distinct or separable from one another. In that case, this being fails to meet one of the necessary conditions for potential non-existence, namely that existence and essence be separable in principle from one another in its being. As such, supposing it to be real or actual, it is incapable of ceasing to exist. Such a being, then, would thereby be a *necessary being*, as this notion is traditionally understood. Thus, we can affirm that the non-contingent being revealed by the essence/existence argument is also a *metaphysically necessary* being, one that is actual in such a way as to not be even potentially non-actual.

In such a being, the identity of essence and existence *explains* its persistence in being—it persists because it is incapable of ceasing to persist. Such a being thus has its being *a se*, i.e., "out of itself" inasmuch as its persistence in being finds its cause or explanation from within itself. In the order of persistent being, then, we find a stopping-point for all explanation in the apprehension of a being of whom it cannot be asked, "What is the cause of its persistence?" Thus, my contingent being finds its explanation in the activity of a necessary being, one for whom the question of persistence cannot be raised.

At this point, of course, the fact that this being exists rather than fails to exist is still merely a surd fact and the question why it exists rather than

---

5. There is more to this notion than merely what is supplied by the notion of non-contingence; see below.

not still an open question. I will address this question in Chapter 10, stopping here only to note that, given that such a being has been apprehended by us and as something real or actual, the question of whether or not it exists is by this point moot. For the same reason, neither can its existence be rejected on the ground that no cause or reason has been provided to explain its bare existence. To those who would substitute the surd fact of the existence of the external world for that of God, treating the appeal to God as somehow superfluous, we need only note that, up to now, we have no reason to suppose that any such world exists, let alone that we apprehend it. By contrast, however, we do apprehend God. Instead, let me stick to the order of exposition by next considering how the necessary being revealed to us by this line of reflection is also an infinite being as well.

From Necessary Being to Infinite Being

Contingent beings are beings in which there is a real distinction between essence and existence and thus are capable of both failing to exist and (even when real or actual) ceasing to exist. Such beings can only be and persist in being when the necessary and sufficient conditions for that state of affairs are real or actual as well. As such, they come to be and pass away because their being is only possible when the proper conditions obtain and cannot continue in their absence. As such, every contingent being is also a *finite* or *dependent* being, requiring the continuous ingredience of other things outside itself both for its coming into being and for its persistence in being. A necessary being, by contrast, since it admits no separation of essence and existence in its being, cannot be affected in that respect by anything external to itself. Since it contains within itself its own cause or reason for its persistence in being—namely the inseparable identity of essence and existence in its being—it does not rely for its existence on any state-of-affairs external to itself necessary for or ingredient in its being. As such, the persistence of that being, lacking any externally necessary conditions, cannot be affected by the removal of any such conditions. Thus, no matter how much things change, its persistence in being will not be affected in any way. In one sense of the term, then, we may designate as *infinite being* any being that is non-dependent or unconditioned, one that persists in being regardless of what happens outside of it because its persistence in being is not dependent on or limited by anything outside itself. The non-contingent being of the Cartesian Cosmological Argument will thus be an infinite being in that sense as well. However, this is only one small aspect of the divine infinity; we now turn to the second and more important aspect of this notion.

In the case of finite being, we noted that the real distinction between existence and essence means that neither is the principle or cause of the other, thereby making it impossible to explain essence by reference to existence or *vice versa*. In a necessary being, however, either existence is going to be the principle of essence, essence the principle of existence, or there will be some further thing that will be the joint principle of both. The first two alternatives have both had adherents in the past. What is called *essentialism* in metaphysics proposes that essence is the principle of existence in the ultimate being. This view has been held by such philosophical notables as Scotus, Suarez, Spinoza, and the Leibnizian forerunners of Kant.[6] On the other hand, the *metaphysical existentialism* attributed to Aquinas by some of his neo-Thomist followers, such as Maritain and Gilson, maintains that existence is the principle of essence in the ultimate being.[7] In one sense, it does not matter to me which of these approaches one takes, since I regard them as ultimately convergent. However, my own preference is for the existentialist as opposed to the essentialist approach, at least insofar as the order of exposition is concerned. In a later chapter, we will discuss Descartes' highly essentialist version of the ontological argument and show how it complements his other arguments for God's existence as well as why he waits until *Meditation* V to introduce it.

According to metaphysical existentialism, then, it is the necessary being's act of existence that dictates its essence i.e., in the identity of existence and essence in the necessary being it is existence, not essence that takes precedence. Thus, existence is the principle of essence with regard to the necessary being apprehended by means of the Cartesian Cosmological argument. As Farrer puts it, what I have been calling a non-contingent being is or exemplifies the essence/nature which belongs to being *as such*, to existence when not arbitrarily constrained or limited by some essence which stands to that act of existence as though it were some sort of external imposition. To put it a different way, the necessary being is the being that expresses the *fullness of being*, i.e., exemplifies or instantiates the essence/nature constituting

---

6. See Etienne Gilson, *Being and Some Philosophers*, 74–128; Gilson maintains that Kant's doctrine of existence derives from this tradition.

7. See Gilson, op. cit., 154–189, in which he gives his exposition of the authentic Thomist (hence, by his lights, true) view of being. See also his many other writings on metaphysics and the *locus classicus* for this interpretation of Aquinas, *De Ente et Essentia*, translated by Joseph Bobik as *On Being and Essence*, Notre Dame, Ind., Notre Dame University Press, 1965.

the highest intensive degree of being, the essence/nature most fully expressive of what existence-as-activity is *as such* or when it is allowed to be itself. ("Surely," says Farrer, "it can somewhere just 'be itself.'")[8]

This is sometimes expressed in Thomist textbooks as the view that when we say that, in God, existence and essence are identical we are at the same time saying that God is the *being whose essence is to exist*. This formula perhaps comes closest to expressing in words the insight being articulated here. At the same time, however, it has a major drawback as well. In saying that God's essence is to exist we (or, at any rate, I) do not intend to suggest that God is nothing but some sort of undifferentiated, structureless act of "pure existence" transcending all descriptive categories. Such an account may apply to the Plotinian One or the Tillichian "Ground of Being" but not to the necessary being I have been describing here. Again, to say these things is not to say that God is nothing but existence-as-activity conceived of in contradistinction to essence, as "pure" or undifferentiated existence. Being itself has a definite essence capable of being captured in a clear and distinct concept, though not perhaps exhaustively or without effort. Nor is it to suggest that God is a kind of common primal "stuff," being or existence-as-activity, out of which all things are made and with which all things are ultimately identical or into which they are somehow absorbed, like Brahman, the Plotinian One or the Hegelian Absolute. The factual existence of God does not rule out the factual existence of things other than and distinct from Himself. The point is not that the necessary being described above is somehow *essenceless*, but that it has a *unique* essence, the essence dictated by, corresponding to, and naturally accompanying existence-as-activity when that activity is permitted to completely express and totally realize itself in accordance with its own internal dynamic. Indeed, it is that very essence/nature which constitutes that internal dynamic and therefore achieves instantiation or exemplification in a unique being in which every potentially for existence-as-activity *as such* is realized to the highest degree possible within a single being.

Once we have deepened our apprehension of necessary being from the point of view of metaphysical existentialism, we are now able to recognize that, just as in explicitly apprehending our own existence we at the same time implicitly apprehend the existence of the necessary being. Thus, in explicitly apprehending necessary being we are at the same time apprehending infinite being *in a further sense of that term*—as a being whose existence is not constrained or limited by essence but instead for which essence is the natural and fullest expression of existence-as-activity. This

---

8. See Farrer, *Finite and Infinite*, 33.

portends the possibility that we might deepen our apprehension of this being even further, by bringing that essence/nature from mere inchoate awareness into the foreground of consciousness as an object of explicit apprehension. The next step, then, is to attempt to characterize that essence in positive terms, to the extent that this is possible for us.

From Infinite Being to Perfect Being

In the previous section, we discovered that, in being aware of a necessary being, we were for the same reason aware of an infinite being as well. A necessary being is so by possessing its own intrinsic principle of substantial unity; in turn, this principle consists in the identity of existence and essence in that being. By contrast to contingent beings that are also finite, i.e., dependent and conditioned beings, a necessary being will be an infinite being, one that is limited neither by anything else nor even by its own essence functioning as an arbitrary limit on its act of existence, as is the case in finite beings. For any such being it will be the case that its essence is merely the expression of existence-as-activity as we encounter it when it is not arbitrarily constrained by some essence imposed on it as though from without. Such a being, then, will at the same time be an infinite being in a further sense as well, one the essence of which fully expresses the nature of being and exhaustively realizes the potentiality of existence-as-activity conceived of as a "self-stretching" reality. By the same token, then, that infinite being will also express the fullness of being by occupying, instantiating, and exemplifying the in-principle highest and best mode of being in an unsurpassable manner. Thus, just as in apprehending a necessary being we are at the same time apprehending an infinite being, in apprehending an infinite being we are at the same time apprehending a *perfect being* as well.

The notions of infinite being and perfect being stand to each other as negative to positive. Infinite being, as the privative prefix suggests, refers to that being's act of existence as unconstrained in its self-expression by any extrinsic principle, hence as identical with existence-as-activity conceived of as realized to its highest pitch. The notion of infinite being refers to the essence proper to that mode of being only negatively as the effect or expression of that unique act of unconstrained existence exhaustively realizing the full potentiality of activity-as-such. The notion of perfect being, however, shifts our introspective attention once again, this time to that infinite being's essence in its own right, according to which we consider it as the unique and ultimate expression of the fullness of being. In turn, we can look at this second notion from two different but complementary angles. On the one hand, that essence is constituted dynamically by that unconstrained act of existing having exhaustively realized the potentiality of existence-as-activity as such; on the other, it can be considered statically as both exemplifying and constituting the in-principle highest and best mode of being and enjoying the attributes or properties belonging to that mode.

So, then, just as the notion of necessary being (i.e., of a being in which existence and essence are identical) proves to be part of the meaning of that of infinite being (i.e., of a being in which existence-as-activity achieves its fullest expression and self-realization), so too does the notion of infinite being prove to be part of the meaning of that of perfect being (i.e., of a being which possesses all of the attributes that properly belong to infinite being). At the same time, the notion of perfect being fills out that of infinite being by providing much-needed specific content to that notion, turning it into a clear and distinct idea, if something less than an exhaustive or comprehensive account of the nature of that being.

At this point, it seems clear that our notion of a perfect being coincides with the Platonic/Augustinian conception of God, often referred to as the God of the philosophers. Thus, by having apprehended and meditated on my own existence and having discovered the *per se* cause of my existence, then meditated on that cause and arrived at the recognition that this being is also a perfect being, we have thereby apprehended that being as God as traditionally understood by philosophers. Thus, the apprehension of the *per se* cause of my persistence is, in fact, an apprehension of God, though it takes a sustained meditation that continually shifts foreground and background, progressively bringing into view each aspect of this multi-layered apprehension in order to arrive at this realization.

However, at this point we face a problem. So far, my apprehension of the necessary being has been solely by means of the fact of my own existence. The Cartesian Cosmological argument brings me to a non-contingent being as the *per se* cause of my individual existence but carries me no further. To attempt to characterize the essence of that being under the additional rubric of perfect being means shifting from the mere existence to the essence of this being, and one may well wonder what justifies us in attempting this. Of course, to characterize perfect being in this way, even if positively, is nevertheless at this point to characterize it vacuously, without any specific substantive content. Furthermore, as Descartes' critics were quick to point out, we have good reasons, from both traditional piety and traditional theology, for supposing that God's essence shares nothing materially in common with that of any creature and that as such that essence transcends our powers of conception. To resolve this difficulty, I need to explain how it is possible for us to apprehend such a being, not simply in its relation to my existence, but also in relation to created being functioning as the *imago Dei*, as the reduced or limited expression of what Infinite Being is the full, complete and total expression. To do this is to reconceive this being as my *exemplary*, not merely my *per se*, cause. Before we proceed, then, we need to explore the relation between finite and Infinite Being and explain how the former can be an image of the latter.

The Metaphysics of Participation and the *Imago Dei*

The question of how creatures can serve as the means by which we apprehend God—as God's image and likeness—is one that finds its answer in the traditional theory of being we have here been presupposing, though this has not always been fully appreciated, even within the metaphysical existentialist tradition.[9] According to this theory, God, as the infinite being whose essence is the ultimate expression of unconstrained existence-as-activity, is thereby *being itself* as well. God does not merely have existence, God *is* His existence, since in God alone is the fullness of being to found. Indeed, God and being itself, i.e. perfect being, are numerically the same thing. In God we find the complete expression of the totality of the existential potentiality of being fully realized in a single reality. We say that God is being itself, or that God is His existence as a way of identifying God as more than merely one being among others. While the assertion that God exists, taken merely as a way of positing the reality of God or reporting the fact that God's essence or nature is instantiated, uses "exists" in the logical sense in which it applies univocally to every reality, no matter how humble, this claim, regardless of how true it is, overlooks the crucial difference between God and every other being. Since there is in God no real distinction between existence and essence (due to the fact that God's act of existence is the principle of His essence) neither is there a distinction in God between God and His being, i.e., His structured activity; God, through exercising His unique act of existence, is a structured

---

9. On the role of participation in Thomistic metaphysics, see Joseph W. Koterski, S.J., "The Doctrine of Participation in Thomistic Metaphysics," in Deal W. Hudson and Dennis Wm. Moran, eds., *The Future of Thomism*, 185–96 and references; see also Helen James John, S.N.D., *The Thomist Spectrum*, 87–107. For an examination of the ontological relation between being and the good from the perspective of analytic philosophy, see Scott MacDonald, ed., *Being and Goodness: The Concept of Good in Metaphysics and Philosophical Theology*, especially the essays by MacDonald (31–55) and the joint essay by Stump and Kretzmann (98–128).

activity by that very fact, hence Being itself. To put it a slightly different way God, through exemplifying or instantiating the *ne plus ultra* of existence-as-activity and thereby the essence appropriate to existence as such, is thus different in kind from all other things. God alone *is* His being; everything else is merely *a* being, exemplifying or instantiated one or another possibility for limited being through exercising an act of existence constrained or restricted by another principle (i.e., essence conceived as arbitrary in relation to that act of existence) serving as an as though external, limiting imposition upon it.

The classic way of putting this is to say that God is identical with His being (i.e., is being itself) whereas things other than God merely *participate* in being, i.e., only partake of being insofar as existence-as-activity is present in them as constrained or limited by essence. Since only God fully exemplifies the essence that belongs to existence-as-activity in its fully completed natural state only God is being itself. Nevertheless, every thing other than God both possesses a limited essence and partakes in a limited way of structured activity-as-such. Thus, every such *thing* is *a* being, i.e., an instance of structured activity, and thus participates in or partakes of what God is, although only in a limited, partial and incomplete way. As such, to the extent that every thing participates in or partakes of being simply through exemplifying or instantiating a limited type, form or degree of being it at the same time *imitates* the God who is Being Itself.

The proper way of conceiving the relation of similarity between God and other beings, then, is captured by the Platonic phrase "participation by imitation." The notion of "participation" indicates a relation of formal similarity between God and other beings consisting in the fact that God, though preeminent and unique in kind, is a structured activity and so are they. As such, they are like God inasmuch as each is a being. However, the qualifying phrase "by imitation" further clarifies this relation of similarity by ruling out the notion that in "participating" or "partaking" of what God is finite beings are *literally* sharing, even in a limited way, in God's peculiar act of existence. To the contrary, God is utterly distinct from his creatures and independent of them. Indeed, it is God who apportions existence to essence and imposes essence upon existence, thus making all things other than Him to exist. Each thing, then, exists in utter and absolute dependence on God while still exercising its own distinct act of existing which realizes its own individuated instance of its essence, the nature it shares with others (whether potential or actual) of its kind. The being of the creature imitates that of God only through being a lesser degree or cut-down version of what God is *qua* being. Still, even this sort of talk can be misleading if improperly understood.

As such, we must also note that the similarity between Gods' being and our own is merely *formal* rather than *material*. Talk about "degrees" of participation by imitation in God's being may suggest that participation is based on partial or incomplete *resemblance* between God and creatures. However, the ontological gap between God and creatures is itself infinite, such that there can be no point of material resemblance between God and any finite being. What God is in Himself utterly transcends the essence or nature of any finite being and precludes the possibility of our forming any concept of God as the result of simply taking some intuitively creaturely perfection and using the imagination to allow it to "expand" until it achieves its highest possible instantiation, manifestation, or degree. Instead, we more properly say that finite beings imitate God, not materially through resemblance but rather *by aspiration* insofar as the individual act of existence in those beings encounters essence as an arbitrary limiting principle preventing it from the further and fuller expansion of activity-as-such.[10]

Thus, the prospect of apprehending God through creatures, including our own nature, requires that the notions of finite and infinite being be so closely related that they are more like the concepts of "left" and "right" or "up" and "down" than between "effect" and "cause" or "explanans" and "explanandum." That some finite being partakes of God's being insofar as it imitates it by aspiration makes sense only against the background of the concept or notion of an infinite being serving as the standard by means of which we are able to recognize differences in degree of being and perfection among finite beings and certain characteristics as perfections both in a kind and across kinds. As such, there can be no "metaphysically neutral" characterization of what a finite being is, by means of which we can motor ourselves, either imaginatively or by means of some sort of inference, from knowledge of our own nature to God as our exemplary cause. If finite beings such as ourselves are going to function as images of God it has to be the case that from the very beginning our apprehension of finite being *as such* occurs against the ubiquitous background of infinite being functioning as the ideal limit of aspiration, or in other words, in one and the same mental act. In this mental act, the apprehension of my own finite being, which is an object of immediate apprehension, is phenomenologically prior or "at the forefront," taking center stage in consciousness, whereas the apprehension of Infinite Being occurs or is present to consciousness as a kind of transcendental background condition making the apprehension of finite

10. See Farrer, *Finite and Infinite*, 15.

being possible and intelligible. Thus, the apprehension of Infinite Being operates in somewhat the same way as space and time do in the Kantian psychology. Being ubiquitous, they are phenomenologically less prominent than the things and events for which they serve as forms of intuition; at the same time, they are both ontologically and epistemologically prior to the experience of those things and events. Further, just as space and time function for Kant as forms of intuition and are incapable of being intuited as such apart from the objects for which they act as forms of intuition, so too is the apprehension of God as the exemplary cause of creatures possible only in relation to those creatures functioning as the *imago Dei*. Although Descartes agrees with the tradition that every being, insofar as it is a being and realizes its nature is an image of God,[11] in this context it is only my own being, which I am capable of apprehending immediately in introspection, that can serve as the *imago Dei* for me. In being aware of myself as a finite being, I am thereby at the same time aware of God as an infinite being; as Farrer puts it, following Descartes, I can be aware of myself as a finite being only if "I am aware of the privation of not being the Absolute being."[12] This in turn requires that I be in prior possession of an apprehension of that being as the background against which I apprehend myself.

If theism is true, of course, there is nothing absurd or unexpected about this. The notion that a being such as myself, created by and utterly dependent on God, should be intelligible in its own terms is not credible. Instead, as Farrer puts it, if theism is true "my God-relatedness enters into my very being"[13] in such a way that "the complete view of myself includes my character as effect of God"[14] such that "the clue to the nature of that Absolute being is, that He is the Absolute of which I am a reduced expression, or the positive characters of my being raised to the mode of absoluteness."[15] Thus, by turning my attention from the foreground of consciousness, where I am "center stage," to the transcendental background of consciousness, I bring God explicitly into view as the infinite being whose reduced image I am.

However, we have not yet stated *how* it is that creatures can serve as the *imago Dei* other than to emphasize that the apprehension of creatures

---

11. See *CSMK*, 340. This passage is from the *Conversation with Burman*.
12. See Farrer, *Finite and Infinite*, 16.
13. Farrer, *Finite and Infinite*, loc. cit; for a parallel passage in Descartes, see *CSMK*, 338; once again, this passage is from the *Conversation with Burman*.
14. See Farrer, *Finite and Infinite*, loc. cit.
15. See Farrer, *Finite and Infinite*, loc. cit. I have quoted these fragments in a different order than they appear in the original text.

is only the leading edge of a multi-faceted apprehension which includes awareness of God as the exemplary cause of our being, access to which is acquired introspectively by turning our attention from ourselves to the transcendental ground of our being. In fine, the inchoate or implicit apprehension of God through creatures, in this case my own being, is accomplished through the acquisition of certain general concepts which we use both in everyday language and in technical philosophy, concepts which on reflection we realize are only imperfectly descriptive of ourselves and properly descriptive only of an infinite being. For example, in being aware of the fact of my existence, I likewise acquire the concept of *being* as structured activity, *existence-as-activity* (what Thomists call *ens commune*) as that which is structured and *essence* as that which does the structuring. In a like manner, even a casual introspective acquaintance with myself reveals to me that I am a "thinking thing" (*res cogitans*), i.e., self-conscious rational subject whose mental contents include beliefs, desires, perceptions, emotional states, etc., and who possesses and exercises agency, both intramentally in the acquisition of "propositional attitudes" and with regard to putatively extramental "behaviors" as well. I therefore acquire the concepts of *consciousness, intellect* and *will* as part of my complement of everyday notions. Having got this far, it is not difficult to see how we could arrive at the concept of the *good* as the object of desire in relation to our faculties, as that which corresponds to and completes or perfects them. In the same way we are able to recognize *degrees of completeness* or *perfection* in relation to our faculties, both in general and with regard with their many specialized employments. In turn, we come to regard the *objects* of those faculties by means of which they are completed as good in the further sense of *valuable*, i.e., *good for us* as perfective of our natural capacities or faculties. Thus, *knowledge* is grasped by us as intrinsically valuable for us insofar as it is perfective of the intellect, and *power* (here interpreted in a metaphysical rather than a narrowly political sense) as a (the?) primary instrumental good (since it is necessary for the accomplishment of any plans or goals we might possess) hence as perfective of the will.

All of these everyday concepts are perfectly general; all of them are likewise abstract. Although we acquire these concepts in an almost unconscious fashion from mere everyday acquaintance with ourselves in conscious experience, these concepts are not limited, either in content or in use, merely to the case from which they are originally and primarily derived. Quite the contrary, we use these concepts to not only make intra-species judgments of relative perfection with regard to ourselves and other human beings, but also make interspecies judgments with regard to relative perfection of kinds, of which the many versions of the "great chain of being" attest. Each of these concepts is therefore at the same time "directional" or *analogical* in use, since it is capable of encompassing *qualitatively different* expressions of the same property, character, or nature as related to one another as degrees on a scale.[16]

More remarkable than this—and crucial to our discussion here—is the fact that despite its being the case that we acquire these concepts through a kind of casual self-acquaintance the *mode* of each of these characteristics as we possess them, regardless of how self-realized we are, is not the top-end of the scale we are employing. For example, in a previous chapter, we were led to recognize that the fact that we exist contingently presupposes that essence and existence are present in us without any intrinsic principle of substantial unity. Since the fact of individual existence is impossible apart from substantial unity, we were forced to recognize that the fact our own existence requires the extrinsic activity of a being serving as the *per se* cause of my persistence in being and ingredient in it. Further, in order to avoid an explanatorily inadequate infinite, vicious regress of such causes, we were forced to recognize that this *per se* cause of my existence was a non-contingent being, one that possesses its own intrinsic principle of substantial unity. Thus, being as we possess it cannot be conceived of as the highest and best mode of being that can obtain or be possessed by any thing. To the contrary, contingent being is inferior, *qua* mode of being, to non-contingent being and no contingent being has title to be called *being in the full and proper sense of that term*. Thus, we are led to realize that the concept of being is neither limited to nor circumscribed in height by reference to the human case in which we originally encounter being and thereby acquire that concept. Therefore, in encountering being in the human case we are encountering it not *de nudo* but instead as an aspect of ourselves as *imago Dei*. In apprehending our own existence as a fact, we acquire a concept of being which is at first vague, uncircumscribed and purely general in meaning. However, once we are able to discern the contingency of our own existence, this leads us to recognize ineluctably that our concept of being is not merely vague, indefinite, or general. This is in fact the concept of perfect being, i.e., of the highest and best mode of being that can be possessed by any thing, *and*

---

16. For Farrer's account of the analogical use of language that bears only a tangential connection to the traditional Thomist "Doctrine of Analogy," see *Finite and Infinite*, 37–48. Farrer there notes the presence within us of an "interior scale" of qualitatively different states or "levels" of conscious awareness that nevertheless are continuous with one another as ground for this conception of things.

was so all along.[17] However, we did not realize it until we reflected upon the contingency of our own existence and arrived at the notion of contingent existence, which is ultimately only intelligible against the background of the prior notion of non-contingent being. Thus, in being aware of myself as being or a being due to the fact of my existence, I am at same time aware, at least inchoately or implicitly, of Being Itself, which is to say that I function for myself as *imago Dei*.

The same holds for all the other concepts I canvassed above. Each of them as we use them in everyday life is (and their more familiar cognates) are vague, general and indefinite with regard to its explicit substantive meaning. Nevertheless, the ways in which we use them recognizes, at least implicitly, their analogous or directional meaning. Further, in the case of each, the degree, or mode of that "self-stretching" reality as it is encountered in the human case, no matter how fully realized we are with respect to human nature, is never the highest or best degree of that reality to which a being could aspire or possess. The full and proper use of the term, then, inevitably refers to the unique, highest in principle mode of that reality which far outstrips the degree or mode of that reality we possess by nature in such a way as to differ, not merely in degree, but in kind from the human case. When we reflect on these notions, then, we realize that these terms, even as we use them in ordinary language apply to us only in a derivative and degenerate way. We are not the paradigm case of being, intellect, will, goodness, or perfection. Quite to the contrary, the full and proper sense of each of these terms can refer only to infinite being, not to any finite being such as ourselves.

Still, we must not be overly disheartened by the discovery that we are not God. After all, each of the foregoing, then, is one dimension along which we participate by imitation/aspiration in the mode of being that constitutes Being Itself and through which we apprehend God as our ex-

---

17. Again, I refer the reader to the passage of the *Conversation with Burman* mentioned in note 10 above. What I have written here seems to me to explain Descartes' point here in the parallel passages in the *Discourse*, *Meditations*, and *Replies*. On the one hand, Descartes denies that I can arrive at the idea of God by extrapolating from my own case, either by simply negating my imperfections (which is no proper concept at all) or by imagining my perfections continually expanding (since there is no guarantee that this will arrive at any terminus and produces only an indefinite idea rather than the idea of an infinite being.) At the same time, Descartes does maintain that we arrive at the *positive content* of our idea of God precisely by a consideration of our own nature as the *imago Dei* in ourselves. The foregoing explains how it is possible for Descartes to hold both of these views at the same time. On this point, see the fine paper by Annette Baier, "The Idea of the True God in Descartes" in Amelie Rorty, *Essays in Descartes' Meditations*, 359–87.

emplary cause. We are, then, at the very least God-like, and more God-like than anything else in the visible creation. In the remainder of this chapter, then, I want to sketch the familiar outline of the traditional account of God as apprehended by means of creatures, in particular, each of us as we are immediately acquainted with ourselves in introspection. I will begin with a general characterization of God as exemplary cause and then briefly look at the nature of God as revealed through myself as *imago Dei*. In so doing, we are made able to grasp how it is that creatures, and in particular, my own being, is capable of being the *imago Dei* and thus serving as the foundation for a limited apprehension of the divine essence itself without, at the same time, annulling the transcendence of the Divine essence.

Certainly, there is no prospect of our having, in this life at any rate, a direct and unmediated apprehension of the divine essence as such. However, all is not lost. As a consequence of the fact that we participate by imitation/aspiration in the divine mode of being, our own nature is capable of serving as the *imago Dei* in yet a further sense. For, in becoming introspectively aware of the ways in which our own finite essence resists the aspiration of existence-as-activity—not merely contingently, but by necessity of our common nature—we are thereby able to conceive of a nature not so limited or constrained and thus arrive at a positive notion of God. The content of this notion will consist in the positive perfections corresponding to the privations afflicting my own act of existence as it is related to and constrained by my essence. In this way, the idea of God as a perfect being can be filled out by listing the traditional divine attributes insofar as these are revealed to me by reflection on my own nature. This, of course, is only a limited perspective on that essence, like a mirror image that reveals only one side of an object from a limited perspective. Nevertheless, it will do for our purposes, which is fortunate since, so far as that goes, it will have to do in any case.

The positive idea or concept of God as our *exemplary* cause is the means by which we apprehend God's mode of being and this idea or concept is, in turn, the complement that precipitates out of our recognition of the contrast between our general or abstract notions of being, intellect, will, and so on and those realities as we experience them in our own case. In this way, then, our essence serves as the *imago Dei* and as the source of the positive content of the idea of God, the means by which we apprehend God. But does this idea or concept, even if derived in this way, really count as an *apprehension* of God, i.e., as a genuine intellectual grasp of God, or is this idea merely a *representation* of God somehow existing in my mind? Either way we go seems to result in dilemma. On the one hand, a concept or idea counts as an apprehension of an external object only if it is the very form of that thing existing in the intellect by means of which the intellect becomes identical (numerically one) with what it knows, albeit only formally and intentionally. However, as Hobbes and Gassendi point out in response to Descartes, it is impossible for the Divine Essence to be contained in the finite intellect.[18] On the other hand, if my idea or concept of God is merely a kind of intellectual image of God, then it hardly counts as an apprehension of God; even a mirror image or the reflection of an external object is something ontologically distinct from that of which it is an image. In that case, aren't we going to be in the same condition as Descartes and Locke with regard to the external world and its denizens, where the gap between effect and cause will need to be closed, not by introspective meditation but by philosophical argument?

My response to this dilemma is to reject both alternatives as spurious rather than to choose between them or to devise some way of going between the horns. On the one hand, it seems perfectly acceptable to me to reply to the first horn of the dilemma by asserting that the *imago Dei* in me (i.e., my act of existence as defeated aspiration in relation to the ineluctable constraints imposed by my essence) *is* the manner in which the divine essence exists in my intellect formally and intentionally to the fullest extent possible for a being with my nature.[19] Remember, my being is a participation by imitation/aspiration in Infinite Being and, though materially and numerically distinct from Infinite Being, still in my own small way what God is formally, i.e., as being, except to a much lower degree amounting to a different mode. This does not prevent me, then, from being formally identical with God to that extent and thus intentionally identical to God to that extent as well insofar as I can be self-consciously aware of that fact. Like Descartes, I reject as a false dilemma the claim that either God's essence must be a perspicuous object for my intellect or it must be utterly transcendent to it. It is in this way that we ought to interpret Descartes' claim (mentioned earlier) that just as I can touch a mountain with my fingertip or see the ocean without it being necessary that I be able to take in its entire expanse in a single glance, I can appre-

---

18. Hobbes, in *CSM*, Vol. II, 125–6 and Gassendi, in *CSM*, Vol. II, 200–201.

19. As Carole Rovane puts it, my idea of God *is* my idea of myself considered as the *imago Dei*—exactly! It is precisely because of this that it can be an innate idea as Descartes defines it, i.e. an idea that I arrive at by the contemplation of my own nature. See her essay "God without Cause" in John Cottingham, ed., *Reason, Will and Sensation*, 100. See also the article by Baier, mentioned above.

hend God without thereby encompassing the entirety of the divine nature with my finite mind.

For the same reason, the concept of God is both apprehension and representation at the same time, thus *merely* neither. My introspective awareness of certain facts about myself—that I exist, have an intellect, am an agent, etc.—is already an implicit, inchoate and primitive apprehension of God inasmuch as it reveals to me certain general concepts (being, intellect, will) which, on examination, turn out to apply properly not to myself, but instead to converge in the notion of a being who is, at one and the same time, infinite being, unlimited intellect and absolute will. As a consequence, reflection on the ways in which my act of existence is limited by nature, i.e., its ontological aspiration is defeated by the constraints of my essence, we slowly clarify that original apprehension until we arrive at clear and distinct concepts both of what I am and what God is insofar as God's essence or nature can be grasped by the human intellect. This latter is a representation or idea in the Lockean sense, but not merely so; it is instead an articulation of that original apprehension, the explicit rendering of what was previously only implicit and inchoate, at once continuous with it and yet superseding it at the same time. This should be sufficient to defuse the second horn of the dilemma.

The Perfections of Perfect Being (with an Appendix)

Reflection on the concept of infinite being leads, then, to the general notion of perfect being. As yet, however, this concept fails to contain any specific content of the sort needed if this notion is to count as a clear and distinct idea or concept of God. How, then, are we to arrive at this content? Given the foregoing, the answer seems clear enough. What we need to do is to reflect on the various ways in which my own nature presents itself as finite and limited, *deny* those limitations of infinite being and thereby arrive at a list of attributes characteristic of perfect being. In this way, our nature as finite being serves as the image and likeness of God by means of which we apprehend Infinite Being as the exemplary cause of our being, as what our being (considered from the point of view of its individual act of existence as activity-as-such) strives to but is unable to realize or actualize due to finite essence acting as an unsurpassable limiting principle.

To put it another way: as Descartes avers—and at this point we have no reason to dispute—the idea of God as exemplary cause of my being is given along with the idea of myself as a kind of complement to it. My own essence, by serving as the arbitrary limit to the aspiration of my act of existence, which constitutes for me the *positive* outline of my own self at the same time constitutes the *negative* outline of what God is, hence constitutes God as *formally* present in me. It thus exists in me as a kind of creator's mark capable of allowing me to be God's image. It is due to this that, in being aware of myself as being, intellect and will, I am therefore, at the same time, inchoately aware of God as infinite being, unlimited intellect and absolute will, somewhat in the same way that in tracing the circumference of a circle from inside I am thereby given the outline of the space outside that circle that I cannot see. Of course, in the analogy just given, I gain almost no information about the space outside the circle; however, if the shape is more complicated, then I am able to form a much richer concept of the complimentary shape it fits. For example, from examining the shape of a key I can arrive at detailed knowledge about the lock it fits. As we have seen, there are many dimensions of finitude blocking the aspirations of my act of existence and from these we are able to arrive at a rich concept or idea of God. My innate idea of God, then, is inseparable from my apprehension of my own essence as being, intellect, will, and so on. Indeed, it *is* that concept, taken first, in relation to its efficient cause (as persistent being) and then, inclusive of this, of its exemplary cause along other dimensions. As such, this idea or concept, far from being merely alien or external imposition by God upon my intellect is inseparable from my very being, whether I am considering my act of existence or my essence.

The various limitations present in ourselves that we deny of the Perfect Being are thus originally identified *negatively* and thus often characterized in negative terms, e.g., words beginning with privatives like in-, im- or non-. However, we are not thereby limited to the results of so-called *apophatic* theology. On the contrary, since existence-as-activity is the self-stretching reality *par excellence*, the directionality supplied by my own act of existence considered as the limited expression of existence-as-activity allows me to analogically apprehend and characterize Perfect Being in positive terms, however haltingly and incompletely. However, this is best demonstrated by actually undertaking the project of attempting to articulate the concept or idea of perfect being in the manner indicated here.

First, from the very fact that I, as finite being, am less than the fullness of being, it follows that I am capable of change. This, of course, is an obvious fact easily deducible from the fact that I do in fact change constantly, even with regard to the contents of my mental life, hence in such a way that it is possible for me to be immediately aware of that fact. My being subject to change is a consequence of the fact that I possess unrealized potentialities endowing me with various capacities for being changed in various ways, as well as because I am subject to ongoing vital processes governing my development in accordance with my nature. However, since God, as infinite being is also *actus purus*, i.e., fully actualizes in every possible respect the positive potentialities of existence-as-activity, God is not subject to change, development, or further perfection. God is therefore both *immutable*, i.e., incapable of change, and *impassible*, i.e., incapable of being affected by anything outside of Himself. One should not suppose that immutability and impassibility make God somehow static, inactive, or incapable of interacting with or responding to a changing world. To the contrary, the mystery of God as *actus purus* is that God is so fully actualized and enjoys such an intense degree of activity in relation to other things that He does not need to change or be affected by external things in order to know, understand and respond to his creatures. As I once put it, long ago: God is always doing whatever He's doing and although it is impossible for us to imagine what this is like, it must be distantly analogous to that sense of being "in command" or "in the driver's seat" which accompanies our having anticipated and taken into account every possible factor prior to the execution of a plan. Not only is there no unrealized potency in God, but (*contra* Hartshorne and other exponents of a limited god) God needs no unrealized potency in order to be perfectly and completely related to His creation through its being utterly dependent upon Him in every aspect of its being.

Another aspect of finitude as I find it in myself is due to my temporality. There can be no doubt that I am a temporal being, as the changing succession of thoughts in my conscious experience infallibly attests. Nor can this be a mere illusion, since, as Peter Geach points out in his book on McTaggart, the conscious illusion of time requires a real succession of thoughts in consciousness, which is itself impossible unless there is actual temporal succession occurring there.[20] In a like manner, the fact that I am subject to time also makes me a complex being, since the events of my mental life, by being subject to coming-to-be and passing-away in

---

20. See Peter Geach, *Truth, Love, and Immortality*, 101–2. The relation of God to time is obviously a significant and difficult question. I know of no plausible solution to the many difficulties that arise here. I can only say that my own view is that, although time is a genuine phenomenon it is only subjective, i.e., a feature of consciousness, and while it reflects genuine ontological and causal relations in the external world, there is no genuine temporal succession in nature. We might say that the Cartesian Cosmological argument proves that there is a necessary being whereas the argument of the present section proves that this being is God as traditionally understood.

time, are therefore only externally related to one another as discrete parts of a whole. (This will be true even if time is a continuum rather than composed of discrete, externally related moments.) By contrast, God as perfect being will be both *timelessly eternal* and *absolutely simple* and as such subject neither to temporal succession in consciousness nor possessed of any temporally discrete parts. To the contrary, God will enjoy, as Boethius puts it, "simultaneous possession of every moment of a complete life." Furthermore, God will lack not only temporal parts but also internal divisibility and ontologically distinct attributes: this follows directly from the divine immutability, since any of these forms of internal division or separation would require that God possess potentiality for change. As such, God's divine attributes are at most conceptually rather than really distinct, i.e., relative to our limited powers of comprehension.[21]

We turn next to our most obvious limitations: knowledge, power and goodness. It will come to no one's surprise that we are far from the full exemplification of the any of these qualities, all of which seem to us open-ended in such a way that we cannot even imagine what the highest in-principle degree of exemplification of such properties would be. It is in the inherent limitations of our intellect and will that we become most aware of the fact that we are limited or finite by nature not merely in some accidental or inessential way. Our intellect is passive, capable only of representing extramental reality to me by a combination of imperfect apprehension and analogical comprehension. My will never affects anything directly, but only through bodily mechanisms or tools that it uses as means to extrinsic ends. Further, our will is at the service of needs and desires which we neither choose for ourselves, have much control over and which frequently conflict both with what our reasons tells us would be best in the situation to do and with what would, from the objective point of view, be best for others or on the whole. As St. Paul notes in his *Epistle to the Romans*, "The good that I would do I do not, whereas the evil I would not do, that I do." (*Rom* 7:19) One need not be religious to recognize this common human condition—though one suspects there are many people nowadays, at least in Europe and North America, who suppose that whatever they want is good and whatever they do is at least morally permissible and as such "no big deal."

---

21. Presumably, Descartes would hold that there is Scotistic formal distinction between the divine attributes, whereas I would maintain, along with the Thomistic distinction, that there is only a conceptual distinction *ratiocinantis*, i.e., relative only to the limitations of our powers of conception and not grounded in any way in the divine essence itself. However, nothing hangs on this here.

In any event, a perfect being will not be lacking in any of these areas and will simultaneously be omnipotent, omniscient, fully rational and morally perfect, both in the sense of being perfectly benevolent and incapable of any wrongdoing. However, like all the divine attributes, these qualities need to be integrated into the simplicity of the divine nature as aspects of the divine perfection. This is to say that none of these attributes can be intrinsically defined in the Leibnizian fashion, according to which they are the "highest in principle degree of a property that comes in degrees." Such a conception simply leads to paradox and apparent incoherence and is instructive only in informing us where these "stand-alone" conceptions of omnipotence, omniscience, and so on break down. While any of the divine attributes can be the basis for the theological investigation of the divine nature, since each of them is identical with the divine essence as a whole and thus that essence itself apprehended from a particular point of view, none of the divine attributes is any more central than any other. As such, attempts to make one such attribute supreme and normative for the others inevitably leads to misunderstanding and heresy. The rule to be used in investigating the divine attributes is that anything that has a tendency to detract from the divine perfection must be denied of God regardless of its placing a limitation on one of his attributes. Thus, if attributing to God the power to actually sin, or destroy Himself, is inconsistent with His overall perfection, we do God no disservice in denying these powers to Him. In a like manner, since only a finite being could be prudent or courageous, we do not make God less perfect by denying these virtues to Him. Again, if the divine atemporality rules out the possibility that God knows "what's happening now," all that follows from this—supposing that awareness of "what's happening now" is merely an irreducible feature of the experience of temporal existence and constituted solely by it (as opposed to expressing a non-temporal fact about reality)—is that this is something which, from God's superior atemporal viewpoint, He could know only if He was less than a perfect being. And so on, for the other cases.

Nor does it follow from this that the terms used to name the divine attributes are somehow meaningless. The overall notion of God as a perfect being, i.e., a being who expresses the fullness of being by actualizing or realizing the full and complete potentiality of existence (=activity-as-such) and possesses the essence appropriate to the being whose nature is to be *actus purus* provides us with an overarching rule for the analysis of each particular attribute without constituting a complete or comprehensive analysis of it. Thus, we know that God possesses power to the degree requisite for and compatible with God's overall perfection, the full measure of knowledge possible for a perfect being, and so on. Obviously, to the extent that our apprehension of God is itself partial and limited, it will carry us only so far; it is at this point that the hard work of theoretical investigation of the divine nature, as undertaken by theologians and philosophers of religion, begins in earnest: see the appendix to this chapter, immediately below.

Appendix

The Nature and Role of Philosophical Theology

Some may object that the foregoing makes too much of the nature of God an object of apprehension, at least to the extent that it belongs to the conceptual articulation of our original apprehension of God as the *per se* cause of my substantial unity and thus as necessary in order for me to exist and thus to account for the fact of my existence. In fact, however, the foregoing leaves most of the current debate in philosophical theology untouched. While I have argued that the conceptual articulation of our apprehension of God takes the form a of clear and distinct idea of God as both the *per se* and the exemplary cause of my being, it does not follow that this either eliminates or resolves any of the traditional difficulties attending the concept of God which so exercise theologians and philosophers of religion. Indeed, it simply heightens the interest with which those competent to investigate these matters ought to pursue their research by assuring us that these problems are not merely otiose or simply puzzles generated by an outmoded world view.

It needs to be noted that, despite what the medievals and their modern followers may have thought, direct apprehension is not the sole means by which which we can acquire knowledge. To the contrary, there is also the method of *indirect apprehension* or comprehension, in which we attempt to investigate those objects partly revealed in experience and at the same time as transcending it in many or even most aspects by the use of conceptual schemes, hypotheses, theories, etc. which attempt to *model in thought* the noumenal reality which we apprehend phenomenally. This is the stock-in-trade of natural science, for example, which uses sense-based observation as the basis for the construction of both analogue and mathematical models of natural phenomena. Philosophical theology, operating under the aegis of *fides quarens intellectum*, attempts to do just this same sort of thing with regard to the divine nature considered in itself.

It is to be noted that, in accordance with what was argued earlier, while extremely desirable in itself and valuable for the intellectual life of the believer, success in the pursuit of the object of philosophical theology, i.e., theoretical knowledge of God considered in Himself, is hardly life and death where religious belief is concerned. Even if every attempt to work out the apparent tensions in the concept of God as perfect being revealed to us in our apprehension of ourselves were to seem to fail at some particular point in time, this would in no way undermine our attribution of those perfections to God as revealed to us through apprehension, any more than the failure of every comprehensive scientific theory at some particular point in time would prove that there is no external world or that there is no comprehensive order to the universe capable of explaining the empirical regularities we observe in nature. In such case, the sober course would simply to be to admit the limitations of our intellect; this is even more incumbent on us in the case of God, whom we have every reason to believe is beyond full human comprehension. At any rate, I do not think that we are anywhere near such a drastic state of things and I expect that anyone who has even a casual acquaintance with the strides made by theistic philosophers in the last four decades and an even minimal degree of philosophical objectivity will likely agree with me.

The same holds for the so-called problem of evil as well. The claim that the notion of a God who is omnipotent, omniscient and morally perfect is either incompatible with or highly implausible given the variety and amount of evil in the world is one that looks plausible only from a very limited and partial perspective which reflects far less on God than on ourselves. Given the divine self-sufficiency, the very existence of the universe is an act of gratuitous love directed toward created things. God neither needs nor gains anything for Himself from His creation and His object in creating the universe can be nothing else than benevolence toward what He creates. Although God can have no higher end in creating than to glorify Himself (since there is no higher being than Himself to glorify), nevertheless, since created things are each, in their particular mode of being, reduced images of Being Itself, God's self-glorification in His creatures comes through his perfecting each in accordance with its own essence or nature within the overall economy of Divine Providence as a whole and thus is the very essence of benevolence toward them. At the same time, the overall economy of creation requires that those things that are necessary conditions for the existence of particulars must take precedence over those particulars themselves, up to and including the most basic laws that govern the universe. As such, it may well be that the interests of individuals may sometimes have to be sacrificed as part of the unfolding of the general world order.

Suppose, then, that a necessary condition for the existence of a world containing sentient, carbon-based life forms is an internal constitution that permits and thus occasionally produces volcanoes, earthquakes and tidal waves. As a consequence of this arrangement, the lives of some small fraction of those beings will end prematurely, perhaps in a state of intense panic and severe pain. According to the Principle of Licit Double Effect, the foreseen bad consequences of an otherwise morally permissible or even beneficial act do not make that act morally impermissible provided that those foreseen consequences are neither directly intended nor employed as a means to the end and such that the good to be produced is proportional to the evil permitted. I would argue that all these conditions are met in this case and that therefore God is in no way morally suspect for having created such a world. For the same reason, just as God is not morally obligated not to create such a world, neither is He obligated to prevent these evils from occurring through continual special miraculous interventions in the world. Finally, neither is God somehow remiss in allowing these evils to be distributed by chance rather than in accordance with merit. Much of the *cachet* and poignancy of human life flows from the vulnerability of our lives taken in conjunction with the fact that in this life there are no guarantees. Without this, there would be neither need nor opportunity to care for others, to protect and watch out for them, since we would have a divine guarantee that nothing bad, or, at any rate, nothing really bad could happen to anyone or ourselves.

The notion that good and evil should be strictly distributed in accordance with merit in this life would rob our actions of all their moral worth. If every good act were accompanied by a direct, obvious, and palpable reward, how could virtue be its own reward? Likewise, as DeMaistre puts it, who would steal if he knew his hand would drop off in the commission of the crime? The foregoing point is compatible with what I take it to be the case, i.e., that there is a general though indirect correlation between the pursuit of virtue and true human happiness in this life, as well as between vicious living and misery. However, it nevertheless remains that in terms of the goods of this life virtue and happiness are but rarely correlated. Of course, as Kant also realized, if there is a God, this state-of-affairs would be intolerable unless ultimately rectified. Even so, there is no requirement that God balance the scales in this life. Quite the contrary, it is fully appropriate that the final disposition of our lives should be deferred to the next world, where, as the Gospel of Matthew teaches, we will be rewarded in accordance with our works.

By contrast, the atheist offers us a world in which those states-of-affairs which we perceive as cosmically unjust are not remediable, redeemable nor ultimately compensable. As these events recede into the past, they harden into irremovable blots on the universe, and as mitigation, we are offered only the comforting thought that, from the point-of-view of eventual human extinction and the heat-death of this pointless, deterministic universe, no one and no event, not even Adolf Hitler and the Holocaust, have any permanent significance. As Thomas Nagel[22] puts it, nothing matters and the comic posturing of the Russell of "A Free Man's Worship"[23] and the defiance of Camus in the *Myth of Sysiphus*[24] are themselves symptoms of the problem rather than serious responses to it. If nothing matters, then neither does the fact that nothing matters and those who think it does just don't get it. In response to this, there is nothing wrong, I suppose, with a resolve to just live one's quotidian life and take its insignificant joys and sorrows as they come; however, the cynicism of *The Third Man*'s Harry Lime seems no less rationally defensible as a strategy for living in such a world.

Of course, the mere existence of a theistic God by itself does little to provide us with a solution to the problem of cosmic justice. Only the sort of positive religion that Nagel is so set against that he refuses even to consider its claims can offer us any real hope that something of permanent value may be rescued from the world-wreck. For the Christian, the outstretched arms of Christ on the cross are the ultimate testimony of God's love for us, the full, almost unimaginable extent of that love, and the resurrection of Jesus the proof of the triumph of that love. I can imagine someone regretfully turning away from such a claim, incredulous on the grounds that the proffered beliefs are too good to be true and what they offer too much to hope for. For anyone with a scintilla of human feeling to reject them out of hand, especially in the face of a supposedly full awareness of the amount of evil in the world, is surely unintelligible from the rational point of view. I will not here speculate further on what might explain it.

It does not follow from this that the discussion of theodicy and the construction of formal theodicies is a waste of time or of no value. The experience of evil is a pastoral as well as a theological problem and the challenge of atheology, in this context as well as all the others, gives theistic philosophers and theologians many opportunities to exercise their theoretical

22. Thomas Nagel, "The Absurd," in *Mortal Essays*, 11–33.

23. Bertrand Russell, "A Free Man's Worship," in *Why I am Not a Christian and Other Essays*, 104–117.

24. Albert Camus, *The Myth of Sisyphus and Other Essays*, 119–23.

imaginations and analytical skills. As in all the other cases I have discussed, however, nothing essential to the life of faith depends on the success of their speculations, and even the failure of all their theories need not constitute a reason to abandon the Christian faith. However, lest we wander too far from our main topic, we need to return to our exposition of Cartesian theism.

Is the Idea of God Innate?

We have at last arrived at the concept of God as a perfect being; as such, we have finally reached, only after an extended meditation, the point from which Descartes thought he was able to begin in the third *Meditation*. This arduous effort, however, will have proved to be worth it when we consider what Descartes, beginning from his idea of a perfect being, attempts to do with it. As we all know, Descartes notoriously attempted to prove that this idea was innate and, more than this, to prove that only God could be the source of that idea. Descartes's proof, the first of his three proofs of God's existence, has been universally rejected by philosophers, if for no other reason than the supposedly self-evident principle from which he derives this proof, i.e., there must be as much formal reality in the cause of an idea as there is objective reality in the idea itself, seems if not exactly false at least unmotivated and *ad hoc*. In this section, I wish to consider what might be salvaged from this proof and retained as part of Cartesian theism. Let us begin by considering in what sense the idea of God is innate.

Given the foregoing, it seems clear enough that the idea of God is an innate idea as that notion is technically defined by Descartes, i.e., as an idea which I arrive at simply by contemplating my own nature and myself. As I have reconstructed (not interpreted) Descartes here, an innate idea is simply any idea I arrive at through a process of introspective meditation on my own self as directly given and knowable in consciousness. Thus, to recapitulate once more, in being self-consciously aware of the fact that I am conscious, i.e., of my own *thinking* or *mental activity*, I am thereby made aware of activity-as-such, of which thinking is one mode. Thus, in being aware of the fact that I am conscious in this way, I am also implicitly or inchoately aware of the fact that I exist and when I advert to the fact that I exist, I become explicitly aware of the fact of my existence: *Cogito ergo Sum*. However, I am for the same reason aware that I am more than mere existence-as-such. Insofar as I am, in being aware of the fact that I think at the same time aware that I am a thinking thing (*res cogitans*), I am aware not merely of my individual act of existence, but of that act as *structured*, hence of myself as a *being*, i.e., *structured activity* as opposed to *mere* existence conceived of as activity-as-such. Thus, at the same time that I apprehend myself as a being, I also implicitly or inchoately apprehend within myself a second, further principle, *essence* or *nature*, which is equally constitutive of the fact that I am a being as is existence-as-activity. Further reflection on existence and essence as I find them in myself reveals to me the *real distinction* between these two principles in me, such that, while I exist as the unity of existence and essence, the principle of that unity is not intrinsic to me. I am thereby led to the conscious recognition of the causal ingredience of the action of some power external to my being that constitutes the unity of my being at every moment that I remain in being. In being aware of the causal ingredience of that external power, I therefore apprehend the *per se* cause of my substantial unity, which in turn functions as the efficient cause of my being and, hence, of the fact of my existence. In turn, reflection on this external power leads me to recognize that this *per se* cause of my being can only be a *non-contingent being*, a being in whom there is no distinction between existence and essence or in which these two principles are identical. (To explicate this last was the burden of the previous chapter.) In turn, we also note that such a being is a *necessary being* as traditionally understood, i.e., one whose persistence is a consequence of the identity of essence and existence in that being and thus is explained by that very fact. Such a being exists *a se*, or (as Descartes somewhat clumsily puts it) is cause of itself inasmuch as the explanation for that being's persistence in being is to be found within that being itself rather than as the consequence of the action of some other being. By being necessary in the foregoing sense, this being will also be an *infinite*, i.e., *non-dependent* being capable of persisting in being without regard to any circumstances or conditions external to itself.

To have arrived at the notion of a being infinite and necessary in the foregoing senses (and the affirmation of the existence of that being on the basis of our apprehension of it as causally ingredient in and necessary for my own existence) is already to have arrived at an apprehension of God, although not yet explicitly as a clear and distinct idea. Instead, as I have argued in this chapter, further reflection on the notion of infinite and necessary being in those senses leads us to the characterization of such a being as one in which existence is the principle of essence, such that this being possesses the essence which is expressive of the fullness of being, i.e., of existence-as-activity as fully self-realized in accordance with its own intrinsic dynamism (*actus purus*). In so doing, we thus conceive of necessary being not merely as a being, but instead as *being itself*, thereby arriving at the apprehension of God as *infinite being* in a further sense, i.e. as a being that knows no limitations other than those inherent in being itself grasped as the exhaustive expression of activity-as-such. However, this further notion of infinite being remains merely empty until we articulate its content to the extent that this is possible by contrasting it with our own mode of being, i.e., *finite being*, in which the aspiration of existence-as-activity is defeated, constrained or thwarted by essence acting as a limiting principle. Thus, by reflecting on the modes of being, intellect, will and so on as we possess them against the background of this notion of infinite being, we quickly come to realize that the general notions of being, intellect, will and so on that we possess apply to ourselves only in a derivative and degenerate sense, and that being, intellect, will and so on *properly so called*, and the terms by means of which we express these ideas, in turn apply properly only to infinite being. Our fully articulated notion of infinite being, then, constitutes a clear and distinct idea or concept of God as perfect being and *exemplary cause* of my being as well as its *per se* cause. We have now arrived at the concept of God as depicted by Descartes: the idea of a being that is eternal, infinite, immutable, omniscient, omnipotent, necessarily existent and so on—in short, a perfect being, the God of classical theism.

Having actually traced the origin and development of the innate idea of God from its origins in our self-reflective awareness of the fact that we are conscious to its full-blown articulation in the concept of a perfect being, we have at the same time proven—*pro ambulo*, as it were—that this idea or concept is innate as Descartes technically defines that term. Further, since that concept or idea's being innate in the way I have derived it ineluctably requires a genuine apprehension of God as both my *per se* and my exemplary cause, my mere possession of this concept or idea is at the same time sufficient proof for the existence of the being described by that concept, thus making superfluous Descartes' first third *Meditation* proof for God's existence.[25] Surprisingly, having started from what he ought to have first proven, i.e., that we possess an idea of God as a perfect being, Descartes actually made his task in the *Meditations* more difficult than it really needed to be due to the fact that he was forced to treat his clear and distinct idea of God as though it were *simply present* in his consciousness, i.e., in a merely external way such that it might have been absent without in any way altering his being, nature or conscious life. As such, Descartes is forced to give a factitious proof of the *a priori* origin of this idea in a special act of divine endowment. However, given the foregoing we can see that there is no need to conceive of the concept or idea of God in

---

25. Nevertheless, I will return to this argument; see chapter ten below.

this way. To the contrary, my own being, both as directly apprehended by me in introspection and by means of that apprehension as conceptually articulated in my intellect, is the "image and likeness" of God in me that reveals the extent to which my God-dependence enters into the very core of my being and thereby makes possible the apprehension of God as my *per se* and exemplary cause.

Of course, at the same time that we have demonstrated the superfluity of Descartes' first *Meditation* III proof for God's existence, we have also shown the superfluity of the many criticisms of the proof, both classical and modern, that depend on the notion of the idea of God as merely present in consciousness, regardless of its origin. Thus, the groundwork we have laid is so far useful, if only to eliminate the confusions and evasions that have led Gassendi, Hobbes, Locke, Hume and many others to deny that we possess any such idea or to offer speculative accounts of the (pseudo-)origins of the (pseudo-)concept of God. Having actually traced the idea or concept of God to its origins in the apprehension of God as the exemplary cause of my being, there is no longer any need to consider the objections of Gassendi, Hobbes, Locke, and Hume other than to dismiss them *en passant*. After carefully considering the foregoing, I think no one can reasonably maintain that we neither possess an idea or concept of God or that the idea is merely a pseudo-concept produced by an illegitimate act of abstraction. While I do, in fact, arrive at my clear and distinct idea of God *in part* by reflecting on my creaturely limitations it turns out (as we have seen) that this merely constitutes the one aspect of the conceptual articulation of a prior, implicit or inchoate apprehension of God without which that act of abstraction, for reasons Descartes has already given, would not even be possible. Nor need we tarry over the alternatives that Descartes works so hard to exclude, such as that I might myself be God without knowing it. Lastly, neither need we consider the alternatives that Descartes himself dispatches, such as Gassendi's suggestion that we derive our idea of God from our parents, and so on.

In a like manner, Locke's arguments against the claim that the idea of God is innate are likewise shown to be beside the point for similar reasons as those we have already discussed. For example, Locke's claim that not everyone possesses the idea of God, that not all worship Him, and so on, presupposes the Cartesian view that if I possess an innate idea of God then I must possess this concept or idea as a fully articulated, clear, and distinct idea of God.[26] However, as we have seen, it is possible for one to possess this

---

26. Locke, *Essay*, 99–100. See also the discussion by E. J. Lowe, *Locke on Human Understanding*, 15–33. In my discussion, I apply some of Lowe's criticisms to the case of

idea or concept inchoately or implicitly without conceptually articulating it. Further, if the foregoing is correct, then anyone who is so much as aware that he is a conscious being is implicitly and inchoately conscious of God as well. Thus, anyone who reports that he or she possesses no such concept even inchoately is surely mistaken, however forgivable this mistake may be.[27] Thus, Locke has not demonstrated that the idea or concept of God cannot be innate because it is not universally obvious to all or because it is the case that, as an autobiographical fact about many individuals, active possession of this idea or concept is derived from early childhood training, books and other indirect sources. In principle, anyone could arrive at the concept of God as perfect being in the way I have described above, regardless of how he or she did arrive at it in fact; that this should be the case is completely compatible with the innateness of that concept.[28]

Having now considered the first of Descartes' arguments for God's existence and dismissed the second as superfluous, the seemingly natural progression would be to consider the third, *Meditation* V proof from the concept of God.[29] Proper order, however, would seem to dictate that we not consider this proof until we have justified our faculties of conceptual analysis and rational intuition from which we derive the principles of formal logic, since these are required for that further proof as stated by Descartes. As such, we will defer further discussion of the second and the third arguments for now and turn instead to the epistemological implications of the results of this part of the essay.

---

the idea of God, which Lowe ignores. It appears to be the case that, for Lowe, the strength of Locke's philosophy derives from the fact that it is the first truly "modern" philosophy in that it accepts what I call the autonomy of science thesis (that natural science neither has nor needs any sort of philosophical grounding or interpretation) and is a thoroughgoing naturalistic system in which God plays no explanatory role. Obviously, I do not follow Lowe in these respects.

27. How forgivable this is, of course, will vary from person to person, but I will not take up the matter of culpability for nonbelief here. There are many self-interested inducements inclining us to doubt or deny the existence of God that have nothing to do with the rational warrant for believing that claim. My only point here is that the existence of God is not obvious to our reason and that it is therefore possible at least for one non-culpably to deny His existence.

28. Again, innateness does not mean somehow obvious or knowable *a priori*; all it means here is that it is derivable from a consideration of my own existence and nature as these are revealed to me in introspective meditation.

29. We will return to this argument below; see Chapter 10.

9

God and Knowledge in the *Meditations*

HAVING REVIEWED and interpreted Descartes' account of our knowledge of God's existence and nature, we are now ready to reconstruct his account of the foundations of knowledge as presented in the *Meditations* and other works, in which the same ideas are routinely presented.[1] The universal verdict of philosophers since the time of Descartes himself has been that his attempt to justify our common sense and scientific knowledge claims is fatally flawed and to be rejected as completely unsound. In particular, his attempt to found knowledge on the existence and veracity of God has been rejected as a complete failure, so much so that some scholars have wanted to suggest that Descartes did not really even believe this himself, disguising his true philosophical beliefs behind a veil of theological obfuscation.[2] We are told, for example, that Descartes' arguments for the existence of God are too weak to merit serious consideration.[3] Even more notorious is the so-called "Cartesian Circle," first identified by Arnauld that no amount of ingenuity, whether on Descartes' part or by others on his behalf, seems to have been able to escape.[4] Of course, unless I thought that the interpretation/reconstruction of Descartes I have presented here were capable of removing these defects, I would not have bothered writing precisely this essay. It is now necessary, then, that I demonstrate how it is that the Cartesian program can be carried through, even if not precisely in the manner in which Descartes intended that it should.

1. This includes the *Discourse on Method* (1637) and part I of the *Principles of Philosophy* (1646) which corresponds almost section by section to the *Meditations* (1640). Despite the raft of criticisms devised against the doctrine taught in the *Meditations*, Descartes does not so much as modify even the details of his system.

2. See, for example, Louis Loeb, "Is there Radical Dissimulation in Descartes' *Meditations*?" in Amelie Rorty, *Essays on Descartes' Meditations*, 243–67 and sources cited there.

3. See Husain Sarkar, *Descartes' Cogito*, 117 and references.

4. In *CSM*, Vol. II, 150; the problem, presented in the form of a question, is stated in the fourth set of *Objections*.

First, I hope I have discharged the widely held perception that there is nothing to be said on behalf of Descartes' arguments for God's existence. Although I have admittedly taken very great liberties in reconstructing the Cartesian cosmological argument for God's existence as a continuous meditation on and explication of the content of a primitive apprehension of God ultimately yielding the clear and distinct idea of God as a perfect being, I believe that I have arrived at the results that Descartes intended using roughly the means by which he intended to so arrive and without invoking any ideas to which he would have had insuperable objections. At any rate, whatever the defects of my reconstruction, they are surely not those that Descartes' critics attributed to his own arguments. More than this, I make bold to assert that what I have said on that topic is both plausible and illuminating.

It remains, then, to complete the job, once again in the spirit of Descartes, if not exactly as he attempted to do it. After reviewing the case for veracity as a divine perfection and dispatching the Deceiver hypothesis, I will consider whether the reconstruction of the Cartesian project presented here is subject to the so-called "Cartesian Circle" and conclude that it is not. Having reached this happy result, I shall conclude that what I will call our *primary cognitive faculties* are reliable and investigate the general conditions under which it is reasonable to accept their deliverances. I shall then turn to a consideration the claims to be made on behalf of two further putative sources of knowledge, testimony, and authority, which though not primary are nonetheless indispensable. I shall then turn to the problem of error as discussed by Descartes and Gassendi and argue that Descartes' response to Gassendi is defensible. This will lay the groundwork for the next and final chapter, in which shall consider Descartes' other proofs for God's existence.

Why—and in What Sense—God is not a Deceiver

God, as perfect and self-sufficient being, has no inner defect, lack, or need that would force or require Him to create the universe to supply; nor is God under any compulsion, natural or otherwise, to create the universe. As such, God can have no other motive for creating the universe than gratuitous love for what He creates for its own sake, not for His own. As such, it is inconceivable that God could wish anything but the best for the creatures He has brought into being out of nothing. Although the very gift of existence is itself by far the best gift that He could give them, God also wishes for every one of His creatures the highest degree of good they can enjoy within the overall economy of God's providential plan for His creation. In turn, this good turns out to be identical with the perfection of each thing in accordance with its nature or essence, by means of which it most completely participates by imitation in the divine nature of which it is an image. God, then, desires that each of His creatures flourish by exemplifying its nature or essence to highest possible degree. God permits this primary end, expressed in His *antecedent* will, to be defeated in some instances for the sake of the perfection of His creation as a whole, the object of His *consequent* will, the details of which we have no prospect of understanding.

Human beings, like other creatures, have a nature or essence; from introspection, we know that among the characteristic elements of that nature or essence are our capacities for consciousness, self-consciousness, intellect, and will. God has endowed us, in and through that nature, with a number of cognitive faculties whose putative object is the knowledge of reality. Since, as with all His creatures, God wills that we should be perfected with regard to our nature or essence to the extent possible, God thereby also wills that we should exercise our cognitive faculties in the pursuit of knowledge of reality to the extent possible using those faculties. As such, it is incoherent to suppose that, in endowing us by nature with such faculties, that God would have endowed us with faculties that are intrinsically flawed or incapable in principle of achieving their objects. For God to have done this would be for Him to have endowed us with a nature incapable of functioning as the image of God because incapable of being perfected in accordance with its object, thus defeating the only purpose for which such a Being could conceivably have given us those faculties in the first place.

This is more than to say, as Descartes does, that God is not a deceiver. God is undoubtedly veracious but, as Joseph Priestly pointed out, it does not follow from this that God is debarred from deceiving us, since perhaps there might be a good reason, not known to us, for God to deceive us in some matter or other for our own benefit. I am far from claiming that Priestly is right about this. Even if he is, however, when Descartes says that God is not a deceiver, we ought not to read him as claiming categorically that God can never deceive us about anything under any circumstances. Instead, all Descartes intends is that God not be a *global deceiver*, i.e., one who has designed and endowed me with irremediably flawed cognitive faculties; this requires, in turn, that my cognitive faculties be *reliable in principle* and *self-correcting*. This does not require that my cognitive faculties are infallible or even that all error is avoidable in fact; all it requires is that any errors that I do fall into be avoidable, detectable, and eliminable in principle using the very cognitive faculties that belong to me by nature.

Thus, for example, it is inevitable that I make arithmetic mistakes, when I successively add long columns of numbers or make astronomical observations, no matter how hard I try to be accurate. Nevertheless, each of the mistakes I make is in principle avoidable and can be detected, and eliminated using exactly the same operations, i.e., addition or observation, by means of which the mistake was originally made. Such errors, then, do not prove that there is anything flawed or wrong in principle with my cognitive faculties or give me any reason for supposing that they will not lead me to the truth if I use them properly. Therefore, given that I have been created by God and simply by existing participate by imitation in the Divine Nature (which possesses omniscience as one of its inherent and inseparable properties), in making me a cognitive being God both directs me toward and desires that I pursue and possess truth, i.e., the knowledge of reality. As such, we have ample reason to believe that our cognitive faculties are reliable and, if properly used, will conduct us to truth.

Dismissing the Deceiver

Given that God is a perfect being, it is logically impossible that God be a deceiver, since for God to be a deceiver can only be the consequence of lack of power and knowledge, malice, or incompetence on God's part, none of which is conceivable if God is a perfect being. Upon reflection, then, the very notion upon which the deceiving God hypothesis is based turns out to be self-contradictory. That is to say, the two notions "perfect being" and "deceiver" can no more be conceived together in the case of God than can the notions of "square" and "round" in the case of a plane figure: "deceiving God" falls into the same class of self-contradictory notions as that of "square circle," since, as we noted earlier, intrinsic epistemic possibility is a necessary condition for logical possibility and no self-contradictory being (i.e., no being for which it is the case that it is inconceivable in its very conception), can be a logically possible being. Our earlier acquiescence in the apparent coherent conceivability of this notion was a consequence of the fact that we had not yet fully apprehended the clear and distinct idea of God as a perfect being. Instead, we thought of only one divine attribute, omnipotence, in isolation from the other aspects of the divine nature and tacked on the notion of "deceiver" to it; however, given the unity and simplicity of the divine nature, such a procedure is illegitimate. Neither need we worry that such a being might exist in addition to God. It is patent that there can be at most one omnipotent being, since the supposition that there are two such beings would either entail that they are equally powerful, hence that neither is omnipotent or that one is more powerful than the other, in which case it could not be the case that both are omnipotent. Since to be omnipotent (in whatever way we ultimately analyze this notion) belongs to God because of His perfection, we can be certain that only God is an omnipotent being and thus that there is only one God. Given that God exists, then, so too does a uniquely omnipotent being, a perfect being for which it is impossible that He be a deceiver. The logical possibility of such a deceiver, then, is ruled out upon reflection and along with it the skeptical challenge based on that scenario.

Similarly, God would not permit there to be an Evil Genius or any other external power capable of systematically undermining the reliability of our cognitive faculties. Thus, having proven that God exists, we can simply dismiss the Evil Genius hypothesis as Descartes does because the very possibility of such a being is inconsistent with the existence of a veracious God. Thus, it turns out that the Evil Genius scenario does not represent a logically possible state of affairs.

Descartes himself dismisses his Evil Genius hypothesis as merely "hyperbolical," extreme and extravagant, but does not explain what he means by this. In a more modern idiom, we might say that, for Descartes, the Evil Genius hypothesis represents merely an *epistemic*, rather than a genuinely logical, possibility. Something is epistemically possible relative to what one knows. Further, epistemic possibility is a subjective, person-relative form of possibility and as such opposed to objective modalities like logical and physical possibility, which characterize states-of-affairs independently of anyone's knowledge. Since epistemic possibility is a necessary condition for logical possibility, there is a presumption in favor of the logical possibility of whatever is epistemically possible. However, epistemic possibility does not guarantee even the logical possibility of the state-of-affairs conceived of as epistemically possible, as the example of Goldbach's conjecture shows. Therefore, having proven the existence of God, and having come to realize that the existence of the Evil Genius is excluded by the state-of-affairs represented by God's existing, we are relieved to find that the epistemic possibility of the existence of an Evil Genius does not represent a logical possibility after all. This most troublesome of all skeptical hypotheses can finally be put aside as spurious and silly.

In chapter two, I outlined a method by means of which Descartes could accomplish the project of eliminating the foregoing Deceiver hypotheses without circularity. First, we adopt the principle that whatever I clearly and distinctly perceive/conceive is true as a methodological principle intended to guide our inquiry based on its role as a necessary condition for my being able to grasp the elements of the *Cogito*. Using this principle, we provisionally accept as true anything that we clearly and distinctly apprehend with intrinsic certainty, i.e., which is such as to be indubitable or incorrigible based on the content of an act of clear and distinct perception. As I noted, some of these also possess extrinsic certainty, i.e., are such that the very possibility of apprehending that content excludes the possibility of demon-deception, whereas others do not; in the latter cases, the deceiving God hypothesis continues to present a ground for doubt, albeit only a negative one arising from its not having been positively "trumped." The hope is that, by means of a series of steps, each of which is itself intrinsically certain and joined to those that precede it by links that are themselves both intrinsically certain and certainty-preserving, we might arrive at the apprehension of something that provides a general positive ground for eliminating the possibility of an Evil Genius. This, of course, is the apprehension that God exists and is a perfect being, hence a veracious one who is neither a deceiver nor such as to permit an Evil Genius to exist. Thus, my apprehension of God's existence as intrinsically certain, when conjoined to anything else of which I am intrinsically certain, creates something that is both intrinsically and extrinsically certain, thus eliminating the possibility of demon-deception with regard to those propositions. This, in turn, vindicates the principle that whatever I clearly and distinctly perceive/conceive is true and provides a ground for converting my tentative acceptance of whatever is yielded by the application of that principle into firm and abiding acceptance, i.e., *positive* or *dogmatic* belief. Since the claim that whatever I clearly and distinctly perceive/conceive functions neither as a premise in an argument nor as something itself grasped as intrinsically certain, there is neither circularity nor anything question-begging about the foregoing procedure. Further, since a favorable outcome was not and could not be guaranteed in advance, its results count as a *genuine discovery*, just like the results of the application of the standard scientific method.

The rest of chapters three to eight apply this method, relying not on formal deductive argument, as it is often supposed that Descartes did, but instead (and arguably more in the spirit of Descartes than the standard interpretation) by means of a sustained and guided introspective investigation on our own nature, a set of philosophical meditations constituting an *itineram mentis ad Deum*. We started from examples of mental contents, such as *I am appeared to redly* or *I doubt*, in which content and object are identical, thus making them both intrinsically and extrinsically certain for me. From these demon-proof subjective facts, we were able to arrive at the apprehension of the objective facts that I think and I exist, the elements of the *Cogito*, in the following manner. Given that I am aware of anything, including my mental contents, it follows immediately that I am aware, hence that I possess conscious awareness of which those mental contents themselves are modes of awareness; by means of this I arrive at the notion of *awareness-as-such* (mental activity) as that which possesses those modes. For the same reason, given that I recognize awareness-as-such as necessarily implicated in my awareness of any of its modes, I likewise come to possess the notion of awareness-as-activity, of conscious awareness as something real or actual. In turn, I arrive at the recognition that I exist, i.e., that in possessing conscious awareness, one mode of activity, I likewise possess activity-as-such, the entitative principle of existence in things of which conscious awareness is but one possible mode. Each of the foregoing is an example of the EOG relation, here taking the form of the relation of a mode to what it modifies. Since my apprehension of the mode is impossible apart from the actuality/reality of whatever that mode is a mode, direct and immediate apprehension of the one is also indirect or mediated apprehension of the other, yet not less intrinsically certain for all of that. Indeed, both *I think* and *I exist* are extrinsically as well as intrinsically certain for me.

At the same time, my apprehension of myself as both conscious and existent would be impossible unless it were possible for me to introspect the contents of my own consciousness, which in turn requires that consciousness be capable of being its own object. This, in turn, requires that I be a self-conscious, rational subject capable of directing my attention in such a way as to make mental contents as such objects of awareness. In being aware that I exist as a self-conscious rational subject, I am also aware of myself as a *thinking thing*, a *self* or *ego* engaged in mental activity. It is to this that the "I" in "I think" and "I exist" refers. Awareness of myself as a thinking thing also involves awareness of myself as a thing or *being*, i.e., a *structured activity* composed of two entitative principles, existence (i.e., activity-as-such, that which receives structure) and essence (i.e., the immanent, structural principle making a thing to be what it is). To the extent that my essence is revealed to me in introspection, my essence is to think, i.e., to be conscious, or at any rate capable of both conscious and self-conscious awareness. Although this need not exhaust my essence, it is certainly essential to me in such a way that no account of my nature which ignores my status as a conscious being can be adequate to the facts of the case, facts that we grasp with incorrigible certainty.

Although there is no in principle reason that prevents my self-conscious awareness of myself as both conscious and existent from being a ubiquitous feature of my awareness, it remains that my self-conscious awareness of these facts is merely intermittent; this, in turn, reveals to us that these facts are constituted independently of my self-conscious awareness of them. With this realization, we leave the confines of mind as such and enter into the realm of metaphysics, of meditation on myself as *being* insofar as this is revealed to me by introspection. According to Descartes, one of the things I discover about myself *qua* being is that I am a *contingent being*, i.e., one that fails to contain within itself any intrinsic principle accounting for its *persistence in being* (i.e., its continuous existence through time). Expanding on this, we may say that to be a contingent being is to be, at one and the same time, both a real or actual entity and yet potentially non-existent, i.e., really capable of non-existence at each moment that it exists. Although I apprehend the fact of my existence with incorrigible certainty, it remains that this is a contingent fact both in the sense that it need never have obtained and in the sense that it could cease to obtain at any moment. If my existence were non-contingent at any moment, then my non-existence at that time would likewise have to be inconceivable at that time, at least insofar as it was clearly and distinctly apprehended. If it is possible for me to clearly and distinctly grasp my own existence without its being inconceivable that I fail to exist, then it is just as clear and certain that to be non-contingent does not belong to the mode of being that belongs to me by nature.

It remains, then, to identify that aspect of my being responsible for my radical insufficiency to account for my own persistence in being. Following Farrer, I claimed to find this in the *real distinction between existence and essence*, the twin entitative principles constitutive of my being. Since neither is the principle of the other, nor mere characteristics of some third thing in which they both inhere, they are present in my being without proper unity, i.e., without the capacity to constitute the unity of a single being. Since I am incorrigibly aware of my own existence, however, it clearly follows that I possess such unity at any moment I contemplate that fact, since this is a necessary condition for the very possibility of that awareness. In thus being reflectively aware of the *paradox of contingent being* (i.e., that I possess substantial unity in fact but not in virtue of the fundamental entitative principles of my being) I thereby realize that ingredient in my awareness of my substantial unity is an awareness of the operation of some extrinsic principle making up the difference between what I am in fact and what I am capable of contributing on my own to constitute that fact. I thus come to recognize that, in being contingent in the sense distinguished above, I am likewise contingent in the further sense that I am a *dependent* being as well, i.e., dependent for my being on the operation of something other than myself.

Is it possible for me to know anything about the being or beings upon which I depend by further reflection on my own nature as revealed to me in introspection? I claimed that we can. First of all, such a being must be the *per se* cause of my existence, i.e., sustain my existence at every moment that I exist; only this would account for the phenomenon of persistence I experience whenever I contemplate the fact of my existence. Secondly, only a *non-contingent being*, i.e., one possessing substantial unity in its own right, could possibly be the *per se* cause of my existence. Not even an infinite number of contingent causes of substantial unity could account for my persistence any more than an unanchored chain of infinite length could explain how a ten-pound weight could be suspended three feet from the floor. At a bare minimum, this requires that the being in question not be contingent in the foregoing sense, i.e., be such that existence and essence are not distinct but rather *identical* in that being. Thus, in being aware of the ingredience of the activity of the ultimate *per se* cause of my existence as a consequence of being aware of my substantial unity at every moment I contemplate my existence, I am at the same time aware of that activity as the activity of a non-contingent being. Of course, this may only be evident to me on reflection and that activity may be mediated by that of other contingent beings.

More than this, however, such a being will also be a necessary being in the sense that it will be one that possesses substantial unity in its own right, by nature rather than as something received from an external cause, hence in such a way as to require no external cause for its persistence in being. So, we next turned to a consideration of what it means to be a necessary being so described. In articulating this notion, I suggested that such a being would be such that it expresses the *fullness of being*, i.e., possesses the essence appropriate to existence, i.e., activity-as-such, when not constrained by any principle other than or external to itself. For such a being, existence is the principle of essence and exhausts every potentiality of activity-as-such, thus realizing itself as *pure act*. Viewed negatively, I conceive of this being as *infinite* or *unlimited* being, one not dependent on or affectible by anything external to itself; positively, I conceive of it as *perfect being*, or God as understood by classical theists. Thus, in being aware of a non-contingent being as the *per se* cause of my existence, I am also, upon reflection, aware of that being also as necessary, infinite and perfect. I am thus led to the realization that in apprehending the *per se* cause of my existence I am at the same time apprehending a perfect being and that, as such, God as well. In apprehending my own existence as contingent, I am thereby led by degrees to the recognition that this apprehension is, at the same time though less obviously, an apprehension of the perfect being, God, whose creative causality is ingredient in my very existence. Therefore, *God exists*.

The positive content of my notion of God as perfect being is derived from my contemplating my own nature as contingent being in relation to that of God as perfect being. Since I am a contingent and dependent being, I am likewise a limited being, one whose act of existence is arbitrarily constrained, both by nature and by circumstances due to the limitations imposed by essence. To the extent that I, *qua* finite being, realize myself as being (structured activity) within the constraints imposed by nature and circumstances, I participate by imitation in what God is as pure act expressing the fullness of being. Given the infinite gap between God's mode of being and my own, this is insufficient to produce any material resemblance between myself and God. However, to the extent that I recognize my act of existence as arbitrarily constrained by my essence and note the ways in which the aspiration of my act of existence is defeated by the intrinsic limitations of that essence, I at the same time apprehend myself as defeated aspiration, thus participate by aspiration in God's mode of being. This in turn is possible, as Descartes says, only if in apprehending myself I at the same time apprehend God as the background against which I am able to recognize myself as limited, not just in relation to others of my kind or even individuals of other kinds, but by nature. Therefore, the entirety of the foregoing supposes that my own nature functions from the very first as the *imago Dei* in me and in that sense exists in me as an innate idea, i.e., one that I acquire from the contemplation of my own being. This, I noted, can be confirmed by noting that many of the terms we use in ordinary language, such as being, truth, power, knowledge, intellect, will and so on do not have these things as they exist in us as their primary referents or focal meaning but could properly and fully apply only to the perfect being, God. In a very real sense, then, the apprehension of God is implicated from the very first in the rudiments of self-conscious awareness, however crepuscular and inchoate this awareness may be and however much it may be in need of the articulation necessary to make that awareness occurrent and explicit.

All of the links connecting the foregoing claims are themselves instances of the EOG relation. In the case of the recognition of necessary being as the *per se* cause of my contingent being, we have a case in which the EOG relation takes the form of existential dependence of one being on another by whose activity that being is conditioned in some manner. In the case of the comparison of my own being with that enjoyed by the necessary being on whose causal activity I depend, the EOG relation obtains between different aspects of the modes of being compared, beginning with those most accessible to introspection and progressing by degrees to those less obvious to us but still necessarily implicated in our awareness of those that are. Thus, in our own case we are able to progressively deepen our awareness of ourselves as contingent, dependent and then as finite. In the case of necessary being, we were further able to recognize that such a being must also be infinite and perfect, indeed, must be God as conceived by classical theists.

To summarize, then: I claim that each of the following facts is apprehended by us as intrinsically certain by means of the directed, reflective use of meditative introspection described above and that each of the links connecting these facts is an example of one or other variety of EOG relation, each of which is itself apprehended with intrinsic certainty.

1. The occurrence of a subjective fact such as that *I am appeared to redly* or *I doubt the veracity of my senses*.
2. I think (i.e., possess conscious awareness).
3. I exist.
4. I am a thinking thing (i.e., a self-conscious rational subject) or being.
5. I am a contingent being.
6. A necessary being exists as the *per se* cause of my contingent being.
7. This necessary being is also an infinite and perfect being, i.e., God.
8. God is not a deceiver; therefore, no omnipotent deceiver exists.
9. God would not permit the existence of an Evil Genius.
10. Therefore, no Evil Genius exists.

I have done a great deal of summarization and restatement of views defended in this essay throughout the course of writing it, which has made this book undoubtedly longer than it could and perhaps ought to have been. Nevertheless, my prolixity has been in aid of accomplishing the Cartesian project under the aegis of the method outlined by Descartes in the *Discourse*. The reader is invited, indeed, challenged to do the same and either confirm or disconfirm the results I claim to have produced using that method. By the same token, those readers generous enough to give me a bit more rope to hang myself may go onto consider some further applications of that method.

Doxastic Voluntarism

Doxastic voluntarism is the view that we have effective free will concerning the objects of our belief, i.e., that believing is a matter of free choice or at any rate capable of being the object of such choice. The contrary view, I suppose, we could call *doxastic determinism*, according to which my beliefs are caused by forces outside of my control and are not changeable at will. At best, I am able to change my settled beliefs only by some indirect means, such as constant exposure to the evidence for a contrary belief or immersion in the life of some community that holds that contrary belief. Apparently, under some conditions, I may be motivated to undertake such a program of belief-change; one inevitably thinks here of Pascal's advice to his libertine friends whose self-interested rationality has persuaded them that atheism is a sucker bet and religious belief where the smart money goes, but who find themselves incapable of genuine religious feeling. "Take masses and holy water," he tells them; practice the faith, associate with religious people and eventually you will get in the swing of things. I know of no one who explicitly defends doxastic determinism and doubt that anyone would do so if they were to reflect even briefly on its obvious and multiform disadvantages. Nevertheless, critics of doxastic voluntarism abound, which leads me to believe that they have not considered those disadvantages. Therefore, I will take some time to review them now, since Descartes, apparently alone among the major figures of the early modern period, seems ineluctably committed to doxastic voluntarism, so much so that his account of error cannot work unless it is true.

First of all, then, if doxastic determinism is true, then my beliefs are caused by forces outside of my control, forces that quite possibly are only tangentially related to the truth of those beliefs. Critics of doxastic voluntarism, all of whom come out of the externalist/reliabilist tradition in contemporary epistemology, usually write as though our beliefs are generally caused by processes which guarantee the truth of our beliefs, such as perceptual exposure to the external world or argument and evidence in theoretical contexts. This suggests that verisimilitude and mode of causal production ("belief producing power") must be somehow correlated. As such, this mode of causality is inherently rational. Would that this were so; however, it is obviously contrary to the facts. If the foregoing were correct, then it could rarely if ever happen that two scientists, philosophers, theologians, etc. could consider the same evidence, arguments, etc. and yet disagree with regard to the truth or implications of the claim supported by those arguments or evidence. Yet it happens more often than not that those intellectuals who have been exposed to exactly the same arguments and evidence disagree about whether the claim supported by that evidence or argument is true or not. The natural way of describing this is to suppose that one of them finds the argument/evidence convincing whereas the other does not. How can this be, if the mode of causality involved here is inherently rational?

Secondly, given that this is the case, how could anyone ever arrive at the multitude of irrational, even crazy beliefs that abound in all ages and among all manner of person, whatever their social class and degree of education? There are numerous individuals who affirm the truth of astrology and "astral influence," who believe in Sasquatch, the Loch Ness monster, the veracity of the *Protocols of the Elders of Zion*, and who seem impervious to the arguments and evidence against these claims. Similarly, it is impossible for one seriously to consider Zeno's paradoxes, the master argument of Diodorus, Bradley's and McTaggart's arguments against the reality of time and the existence of relations without being impressed by their apparent soundness; yet hardly anyone is persuaded to believe the conclusions of these arguments. Thus, the apparent equation of evidence with "belief producing power" seems obviously suspect. Nor does the rationality of belief obviously seem to track "evidence and argument" in all cases. It seems perfectly rational to reject such claims as *motion is impossible, time is unreal*, and *there are no relations* despite the fact that one feels the force of the arguments for those claims and has no ready refutation of them. Neither belief itself nor the rationality of belief seems to track entirely with "belief producing power" experienced as a *felt tendency to believe* a certain proposition based on evidence or argument.

Even if such a view were not obviously false, it remains that the supposition to the effect that argument and evidence have some form of direct "belief producing power" *just as such* is contrary to the very notion of rational belief, hence not possible as an explication of it. Either we conceive this "belief producing power" as independent of the truth/verisimilitude of the propositional contents (say) that possess this causal power or it is not. If it is independent, then it is at best accidental that belief producing power and truth/verisimilitude are connected, and we have no reason to believe this in any particular case, and thus no reason to suppose that it is the case that these two things are genuinely correlated. On the second supposition, then it is precisely as valid and sound reasoning or compelling evidence that these propositional contents exercise their belief producing power. However, we can only have reason to believe that this is the case if we are in a position to judge the cogency of that reasoning or evaluate that evidence independently of the influence of its belief producing power so as to determine the degree of correlation of the two. This, however, is to credit ourselves with an ability that we cannot have if doxastic determinism is true. For if doxastic determinism is true, presumably it is the case that my judgments of the cogency of reasoning and worth of evidence are themselves the primary effects of the belief producing power possessed by those propositional contents as it is exercised by those contents in relation to my intellect. If so, these judgments do not represent an independent evaluation of that cogency or evidence of the sort needed to establish that these two are ordinarily correlated. Suppose, then, that these judgments are not directly the effects of the belief-producing power of the arguments or evidence under review and thus have the requisite independence to count as genuine judgments of the arguments and evidence in question. It nevertheless remains that, if doxastic determinism is true, this requires that these judgments (which are themselves beliefs, albeit second-order beliefs) be the causal product of some evaluative mechanism which exercises belief-producing power, either directly and hence accidentally, or through some sort of comparative process that operates independently of the impact of that belief-producing power. In the first instance, we have not advanced over the original situation we envisaged; in the second, we are clearly off on an infinite regress. No matter how we twist and turn, if our beliefs are not objects of free choice but rather the causal products of some process beyond our control, we can never have any reason to suppose that they track reality.

The moral of the story is that no mechanical causal process, no matter how well it tracks reality, can constitute human rationality. We can rationally believe that there is such a process only if our judgment that such a process exists can be made independently of its operation. If that process or some surrogate for it is operative in the case of every exercise of our capacity for judgment, then that capacity can never stand in judgment of that process; as such, that process will perpetually lie beyond its evaluative grasp. In that case, however, we can never have any reason for supposing that there is such a process, since there is no way to achieve the cognitive independence required in order to confirm the judgment that it exists. Such a conception of rationality is therefore self-undermining, since if it were true we could never have any reason for believing it to be so and no grounds for supposing that we are rational in the sense defined by that conception. In that case, we could have no reason to believe that any exercise of our rational faculties is reliable or trustworthy, including those by means of which one arrives at a belief in doxastic determinism. Indeed, the doxastic determinist is debarred from even so much as the attempt to criticize the argument I have given here, since to do that would suppose that he or she possesses the ability to evaluate the arguments and reasons I have given independently of their belief-producing power. This, as we have seen, is not possible if the doxastic determinist position is true.

The notion of freedom, then, is built into the very notion of rationality itself such that rationality is inconceivable apart from it. If this were not so, it would be useless even to discuss the "ethics of belief" and our epistemic or doxastic obligations, since what we believe and that we believe it would not be in our effective control. It would be useless to exhort people to be rational, apportion belief to the evidence, exercise objectivity and so on; such exhortations would make no more sense in relation to our intellects than they would if they were directed to a calculating machine and would in any case be either unnecessary or impossible to obey. It would reduce rational discussion and the very making of arguments and marshalling of evidence to a mere expression of the ways in which causal forces have laid their heavy hand on our intellects, and express nothing more than an induced disposition to say certain things in order to causally effect the beliefs of others, perhaps as the consequence of an ongoing fight for survival among "memes."[5] This, of course, is the death of rational discourse and with it, of science and philosophy as well.

There are, so far as I know, no explicit defenders of, or exponents of, doxastic determinism. There are arguments against doxastic voluntarism, though they are uniformly weak. Bernard Williams, for example, claims that doxastic voluntarism must be false because, if we could simply choose to believe whatever we like, then we could simply choose to believe something that we knew was false.[6] Well, by "belief" I simply mean the intellectual act of assent to the truth of a proposition, so if I know that a particular

---

5. For an exposition of this intriguing but ultimately fruitless position, see Dennett, *Consciousness Explained*, Cambridge, Mass., Bradford Books, 1991, and references.

6. At any rate, I think this is what Williams argument amounts to; what he actually says is that, if I could acquire a belief at will, I could do this irrespective of whether or not it was true and even know that this was the case and that this is impossible since to believe something is to assent to its truth. But this is not even remotely impossible in cases in which I do not know one way or the other whether the candidate-belief in question is true or false and I can see a plausible case for either side. I direct the reader to William's article "Deciding to Believe" in his *Problems of the Self,* 13–51; see especially 48.

proposition is false, it follows that I also believe that this is the case.[7] In that case, it would be a doxastic contradiction for me to both assent to and dissent from the same proposition at the same time, something evidently impossible for me. But the fact that my freedom is limited by the laws of logic is hardly a proof that I have no such freedom, any more than the logical impossibility of certain actions (e.g., creating square circles) proves that God is not omnipotent.

More commonly, critics of doxastic voluntarism point to the fact that it is not possible for me to willfully assent to just any outlandish proposition willy-nilly as proof that we have no power of choice over our beliefs. So, for example, it is claimed that I cannot, just by an act of will, believe that I was born on Mars; indeed, that I cannot do so even in the face of a substantial inducement, such as a million dollars.[8] Again, only a Sartrean existentialist would want to claim a freedom as extensive as this. It is quite enough that I should have freedom of choice with regard to beliefs that I have some inclination to believe or refuse to believe. Nor is it true, as Alston argues that, given that I cannot freely believe that I was born on Mars, I necessarily must believe that I was not.[9] The contradictory of belief is non-belief, which can be constituted either by dissent from or by suspension of belief. While it may be psychologically impossible for me freely to choose to believe that I was born on Mars, I can certainly suspend judgment on the matter by considering a skeptical hypothesis based on the movie *Total Recall*. Suppose that, in fact, I *was* born on Mars, but an evil scientist has "reprogrammed" my memory so that I have no inclination to believe and every reason to disbelieve that fact. Since this is both intrinsically and extrinsically epistemically possible, hence presumptively logically possible, and as I have no argument that excludes this possibility, it is also metaphysically possible as well. In my own case, at least, I can report that this is sufficient to make suspension of belief in this case a live option and thus psychologically possible for me; I think this will be so for many other persons as well.

7. Others, such as Jeff Jordan, following Alston (see his "Belief, Acceptance and Religious Faith" in Jeff Jordan and Daniel Howard-Snyder, *Faith, Reason and Rationality*, 3–27) restrict the term "belief" only to those propositions that are held strongly, over a long period of time, or habitually; see Jordan, *Pascal's Wager*, 204. I have no quarrel with the trivial claim that beliefs of this sort are going to be harder to change. However, I am talking here about the initial acquisition of belief and, at any rate, I can assent to a proposition at many levels of commitment (tentatively, conditionally, in the face of doubt or even contrary evidence); there is nothing paradigmatic about firmly held belief.

8. Alvin Plantinga has made this claim many times, for example, see his "Reason and Belief in God" in Plantinga and Wolterstorff, *Faith and Rationality*, 34.

9. See Alston, *Beyond Justification*, 63.

More generally, the extent of our psychological freedom of choice with regard to belief corresponds precisely to the limits of Cartesian methodological doubt, as should be familiar to anyone who has read the first *Meditation*. Since the deceiver hypothesis allows us to cast doubt on all contingent propositions derived from the senses, memory, induction, inference and even *a priori* truths insofar as their content does not exclude the possibility of demon-deception, there are no beliefs of this sort that we are *compelled* to believe, i.e. about which it is psychologically impossible for us to suspend belief. The only substantive beliefs that cannot be undermined in this way are those that constitute the Augustinian triad: I exist, I know and I love/desire. But, given that any belief about which it is psychologically possible for me to suspend belief is one that I am not compelled to believe, I am free with respect to the affirmation of that belief so far forth, even if it is not the case that I can always choose to affirm it by a mere act of will. By the same token, I can entertain any proposition as a potential belief for which I can have any ground, however unlikely, for supposing that its contradictory might be false. As such, whenever I either assent to or withhold assent from a proposition in such circumstances, I do so freely in such a manner that I can be held culpable for what I believe.[10]

Earlier in this section when I was using the term judgment, I was using it in a non-technical sense in which it refers to a power of rational judgment that we all possess as part of our native intellectual ability. Rational judgment, in this sense, is the outcome of a process akin to deliberation in the case of action, and the judgment itself the analogue of the act of choice. As such, it is the taking of a decision similar to that made by a judge in a courtroom with regard to guilt and innocence, only in the case of rational judgment it is the truth and falsity of propositions that is being judged. Earlier, however, I used judgment in another, technical sense derived from medieval cognitive theory, according to which a judgment is a spontaneously occurring propositional content accompanying the operation of another cognitive faculty such as sense perception or memory. Thus, my perceptual experience that I am (putatively) addressing a room full of people on the topic of doxastic voluntarism is accompanied by my awareness of a propositional content to that effect along with a disposition (akin to a desire in the case of an object of action) to believe that propositional content. In a like manner, my (putative) memory that I spoke on this same topic to another group of people yesterday is accompanied by a propositional content to that effect and a similar disposition. It is

---

10. The reference to grounds here is deliberate since, as I have noted, there are both rational and non-rational grounds for belief.

judgments in this second, technical sense that are the objects of judgment in the first sense distinguished above. It is these spontaneously occurring propositional contents accompanied by a felt tendency toward belief that are the causal products of external stimulation and the objects of the kind of rational judgment that is the foundation for belief. In the counterexamples to doxastic voluntarism presented above, the candidate beliefs in question are not the products of judgment in this sense, simply propositions taken at random for which I have no felt tendency to believe and indeed, a strong contrary disposition to reject. The fact that such propositions are not objects of potential belief proves nothing, since as we have just seen, there are plenty of potential beliefs, including contrary ones on the same topic, concerning which a broad range of potential propositional attitudes can be applied by me in the act of free judgment. Many of these, while rational insofar as they are the product of the free employment of intellect may be less than normatively rational in relation to our epistemic obligations. Such attitudes include belief, rejection, doubt, suspension of belief, hope, wistful regret ("Would that it was so!") and so on. My rational judgment amounts to a decision to attach one or more of these propositional attitudes to judgment considered as a spontaneous propositional content and my actually doing so constitutes that propositional content as something that I believe, don't believe, doubt, suspend judgment over, hope is true or wish were true without believing it, and so on. Of course, it needs to be noted that in most cases I readily acquiesce to my spontaneous judgments without any of the rigmarole that I have been describing, since I have instinctual and habitual dispositions to belief in the face of certain sorts of stimulation which, while resistible, are such that in general I see no reason and have no tendency to resist.

So, then, the fact that not every propositional content is an object of belief for me does not disprove the claim that there are a substantial number of such contents that are such or that I am largely free with regard to what I believe, especially about important and substantive theoretical matters of the sort interesting to philosophers and scientists. Neither does the fact that I cannot change my entrenched beliefs at the drop of a hat simply by "changing my mind" provide significant support for doxastic determinism. Like any habitual behavior, be it the smoking habit or the unconscious tendency to utter the syllable "um" every few words when one speaks, entrenched beliefs, even after we have determined to reject them, have a natural tendency to re-assert themselves due to their profound degree of penetration into our cognitive structure. These may prove difficult to give up without effort and continual reflection on the evidence to the contrary, although more commonly one simply finds that one's entrenched beliefs have changed over time, the old ones having been "worn away" imperceptibly by contrary influences. However, this is hardly the case for most of my beliefs, which it remains easily within my power to discard in the face of contrary evidence—so much so that rationality requires that we be prepared to resist the tendency to change our beliefs willy-nilly, lest we be guilty of intellectual frivolity or light-mindedness.

This should be sufficient defense of doxastic voluntarism. Descartes takes it for granted that we have substantial direct control over our beliefs as part of the normal operation of our free will. As we have seen no reason to doubt that this is the case, let us now turn to Descartes' discussion of the nature of error and God's complicity in its occurrence.

Descartes on Error and Evil

Given that belief, especially in substantive theoretical contexts, is under the control of free will as exercised in rational judgment, our belief-commitments are appropriately regarded as the object of normative rules governing the proper and improper use of that faculty. In such case, we have an alternate possible explanation for erroneous belief besides some sort of defect or imperfection in our cognitive faculties. Instead, error and false belief could be the result of our failure to properly use or the positive misuse of our cognitive faculties. As such, the source of error will lie in the individual possessing those faculties rather than the Being who endowed us with those faculties, in which case that being simply permits me to fall into error as a result of my own free choice. All this will be so just in case every sort of common error pointed to by the skeptic could be avoided in principle by the judicious use of the intellect or, even if somehow unavoidable, at least detectible and eliminable in principle by the ordinary use of one or another of those faculties. This will absolve God of any direct responsibility for my cognitive errors and thereby show that God is not a deceiver, thus providing a Cartesian theodicy along Augustinian lines, i.e., a version of the "free will defense."

It is to be noted that Descartes is not committed here to the claim that it is possible for a judicious intellect to avoid all error; obviously, we are finite beings with limited powers of attention and concentration and it is inevitable that we should make errors and mistakes despite our best efforts. Descartes is only committed to the claim that every error or mistake we fall into could have been avoided in principle on those occasions in which they occur. This can be done either through taking more care, paying better attention, refusing to employ one's cognitive faculties on that occasion, or, if forced by circumstances to employ them, to do so with full awareness of the fact that one's judgment (in both senses) may not be trustworthy. As far as I am aware, there are no false beliefs that cannot be accounted for in this way. Nor should we expect there to be any counterexamples to Descartes' account, since such cases would involve errors neither avoidable nor detectable using our cognitive faculties and it is quite impossible that we should be capable of knowing that such errors occur, since only divine revelation could inform us of them.

It is to be noted as well that there are other, non-rational influences operating on our intellects, such as desire, passion, imagination, self-interest, tradition, fashion, love of novelty, intellectual pride and so on. These have a tendency to either add to or detract from the inherent attractiveness of certain propositional contents as they appear to us in the form of spontaneous judgments and are thereby capable of seducing us into erroneous beliefs.[11] Of course, we recognize that our beliefs should be determined primarily, if not solely by argument and evidence. It is therefore incumbent upon us to develop the intellectual virtues, i.e., habits of thought that neutralize and compensate for the distorting influence of non-rational motivations to believe. Similarly, beliefs that are solely or largely motivated by such non-rational factors are suspect and are adopted at one's peril. Once again, God can hardly be blamed for errors of this kind.

As against Descartes, Gassendi[12] notoriously maintained that the foregoing does not in fact completely absolve God of the charges against Him. After all, God could have made me more perfect than I am, indeed, could have made me so that I was infallible in the employment of my cognitive faculties. That God did not make me as perfect as He could have argues against either the divine power or the divine benevolence, both of which are blasphemous suggestions. Descartes, then, has failed to show that God is not a party to my cognitive errors and thus has failed to completely absolve God from responsibility for them. God could have prevented those errors from occurring by giving me better faculties or in-

---

11. Despite what Clifford and others have maintained, rational considerations are not the only considerations that bear on virtuous belief. A parent or a spouse should not be as easily convinced of the guilt or infidelity of a child or a marriage partner as an objective observer with no stake in the matter would be. Neither should a defense attorney in court. There are limits to credulity even here, but certainly, we would look askance at someone of the sort who could be persuaded of these things on evidence that would convince disinterested bystanders.

12. See Gassendi, fifth *Objections*, *CSM*, Vol. II, 214–21 and Descartes' fifth set of *Replies*, *CSM*, Vol. II, 257–60.

tervening to prevent those errors; the fact that he did not and does not do so makes him complicit in their occurrence, not merely passively permissive of them.

It seems to me that Descartes' response to this is perfectly satisfactory. God does me no wrong in not making me more perfect than I am, so long as He does not make me in such a way that my cognitive powers are insufficient for the task for which He has given then to me. Given that Descartes has justified the claim that our cognitive faculties are free from any systematic defect or malfunction, God has given me everything that I am owed insofar as I am a cognitive being in order that I may use my cognitive faculties for the ends for which I was given them. We can speculate about why it is that God did not give me more powerful or error-resistant cognitive faculties, but this is largely idling and in no way motivated by a genuine theoretical worry about the divine benevolence.

At any rate, given that our cognitive faculties are sufficient unto the day for the pursuit of knowledge, the next topic must be the reliability of my cognitive faculties as they function in their ordinary use. The veracity of God has eliminated the grounds for skepticism and discharged the suspicion that there might be something systematically flawed with regard to my cognitive faculties. However, this general guarantee of their reliability is not sufficient by itself to support particular rational judgments in particular cases, since as we have seen error is still possible. We need, then, to turn to a discussion of the conditions governing the employment of our cognitive faculties in ordinary cases. Although it is impossible to do this in any thorough or systematic way, I will at least attempt to sketch the general outline of an account of the nature of epistemic justification.

The Employment of Our Basic Cognitive Faculties

Let us begin with what I will call our *basic cognitive faculties*, which are distinguished by the fact that they are sources of spontaneous judgment in the course of their ordinary, ineluctable operation. These faculties will be such that the propositional contents to which they give rise are simply expressive of the content of the non-propositional cognitive acts whose intentional objects are *facts*, i.e., states-of-affairs existing in relation to consciousness such that they are capable of serving as the truth-conditions for propositions. Since we have already discussed introspection and defended the claim that its clear and distinct deliverances are incorrigible and infallible for me, we will not consider it any further here. Instead, we will consider the claims of those basic cognitive faculties whose standard intentional objects transcend consciousness, either in whole or in part, thus are ontologically distinct, in some sense, from the intentional contents of the mental acts by means of which we apprehend them. I reckon these faculties to be the following: *sense perception, rational intuition, memory,* and *spontaneous induction.* Let me briefly discuss each of these.

Of sense perception, I have already spoken at length and only need here briefly recapitulate what I have said before. In sense perception, structured *qualia* present themselves to me as independently existing external objects that are at the same time the contents of an act of perceptual awareness. As such, sense perception is no mere representation of those objects, or such representation plus a feeling of causal dependence on something external as its cause; instead, it is a *putative apprehension* of those objects. We would have no reason ever to doubt that such apprehensions were genuine except for the facts about perceptual error and hallucination that inform us that sometimes things appear to be other than they are and that putative sense perceptions can occur even in the absence of external objects. Thus, the deliverances of the senses, even on their own terms, are neither incorrigible nor infallible for me despite their apparent immediacy.

Rational intuition is the faculty by means of which I putatively apprehend forms of *a priori* knowledge, including conceptual truths, the fundamental principles of mathematics and logic and other self-evident principles such as that nothing can be both red all over and green all over at the same time. These principles present themselves to us neither as linguistic conventions nor as merely "true by definition;" to the contrary, like the Three Laws of Thought and the Principle of Sufficient Reason they present themselves to us as facts about the nature of things, as necessary conditions for anything to even exist, let alone be an object of apprehension. Nevertheless, many of the objects to which these truths refer, such as numbers, geometrical figures, arguments, possible worlds, universals and so on are *abstract* objects that can be known by the intellect but not through the senses. As such, the acceptance of *a priori* knowledge at face value does seem to commit one to a more complex ontology than many more abstemious philosophers have been wont to accept. However, that is no reason by itself for resisting the deliverances of this faculty. Nevertheless, it cannot be claimed that this faculty is incorrigible or infallible; not all apparently *a priori* truths turn out to be so in the end, as the career of nineteenth and early twentieth century Idealism shows and not all putatively *a priori* truths (such as the aforementioned Principle of Sufficient Reason) are universally recognized as such by everyone. Therefore, once again, the deliverances of this faculty are only *prima facie.*

Philosophers have unjustly neglected memory.[13] When we consider how extensively memory is integrated into the very possibility of knowledge there is scarcely anything, including inferential knowledge, which does not presuppose the veracity of memory. Yet no faculty is more prone to error, as both common sense and scientific studies have shown, than memory. Although there are several forms of memory, the most basic and common variety of memory is experiential memory by means of which we review the experiential content of the past experiences in our lives and, in that sense, "re-live" those experiences. For most of us, however, the passage of time dims and dulls these experiences, causing us to lose a good deal of the content of those experiences. At the same time we often quite innocently "fill in" the content of those experiences thus distorting the actual memories themselves. Although our memories of everyday recent events are generally reliable, it remains that memory is hardly incorrigible and infallible for us.

Finally, there is what Hume called the habit of induction, as opposed to the more formal sort of inductive reasoning studied by logicians. This faculty is a source of spontaneous, almost instinctive judgments based on past experience taking the form of an anticipation or expectation of some future event upon observing some current one. Although Hume's attempt to reduce inductive reasoning to the operation of this faculty is probably not to be credited, it nevertheless remains that most of our inductive judgments derive originally from the operation of this faculty and that unless this faculty is reliable in the main we will have no likelihood of justifying any inductive inferences.

Given that there is no Deceiver and that the veracity of God guarantees that my cognitive faculties are reliable, i.e., such as to produce true belief when used properly, we can now state the conditions under which the judgments generated by these faculties possess warrant for me:

1. I clearly and distinctly perceive (etc.) that F, where F is some fact about reality.

2. I judge that P, where P is a proposition articulating F as the content of my act of perception (etc.).

3. The *prima facie* best explanation for my F-experience is that I am actually experiencing F.

---

13. But see the excellent little book on this topic by Don Locke entitled *Memory*, Garden City, NY, Anchor Doubleday Books, 1971.

4. My F-experience is not defeated or overridden by other considerations, such as contrary experience or well-established theoretical knowledge.

Under such conditions, my belief that P is *warranted*, i.e., epistemically justified for me and thus, if I actually do believe it (i.e., believe as I am prompted by judgment) that proposition becomes something that counts as knowledge for me. Of course, even these conditions do not guarantee that I can never be wrong in affirming P; however, the fact that my faculties are reliable and self-correcting insures that, if I am mistaken, it is possible in principle that my error can be detected, in which case I can simply revise my belief. Similarly, the longer I go without finding any reason to doubt the truth of P, the more reasonable it is for me to persist in believing it.

The Proof of the External World

While individual contingent propositions are warranted and yet fallible in principle, there is a set of propositions that expresses, not so much the contents of specific acts of apprehension, but instead our general confidence in our cognitive faculties. These faculties exist in us as general dispositions to interpret our experience *realistically*, i.e., as revealing to us a real world that, while independently constituted and partly transcendent to experience/apprehension, nevertheless also exists *in* experience as an object of experience for us. These dispositions are, so far as I can tell, universal in all human beings, regardless of their acquired philosophical or religious beliefs, and likely result from the fact that the vast majority of our everyday judgments involving our basic cognitive faculties are warranted for us. The propositions expressing these dispositions we may rightly call *first principles*, the underpinnings of our common-sense picture of the world. These first principles include the following:

1. Sense-perception is a good guide to the nature of the objects of experience.
2. Memory is a generally reliable guide to the lived past.
3. The inductive habit is a reliable guide to the likely course of future experience.

There are other first principles, but these should be adequate—and sufficiently controversial—for present purposes.

Unlike the specific judgments prompted by our basic cognitive faculties, these first principles cannot be refuted or defeated by just any sort of contrary evidence. In particular, they cannot be overridden by a few counterexamples or false judgments. Instead, they can only be refuted or defeated by numerous counterexamples or evidence of some sort of systematic flaw. Undoubtedly, if any of our faculties were such that the spontaneous judgments to which they prompt us were routinely overturned by further experience or theoretical knowledge, such that the beliefs founded on those judgments were usually and routinely found to be mistaken and the expectations formed in accordance with them defeated, we would have long since ceased to believe the foregoing propositions. Given that this is not the case—and elsewhere I have argued that there is simply no prospect of our discovering that it is—we have no sufficient reason, drawn from experience or well-confirmed theory, for supposing that any of these propositions are false.

However, that by itself is not sufficient reason for supposing that they are true and it is here that Descartes' theistic epistemology comes into play. It seems clear enough that we are led ineluctably to the aforementioned first principles by the natural light of reason and that the general tenor of experience confirms and reinforces the dispositions corresponding to and expressed by those principles, which in turn are accepted uncritically by common sense. As over against the testimony of experience, there are only the traditional skeptical doubts and perhaps, a few *a priori* arguments developed by philosophers and generally regarded as inconclusive. Still, are we justified in claiming the pre-critical certainty about these propositions that we ordinarily feel about our cognitive faculties?

I think that we are. Given that there is no Evil Genius and that God is not a deceiver, He could not permit it to be the case that I was systematically and fundamentally misled by the cognitive faculties He has given me as my primary source of knowledge of reality. Nor, I think, would it be the case that God would have made it so difficult to use those faculties in order to discover the truth that only a few philosophers or scientists would be capable of discovering anything worth knowing about the nature of things. For God to do this would make Him either complicit in a massive deception (and further, one which it would be impossible for me to discover, even in principle) or make my cognitive powers largely useless to me as a guide to everyday belief. Therefore, since we have "Demon-proof" knowledge of God's existence and that God is a perfect, hence veracious being, we have at the same time a divinely grounded epistemic certainty that an external world exists and that the foregoing first principles are true.

We need not fear, then, that any future experience will crop up that will rob us of these primary guides to warranted belief.

Inference, Authority, and Testimony

Concluding this Chapter let me consider what is to be said on behalf of three of other sources of belief: the non-basic cognitive faculties of inference, authority and testimony. Each of these is also a major source of belief, indeed, the latter two together are by far the sources of more of our beliefs than all the rest of our cognitive faculties put together; their being non-basic does not make them less important than our other faculties.

The basic principles of inference, such as the fundamental patterns of deductive reasoning, are derived from our faculty of rational intuition and derive their warrant from their putative self-evidence supplemented by the evidence provided by mechanical testing procedures (e.g., truth-tables). Indeed, the branch of philosophy known as formal logic provides us with a complete and consistent axiomatic presentation of the first-order predicate calculus allowing us in principle to provide a proof of validity for any valid deductive argument. This insures that any proposition so derivable is warranted for us, since it is derivable from propositions themselves warranted for us by rational intuition. Thus, it is reasonable to accept the conclusion of any valid and sound deductive proof, i.e., any proof that has been certified by the procedures of deductive logic. Again, the divine veracity guarantees that there is nothing irremediably flawed in any of my cognitive faculties, including my powers of inference. Thus, inference *when used with due care* will reliably lead us to correct results and is also self-correcting, so that errors in reasoning will not simply be discoverable in principle but generally will be discovered in the course of review using the same techniques and principles used to generate them in the first place. The results of the use of inference, then, are warranted for us and should be accepted unless some reason arises as to why they should not be, such as, e.g., the commission of an informal fallacy.

Of course, not all inferences are deductive inferences. Many forms of inference, such as those involved in arguments involving generalization, e.g., enumerative and statistical inductions and statistical syllogisms, are intended to confer only probability rather than certainty on their conclusions. In a like manner, many particular causal judgments, such as those isolated and justified by Mill's Methods are effectively justifiable only with probability rather than the sort of certainty provided by formal deductive reasoning; the same holds true for analogical reasoning. Fortunately, logicians in the last forty years have been taking these modes of reasoning more seriously and have worked to provide canons and guidelines to help us use inductive reasoning to justify universal generalizations, statistical generalizations, particular causal claims and the conclusions of analogical arguments. I have nothing here to add to those researches; let me simply express my confidence that what we now call the logic of induction is advanced enough to give us good reason to suppose that many of our everyday inductive judgments are warranted. Given that we have the divine guarantee that our cognitive faculties are basically sound, we are justified in accepting those warranted propositions as reasonable beliefs.

Authority is the source of an overwhelming amount of our factual and theoretical knowledge; as such, unless beliefs based on authority can be warranted for us, we cannot have any confidence in any belief concerning anything that we have observed or proved ourselves. There is no space here to discuss this matter in any detail; let me just propose the following, without comment, as conditions for any claim based on authority to possess warrant sufficient to justify rational belief:

1. The authority in question must be *cognitive* authority, i.e., the claim to authority must be based on knowledge or expertise.
2. This authority must be exercised within the expert's field of competence.
3. The exercise of this properly credentialed authority must be *disinterested*.
4. The expert's judgment must generally agree with that of other competent experts in the field.

Although this obviously needs much more explication, I shall take it that these claims are neither so vague nor controversial that they cannot be expected to win provisional assent.

Testimony is obviously another major source of belief, and one which is implicated in nearly all cases of belief based on authority, since, after all, the expert's judgment presupposes his veracity and reliability just as much as his expertise. Unless testimony is generally acceptable by us, not just pragmatically but with warrant, we will once again find ourselves unable reasonably to believe most of what we think we know. Obviously, much is required in order to lay out fully the relevant warrant-conferring conditions in the case of beliefs based on testimony. Let me simply sketch the outline of an account of warranted belief based on testimony:

1. The report must terminate in an actual witness or witnesses to the event for which the report constitutes testimony.
2. The witness or witnesses must be competent and generally reliable observers.
3. The event testified to must be at least logically consistent with, and ideally fully coherent with, the whole body of our general knowledge.
4. The claim testified to must not be defeated by the facts or evidence bearing on the case, including the fact that anticipated corroborative evidence fails to turn up despite our best attempts to search it out.

This last condition, of course, is justified by the general confidence in our other cognitive faculties derived from the divine guarantee provided by His veracity. Thus, our failure to discover projected corroborative evidence does undermine a claim to testimony even on the part of otherwise competent witnesses.

Of the concept and canons of explanation, especially in theoretical contexts, I have here said nothing. Part of the reason for this is that explanation belongs to a different cognitive faculty I have not had occasion to discuss and of which Descartes had only the barest inkling. Having rejected faculty psychology, Descartes attempts to make due with just apprehension, failing to distinguish different mental contents as the products of different cognitive powers. Because of this, he is led into the Cartesian Circle, since he is unable to distinguish what is grasped clearly and distinctly by introspection from what is apprehended clearly and distinctly *simpliciter*. Even inference for Descartes is less a matter of formal logic than it is a series of intuitive apprehensions of immediate relations of truth-dependence among propositions joining the remotest premises to the ultimate conclusion.[14] Be that as it may, this other faculty is what we might call *comprehension* or *theoretical understanding*, in which we attempt

---

14. As I believe a close reading of the *Discourse on Method* will show; see also *Principles of Philosophy*, section 204. We must remember that Descartes lived before the modern notion of formal logic existed and that our construal of Aristotelian syllogistic as an inferior sort of formal logic is anachronistic. For more on the state of logic and method in the seventeenth century, see the essays by Gabriel Nuchelmans and Peter Dear in Daniel Garber and Michael Ayers, *The Cambridge History of Seventeenth-Century Philosophy*, 103–77. For Descartes' views on logic, see Stephen Gaukroger, *Cartesian Logic, passim* and Gary Hatfield, *Descartes and the Meditations*, 33–42. For Descartes' views on mathematical method in contrast to that of traditional logic, and its role in the *Discourse on Method*, see Hatfield, *Descartes and the Meditations*, 8–15.

to indirectly apprehend external reality by means of theoretical constructs (hypotheses, models, etc.) suggested to us by material or mathematical analogies and which we try to confirm using observation, experiment and/or inference to the best explanation. Even to attempt to sketch this notion would take us too far afield here, although I do intend to deal with this in detail in another place. For now, then, let this stand as our account of the epistemological implications of Cartesian theism.

10

Descartes' Arguments for God's Existence

A Vindication

DESCARTES GIVES three arguments for God's existence in the *Meditations*, arguments that philosophers have almost universally dismissed with contempt. Given the foregoing, however, we are in position to appreciate the basic soundness of Descartes' arguments for God's existence, despite the flaws inherent in his own presentation of them. I shall consider the arguments, not in Descartes' particular order but in one that best reflects my exposition to this point.

Descartes' version of the cosmological argument in *Meditation* III is clearly the precursor of the argument from the "real distinction" between essence and existence I have called the Cartesian Cosmological argument and so superseded by it, despite the fact that Descartes rejected the doctrine of the real distinction, at least verbally. I have argued, however, that this is what Descartes needs in order to carry his argument to a successful conclusion. There is no reason, then, to reformulate it here. If the essence/existence argument is sound, then so is Descartes' proof. However, Descartes presentation of the argument presupposes much of what he needs to prove, such as that we have a clear and distinct innate idea of God and that we are contingent beings in some sense that requires the existence of a *per se* cause for our persistence in being. Given the analysis of the last three chapters, I hope I have filled these *lacunae* and provided a proper Cartesian foundation for these claims. It remains, then, to consider more carefully the remaining two proofs for God's existence offered in the *Meditations*.

The Argument from the Mere Possession of the Idea of God

In the case of Descartes' first, central, and universally despised proof of God's existence from the very fact of our possession of a clear and distinct idea of God, we find an argument in need of major rehabilitation. By this point, I hope I have said enough to establish the claim that Descartes takes for granted, namely that we have a clear and distinct idea or concept of God as a perfect being. In the Cartesian Cosmological argument, I showed how beginning from an apprehension of one's own existence, one is able to apprehend and appreciate the fact that one is a contingent being. From this result, one is thus able to apprehend the ingredience of the conserving power of a non-contingent *per se* cause, and then rise by degrees to recognize that cause as a necessary, infinite and finally, as a perfect being. We then focused on God as our exemplary cause, as the being in which the aspiration of existence-as-activity is actualized fully and completely and in comparison to which the aspiration of my own existence is thwarted by the metaphysically arbitrary limitations of my essence. In this further role, the notion of God functions as something like a Kantian *regulative idea*, as that which complements our idea of ourselves as limited being, constituting the unimaginable (though not unintelligible) ideal for being as such (or *qua* being) that is frustrated in our own case. Its content, then, is *directional* in relation to aspiration rather than captured in a specific intuition of that being as it exists in itself, a state that evidently transcends both our power of apprehension and imagination.

I have also contended, as does Descartes, that this idea must precede our awareness of our own limitations as such. Unless the directional content of this idea were inherent in the very aspiration of our being as its goal, we could not recognize the limitations inherent in our essence as finite being as limitations in relation to the activity of existing. Rather, either these would seem to us to be mere nuisances or as otherwise perfectly natural to us, which when viewed from one perspective, they certainly are. Human beings could not exist as human beings without possessing the characteristic limitations determined by their common essence. Our recognition of these limitations as limitations cannot merely be with reference to our own nature, but instead with respect to being itself, the ideal for structured existence that our mode of being falls far short of realizing. Nevertheless, this idea, while merely gesturing in the direction of what it is actually like to be a perfect being still possesses enough content to serve as the basis for an outline of what such a being must be like, hence as sufficient to ground a set of general rules to govern the theoretical investigation of the divine nature and to determine what, in such investigations, is in or out of bounds. It thus amounts to a *concept* of God to which the *theoretical conceptions* of God developed by theologians and philosophers of religion have to conform in order to be meaningful.

It does not follow from this that the idea of God is obvious, something that, as Descartes imagines, I might simply stumble over in the course of a casual inventory of the contents of the intentional field of consciousness. Like other regulative ideas, it is in the background of consciousness as a structural presupposition of certain judgments that I make naturally, without thinking about them, as reflected in our ordinary, everyday unrestricted use of terms such as "intellect" and "will." It is only when one turns inward and investigates the metaphysical presuppositions of those judgments that one discovers the more basic ideas and principles presupposed by those judgments. Just as I am able to make deductive inferences prior to understanding the principles of logic, or to use the language of spatial and temporal location prior to my consideration of what space and time might be as subjects of physical inquiry, I am able to recognize in the foreground of consciousness that I am a metaphysically limited being without bringing to explicit awareness the contrasting but necessarily complementary idea of perfect being as that to which all beings (considered *qua* being) aspire and which in finite being is defeated or frustrated. It is nevertheless there and, once again, an idea or concept revealed to us by reflection on our own nature, thus innate in Descartes' technical sense of that term. For inherent in the phenomenon of aspiration itself there is the inchoate sense or awareness of its general direction and hence an anticipation of what the full and complete realization of that which aspires would consist in sufficient enough to inform us that even when one has achieved the fullest possible realization of one's own nature as dictated by one's essence that one still will have fallen far short of what might have been achieved by a different sort of being with a more complete and perfect nature than one's own.[1]

Finally, by reflecting on the various ways in which one experiences one's own act of existing being frustrated or limited by its essence rather than completed in relation to it as aspiration, we are able to provide minimal but sufficient content to the idea of God as our exemplary cause. This thereby becomes normative for how to conceive of God in theoretical terms when theologians and philosophers of religion discuss the divine nature. We thereby arrive at the notion of God as not just perfect being in some purely abstract sense, but more concretely as Supreme Intellect, Absolute Will, and so on, as we will continue to do as we proceed. This is surely sufficient to count as a clear and distinct idea, if not a completely compre-

---

1. On this point, see Farrer, *Finite and Infinite*, op. cit., pages 287–99, where Farrer catalogues various ways in which the phenomenon of aspiration reveals our own nature as the *imago Dei*; for even more such cases, see my *Apprehending God* (unpublished).

hensive one; God's nature remains a mystery (in Farrer's sense of the term) ever capable of being more fully plumbed and analyzed. Nevertheless, I take it that I have vindicated Descartes' claim that we have an idea of God that is as clear and distinct as can be expected, i.e., as is possible in principle given the exalted nature of its object and the limitations of the human intellect. At any rate, I hope it is sufficient for our purpose here, which is to vindicate Descartes' argument for God's existence from one's mere possession of the idea/concept of God as described above. The argument, which proceeds by elimination, proposes to show that only God Himself could be the cause of such an idea in us. Before proceeding to this, however, we need to consider what Descartes considers ideas to be. Since he does not tell us explicitly, we are left to attempt to interpret this notion on his behalf; it is now time to take a closer look at this argument.

The most common conception of what an idea is, especially to those most familiar with the empiricist tradition, is that an idea is a *mental image* of some putatively existing external object, a "picture in the mind" consisting of *qualia*—simple sensory qualities such as individual colors, shapes, textures, tastes, smells, sounds, and so on. As I noted earlier, it is from this perspective that Hobbes criticizes Descartes' claim to possess a clear and distinct idea of God, when he claims there is no such idea given that God cannot be perceived by the senses. Since Descartes responds to Hobbes that not all ideas are mental images, we know that Descartes did not have a simple "copy" or "picture" account of ideas. He is surely right about this, for many of the ideas we discuss, even in our everyday experience, such as space, time, virtue, justice, equality and so on lack sense-derived mental images attaching to them. However, what then can an idea be? To answer this question, let us look at Descartes' seemingly obscure distinction between the formal and objective reality of ideas.

The Distinction between Formal and Objective Reality

In the *Meditations*, Descartes distinguishes between the formal and objective reality of ideas.[2] This distinction, though redolent with scholastic overtones and employing scholastic terminology, appears to be unique to and original to Descartes, despite the fact that he takes it to be familiar enough that he need not explain it in any detail to his readers. For their part, most of Descartes' readers have found it completely obscure and unmotivated.[3] I am hopeful of making it less so.

---

2. See *CSM*, Vol. II, 28–9.
3. For a discussion of the notion of the objective, formal and material *esse* of ideas/

Descartes' distinction takes cognizance of two functions that ideas perform in the cognitive process. First, they are *mental entities* and, more specifically, they are *contents* of certain mental states and acts, such as judgment, belief, doubt, hoping, wishing and so on, all of which constitute propositional attitudes. Consciousness is a mode of activity and the contents of consciousness are that which structure that mode of activity. Ideas, then, are or belong to the contents of consciousness. At the same time, ideas are also that by means of which mental contents represent or intend external objects; it is thus by means of ideas that mental contents are capable of signifying or representing those external objects to us. The formal reality of an idea captures the first aspect or function of ideas, whereas the objective reality of an idea corresponds to the second. We will consider the formal reality first.

The use of the term "formal" here strongly suggests the influence of scholastic cognitive theory on this aspect of Descartes' thought. According to the later scholastics influenced by Aristotle, the intellect, though immaterial in some sense, is nevertheless a kind of non-physical "prime matter" capable of receiving and instantiating all forms. In turn, forms are thought to be both the essences and natures of things existing in substances as their unifying structural principles (this is called *substantial form*) and as accidental properties inhering in the surfaces of those substances (which become known as *accidental forms*). In sense perception, the forms of the object, whether substantial or accidental, existing in things as principles and qualities, are transferred from those objects to the mind and become what are called *species*, i.e., forms that exist in subjects without qualifying them or becoming their natures, "piggy-backing" as it were on those realities from whom they hitch a ride on the way to our intellects. As conveyed by the air and other media, these forms become *species in medio*; as the physical affect of sensory stimulation existing in the organ of sense itself, it becomes a *material species*; and as existing in and apprehended by the intellect it becomes an *intelligible species*. According to a mainstream tradition in scholastic cognitive theory (which, however, was never very fully explicated until the neo-scholastic revival of the twentieth century), again following Aristotle, knowledge is the identity of knowing subject with its external, independently existing object accomplished by means of

---

concepts in the later scholastics (in particular the Coimbrans) see Clemenson, 43–46. My account of how Descartes understood these ideas, which reflects his Galilean physicalism, rejection of substantial forms and commitment to the thesis that external objects in no way resemble our mental images of them, differs greatly from that proposed by Clemenson.

(especially) substantial form.⁴ According to this theory, it is the numerically same form that exists, first in the object as its essence and nature that comes, by a series of transfers, to exist in the intellect as an intelligible species, qualifying the intellect without becoming its nature, hence *intentionally inexisting* or *existing in* that intellect. The intellect *qua* knowing subject thereby becomes formally and intentionally identical with the object it knows by taking on its form, something expressed by Aristotle in his cryptic claim in *De Anima* that, in the knowing act, the subject becomes the object that it knows.⁵ This account explains both how knowledge of an independently existing external world of material objects is possible and also how a mental content can be intentional for us, i.e. because it is the object to which it directs our thought existing in consciousness as a *phenomenon* in one sense that Kant uses this term: the object itself as related to and appearing in consciousness.⁶

Of course, Descartes' Galilean physicalism requires that he deny the existence of both substantial and accidental forms and hence any literal application of the picture I have been sketching to the case of human cognition; further still, Descartes is forced to deny that external objects in any way *resemble* the mental contents that intend them. For Descartes, ideas can be at most non-resembling representations of external objects existing in us because of a causal process rooted in the physical microstructure of material things and terminating in the stimulation of the brain, which in turn produces immaterial ideas in the mind. Such ideas are at best exter-

---

4. See, for example, Joseph Owens's account of this in his *Cognition*, Houston, TX, Center for Thomistic Studies, 1992; originally written in the 1960's. Owens traces this doctrine to Aristotle's *De Anima*; see his *The Doctrine of Being in Aristotelian Metaphysics*, 444, footnote 29.

5. Owens, loc cit.

6. My account here has many points of contact and disagreement with those of Yolton (who asserts that Descartes was a direct realist) and Clemenson (who maintains that Descartes, following the Coimbran writers whose textbooks were used at La Fleche, held a version of Scholastic Critical Realism). I do not have space to air our differences here. I will only here assert (which is not an argument) that neither view can make sense of Descartes's unique "causal principle" used in his first proof of God's existence in the third *Meditation* but that the introduction of such a principle makes perfect sense if what Descartes was attempting to do was re-cast scholastic terminology in a fashion that would allow it to operate in the context of the strong representational realism entailed by his Galilean physicalism and consequent rejection of substantial forms. I am afraid that I must concur with the opinion of Gilson (quoted by Clemenson, *Descartes Theory of Ideas*, 62) that even where Descartes uses Scholastic terminology, the concepts those terms express are his own, not those of anyone else. For more on Descartes's causal principle, see Tad Schmaltz, *Descartes's Theory of Causation*, which came into my hands too late for discussion here.

nally related to the objects they lead us to think about, much as language is capable of representing non-linguistic entities in speech and leading us to think about them without in any way resembling those entities. However, Descartes' ideas are so tenuously connected to the external world that one wonders how the contemplation of ideas could provide any reason for thinking that it exists, let alone provide information about it. In the case of God, however, Descartes hopes to show that our mere possession of that idea proves God's existence and to establish this simply by the contemplation of features of that idea. Descartes' account of the formal and objective reality of ideas intends to allow him to derive a scholastic result without relying on the Aristotelian theory of cognition thought by the medievals to be absolutely essential to the very possibility of knowledge. Nevertheless, Descartes still wants to think of ideas as in some way analogous to forms and as having the same properties and function as forms in cognition, and this despite his having to abandon the claim that, in perception, there is a literal identity of knowing subject and object known. Instead, his Galilean physicalism commits him to the claim that ideas are merely the causal products of wholly physical stimulation of the wholly physical body and its wholly physical sense organs that somehow gives rise to immaterial contents of consciousness signifying external bodies in and to the soul. In place of the material forms of the scholastics, Descartes' strict substance dualism causes him to focus on the contents of mental acts of perception—structured collections of simple sensory *qualia*—as the immediate objects of perception. The idea itself, however, is neither a collection of *qualia* nor a "mental image," i.e., a collection of *qualia* considered as representing something existing external to the mind, but instead the structural principle of unity that ties together that set of *qualia* and individuates it from other mental contents. This form or structural principle is not itself a *quale* but is given along with the *qualia* it structures and unifies. As that principle is apprehended in a particular perceptual experience, it is particular and peculiar to that set of *qualia*. As abstracted from those *qualia*, not as a vague image but as a *concept*, it is expressible in language, definable and hence potentially universal in its application to many cases. Such abstract concepts would be the Cartesian analogue of scholastic intelligible forms.

Given this background, let us now turn to the distinction between formal and objective reality. The distinction turns on the two aspects of the reality of ideas I noted earlier: first, ideas existing as mental contents and second, ideas in their role as signifying external objects and other realities existing independently of consciousness. Since ideas existing in the first way play the same role as scholastic intelligible species, i.e. forms existing in the intellect without becoming its essence or nature, they possess *formal* or *ideal* reality as contents of consciousness. All ideas are equally contents of consciousness and there are no "degrees" of formal reality in this context; the idea of God possesses no more reality, *qua* idea, than does the idea of a stone. However, considered in relation to their objects as their representations to us in consciousness, ideas can be said to differ in *objective* reality in a manner in which I will now endeavor to explain.

Descartes distinguishes three basic kinds of ideas: adventitious, invented, and innate ideas. Adventitious ideas are those that arise spontaneously in the course of everyday experience and which we naturally interpret as coming to us "from outside;" perceptual ideas are one obvious example. Invented or *imaginary* ideas are those produced by the mind itself through the operation of the imagination either voluntarily, as in a daydream, or involuntarily as in dreams that occur in sleep, hallucinations and so on. Descartes takes it to be the case that the causes of adventitious ideas are the non-mental objects in the external world that those ideas signify to us; he also claims that all invented ideas are the products of a recombination of the elements of perceptual ideas stored in the memory and thus ultimately reducible to them. Innate ideas are those that we can arrive at simply by contemplating our own nature, i.e., the introspective examination of the elements of consciousness, such as that of thought or consciousness itself, existence and, of course, God. The purpose of Descartes' proof is to eliminate any other explanation of the origin of that idea.

He does so by making degrees of *objective* reality among ideas correspond to differences in *formal* reality among the objects those ideas signify or "represent." Consider the following list of entities: the idea of a stone, a stone, a carrot, a dog, a human being, an angel, and God. All of these, considered merely as ideas, have the same status as mental contents: all of them possess intentional inexistence and thus the same degree of formal reality. However, the objects they putatively represent differ greatly in their formal reality and are represented as so differing as part of the content of those ideas themselves. The idea of a stone *as such* or *qua* idea possesses only intentional inexistence and thus depends on being thought about in order to exist. Such an idea has a cause but only *subjective reality* as an object of thought; thought about *as such* or *qua* idea, it represents not a stone but only itself *qua* mental content. It is for this reason that, in the case of ideas, content and object are identical and thus can be apprehended with complete certainty. At the same time, the idea of a stone intends or directs us to think about a stone as something existing extramentally and as thus possessing *objective existence*, i.e. as representing something existing as an external object in its own right independently of my awareness of it. It is not ideas, but rather their putative objects, when these are considered as things existing extramentally that possess different degrees of formal reality.

The Degrees of Formal Reality.

Ideas, being mind-dependent, possess the lowest degree of formal reality; all the other degrees of formal reality are greater insofar as the things possessing them possess mind-independent existence. Yet even among these mind-independent things we find qualitatively different levels or degrees of formal reality. For example, an example of redness existing in an external object would possess mind-independent existence (at least conceived of as a structural feature of the physical microstructure of a material thing) yet exist merely as a *property*, dependent for its existence on a subject or *substance* in which to inhere. By contrast, a stone is a kind of substance, and thus of a higher order than a mere property, but an inanimate one with extremely limited powers and capacities. A carrot, by contrast, is an animate being and thus possesses a variety of properties or characteristics that are quite beyond those possessed by stones. In the same way, a dog is also animate but possesses characteristic powers utterly lacking to a carrot, such as the powers of sensation, feeling and local movement. A human being possesses all of the powers of carrots and dogs, yet exceeds them in possessing full-blown self-conscious rationality to the point where this amounts to a difference in kind between human beings and other living things. An angel, who would be a completely spiritual being not limited in its powers or abilities by a body, would exceed any human being in its capacity to know and to act. God, being perfect, would out-excel every being in principle in such a way that it could not even exceed itself. One need not embrace the full-blown "great chain of being" in order to recognize these distinct degrees of formal being in things constituted by real differences in essence.[7]

More than this, although Descartes describes formal reality as coming in degrees, these are not degrees of intensive magnitude on the order of degrees of heat or brightness or sensuous pleasure, where we have a simply, uniform quality that alters along a single, uniform dimension (intensity) with at best varying effects on the perceiver. Rather, the degrees

---

7. In fact, Descartes distinguishes only four levels of formal existence: that possessed by ideas, that possessed by properties, that possessed by finite substances and that possessed by infinite substance, i.e., God.

of formal reality among the things represented by our ideas correspond to differences in kind of which there is no inkling in the ideas that we form of them considered as such, much as is the case with spatial dimensions: point, line, and plane.[8] Consideration of an idea *as such* (i.e., merely as a set of structured *qualia* existing in consciousness) carries with it neither awareness of nor even the possibility of conceiving of an independently existing external object represented by that idea. By the same token, consideration of inanimate nature simply as such carries with it not even a glimmer of what animate nature would be like or capable of. Nor is the type of consciousness possessed by rational, self-conscious individuals so much as hinted at in the sort of consciousness possessed by non-rational beings. Different degrees of objective reality among ideas corresponding to differences in the formal reality in things cannot be explained or accounted for merely as the continuous prolongation or higher intensive magnitude of something common to all those degrees and experienced from the first. Differences in degree of objective reality in ideas reflect differences in kind or mode that cannot be derived by extrapolation from or combination of examples of elements of lower degrees, even if they are ultimately resolvable into them from the point of view of a completed science. As such, differences in degrees of objective reality among ideas cannot be accounted for by the activity of the mind that experiences them. The possibility of such degrees, then, has to reside in their external causes and be explained by differences in formal reality among them.

Thus, we have the basic intuition that informs Descartes' principle that *there must be at least as much formal reality in the cause of an idea as there is objective reality in the idea itself.* Since the degrees of objective reality constitute a series of differences in kind in the ideas of things, so too must the causes of those ideas form a hierarchical series of beings likewise different in kind from one another serving as the causes of those ideas. The sort of formal reality that belongs to ideas as such confers upon them only subjective reality as contents of consciousness. Their intentionality, by means of which they represent external objects to us, suggests to us that they are in some manner or other caused by objects existing externally to us, minimally in the Lockean fashion simply by the facts of their spontaneity and regularity as they occur in consciousness. Our ideas, in turn, represent objects with different degrees of formal reality. Since

---

8. See Edwin Abbot's *Flatland*, New York, Dover, 2007, originally published in 1880. Although this book is often treated as a mere mathematical amusement, it can be provocatively read as a Christian allegory about the problem of expressing the Divine Nature in human language.

these different degrees cannot be accounted for simply by an addition of homogeneous parts to parts already existing (as degrees of heat can be so added); they must be accounted for in terms of the differences between the objects they represent to us functioning in some sense as their causes. Given this, a being with a lower level of formal reality could never be the cause of an idea of something possessing a higher degree of formal reality than it possesses by itself. From an examination of our ideas alone and possibility of our possessing them in the first place, then, we conclude that different degrees of objective reality in ideas require different degrees of formal reality in their causes.

From here, the rest of Descartes' argument follows quite nicely. The idea of God is the idea possessing the highest in-principle degree of objective reality that any idea can represent. Since the idea of God is not an adventitious idea, not being the product of sense-experience, it must be either an invented idea or an innate one. It is not an invented idea, since an invented idea must be arrived at either by an extrapolation from or by a combination of adventitious ideas. Further, our adventitious ideas are all ideas of beings possessing a lower degree of formal reality than that possessed by God and no such idea can properly portend except directionally the content of any degree of formal reality higher than itself. Neither can I be the source of this idea, since the idea of God contains more formal reality than I myself possess. Lastly, neither am I God, since if I were I would possess all perfections and thus would know with extrinsic certainty that I am God: since I don't, I'm not. It remains, then, that the idea of God is an innate idea existing in us in the manner that I suggested earlier, as a Kantian regulative idea. This idea arises in a context in which our own nature, being the image and likeness of God existing in us in the form of defeated aspiration, is apprehended as finite being. In turn, this occurs when that nature is apprehended as the deprivation of the fullness of being that resides only in a perfect being and whose mode of being can only be appreciated as that which lies in the direction beyond the arbitrary limitations imposed on existence-as-such by our own limited essence/nature. Such an idea, then, can only exist if God exists as its cause, since only a perfect being could be the cause of the idea of such a being and only God could possess the formal reality necessary to account for the objective reality of that idea as it exists in us.

The foregoing is consistent with the notion that God shares nothing in common with His creatures. Differences in degree can amount to differences in kind if they are far enough apart; no one would suggest that a human being is not different in kind from a simple, one-celled organism even if one is convinced that the former evolved from the latter. Thus, in asserting that God possesses the highest in-principle degree of objective reality we are not asserting that God lies on a continuum with His creatures in such a way that he resembles them in kind or shares any properties in common with them. Thus, the transcendence and uniqueness of God are in no way compromised by the foregoing argument. Of course, having already shown that God exists in the very process of vindicating Descartes' claim that we have a clear and distinct idea of God, this proof has been rendered largely superfluous, as I have already noted; perhaps its main value lies in its dispatching of an alternative account of how that idea might have come about. At any rate, that will suffice for the discussion of this proof.

The Ontological Argument

Descartes' third proof, the notorious ontological argument, remains to be considered. Seen in the light of the foregoing discussion, the Cartesian Ontological Argument simply reverses the reasoning of the Essence/Existence argument, beginning from a consideration of the divine essence as perfect being and concluding to the necessary existence of a being instantiating that essence. Rather than treating it as a stand-alone argument, I follow Descartes' original presentation according to which the Ontological Argument is ancillary and simply represents additional confirmation for the veridicality of the apprehension of God made explicit by means of the Essence/Existence argument. At the same time, it fills an important *lacuna* in the Cartesian Cosmological argument as presented by Descartes and renders it a genuine demonstration of its conclusion.

In the *Meditations*, Descartes himself treats the Ontological Argument as a stand-alone argument for God's existence, but one whose full import cannot be understood prior to the meditative process that gives rise to his first two arguments for God's existence. The first two he describes as employing the *analytic method* by means of which the idea of God and the fact of my own existence are traced back to their (exemplary and efficient) cause. He calls this approach *a priori*, using this phrase in a sense apparently unique to himself, since it provides not only clear and evident proof for God's existence but does so in such a way that one is able to grasp this truth for oneself in an immediate, certainty-conferring intuition of God. Such a "proof," then, both arrives at an intuition of the cause itself and explains at the same time how my conception of such a cause is even possible in the first place. The Ontological Argument, by presenting a "geometrical" demonstration of God's existence, is *a posteriori* in the sense that it arrives at the conclusion of the argument by deducing it from other, more primitive notions by means of logical deduction. This synthetic approach is inferior to the analytic one, then, for two reasons, one of which Descartes mentions, the other of which he does not. First, as Descartes himself puts it, it is very difficult to grasp these primitive notions clearly and distinctly, and as such the difficulty is compounded by the existence of competing conceptions of these notions and preconceived ideas that prevent us from grasping their true import.[9] Secondly, such a proof depends on cognitive faculties, such as our capacity for conceptual analysis and deductive inference, that are fallible and whose reliability cannot be vindicated until God's existence has been proven. The ontological argument, then, even if a successful demonstration of God's existence, is neither primary nor completely satisfying as a proof for God's existence. However, as we shall see, it does provide a nice capstone to our knowledge of God acquired by apprehension.

We begin, then, from the notion of God as a perfect being, one "greater than which none other can be conceived," even in principle. Such a being will thus possess all compossible perfections, i.e., every property that it is better to possess than not and that is not excluded from the divine essence by being either superseded by some other, better property or as incompatible with other, better perfections that essence might possess. Such a being will also be perfect in the sense that it will possess the in-principle highest and best nature or essence, i.e. the one which most fully and completely expresses *being itself* or *structured activity as such*, in a manner unsurpassable by any being, even itself. Further, as we have seen, only a being whose essence is to exist, i.e., whose essence expresses the fullness of being and exhausts all the potentialities inherent in the act of existence (whether formally or eminently), could possibly be such a being.

Such a being will also be an infinite being, i.e., a being completely unlimited either externally, i.e., by beings or circumstances external to itself or internally, by an essence that limits the self-expression of its act of existence, confining it in ways that are arbitrary relative to that act. Rather, since existence (activity-as-such) is the principle of essence in God, the divine essence is, in truth, simply the fully realized self-expression of that act, the form it takes when completely actualized, hence not separable from it. By the same token, then, such a being will be a metaphysically necessary being as well, one whose persistence in being is self-explanatory due to its status as a non-contingent being, one in which essence and existence are identical and thus inseparable from one another. The burden of the proof,

---

9. See *CSM*, Vol. II, 85.

then, is to show that a being that is necessary in this sense is also a *logically necessary* being, i.e., one whose non-existence is logically impossible.

The argument proceeds as follows: Where X is any possible being (i.e., any being that might actually exist and is not known not to do so) I can only conceive of X as non-existent if I can envisage the possibility that the essence of X fails to be instantiated or exemplified. I can envisage the possibility that X's essence fails to be instantiated or exemplified only if there is a real distinction between essence and existence in X. In God, however, essence and existence are identical such that there is no real distinction in God between essence and existence. Therefore, I can neither envisage the possibility that God's essence fails to be instantiated or exemplified nor conceive of God as non-existent.

To the response that "what holds of the conceptual order need not hold of the order of reality," it is enough to note that this objection simply begs the question against the argument. In addition, the claim in question is simply false. No one, I take it, would seriously assert that a statement such as *2+2=4* or *all triangles have three sides* hold of the conceptual order but need not hold of reality. Nor is the falsity of this claim restricted only to "analytic" propositions: a negative existential such as *there are no square circles* holds of reality just as much as it holds of the conceptual order.

Nor is this a case of inconceivability in the conceiving rather than inconceivability in the conception. What the argument reveals is that a necessary condition for the non-existence of anything is that essence and existence be really distinct in that thing, since to conceive of anything as possibly existent but not actually so requires that existence be separable from essence. In the case of God, however, this necessary condition is not met, thus making God's non-existence inconceivable due to its *extrinsic epistemic impossibility*, which I have argued elsewhere is sufficient for logical impossibility in cases such as these. As such, I have not claimed that God's existence is self-evident, either in itself or to us, nor have I claimed that God's non-existence is intrinsically epistemically impossible (i.e. self-contradictory, like the notion of "square circle"). The fool has said in his heart "There is no God." He has not uttered nonsense in so doing, but the Ontological Argument does override the presumption in favor of the logical possibility of God's non-existence, thus eliminating it from further consideration.

The immediately foregoing suggests a second, metaphysical form of the Ontological Argument, which dispenses with the talk of what is conceivable and speaks straightforwardly about things themselves, as follows. A necessary condition for the non-existence of any metaphysically possible being (as above characterized) is that its essence fails to be exemplified or instantiated. A thing's essence can fail to be exemplified only if there is in that thing a real distinction between essence and existence. However, in God essence and existence are identical in such a way that there is no real distinction between essence and existence. As such, God's essence cannot fail to be instantiated or exemplified. By the same token, then, God's non-existence is impossible, from which it follows that God actually exists.

The illusion that God's essence is conceivable apart from His existence is produced (and abetted) by our tendency to think of the divine essence as a collection of properties specifiable independently of God's existence and intuitively belonging to the Deity on general grounds of perfection or worthiness of worship. In fact, however, our concept of God as a perfect being is largely plastic, a mere Kantian regulative idea that cannot be rigidly identified with any specific theoretical conception of what that those perfections happen to be and how they are to be interpreted. The tendency to employ a kind of precisive abstraction and thereby arrive at a notion of perfect being that consists of a list of properties confuses our apprehension of God (which does not include a direct awareness of the divine essence as such) with the activity of comprehension, where we attempt to indirectly apprehend that nature or essence by constructing theoretical models of that reality. To confuse these two projects—both of which are completely legitimate within their own spheres—creates a gap between God *qua* perfect being and His act of existence, one which seemingly necessitates some sort of bridge principle to connect them. As Descartes reads Anselm, for example, Anselm claims that, since it is better to exist in actuality than it is to possess mere possible existence, we must attribute actual existence to God.[10] Descartes explicitly denies this assertion, claiming instead that it is necessary existence that belongs to God uniquely by nature and that his version of the Ontological Argument derives from an analysis of the unique concept of God. However, Descartes does not explain precisely how the notions of Divine perfection and necessary existence are connected to each other, which naturally leads one to suspect that Descartes' view is that necessary existence is itself a perfection, hence belongs to God as one of His essential properties. Although Descartes never explicitly asserts this, it is probably the most natural reading of his text. At the same time, it invites the same objections (*mutatis mutandis*) to his own argument that Descartes apparently thinks are decisive against that of Anselm.

The foregoing idea, however, gives us another way to read Descartes and to reconstruct the Ontological Argument, one that does not depend on treating existence as a property or perfection as such. Instead, we can think

10. In *CSM*, Vol. II, 84–5.

of the divine essence as the fullness of being, i.e., the essence, whatever it may be, appropriate to that concrete being in which all of the potentiality of existence-as-activity is exhaustively realized in a single, complete and eternal act. We then proceed to reason back from there to the thesis that only a being in which existence and essence are identical in such a way that existence is the principle of essence and dictates its form could be such a being. From there the argument proceeds.

Some scholars, however, maintain that Descartes did not have anything like the foregoing argument in mind, since they claim that Descartes rejected the doctrine of the real distinction in favor of the doctrine that there is only a distinction of reason between existence and essence in concrete existing substances.[11] Whether this is so is a complex scholarly issue that cannot detain us here, since Descartes, though on record as having rejected this doctrine never discusses it directly, so we do not know how he understood this doctrine and hence in what sense he rejected it. We need note here only that, as has been pointed out by others, the supposition that Descartes' adopted the Suarezian position on the relation of existence and essence in created being undermines the Ontological Argument by leaving Descartes, open to Gaunilan "perfect island" objections.[12] As such, even if Descartes did not endorse the doctrine of the real distinction as I have characterized it here, it is certainly consistent with his overall position, and a better choice than the one he made with regard to this issue.

Still, one may be dissatisfied with the foregoing proofs on the ground that it assumes that God is a possible being in a rather stronger sense than mere logical possibility, i.e., as a being that might actually exist. However, these two notions can be easily bridged. Given the conception of God as a perfect being, God's existence is going to be intrinsically epistemically possible, since there is no contradiction in the notion of a being whose essence is to exist. It will also be extrinsically epistemically possible since God, being perfect, is also an infinite being as well, such that no concatenation of external conditions could possibly conspire to prevent God's existence; such a being will therefore be presumptively logically possible as well. Further, since the physical laws of nature will be included in this notion of external conditions, God will be (in this sense) a physically possible being as well. However, whatever is possible in all these senses and not otherwise known not to exist is also a metaphysically possible being as well.

---

11. Secada quotes Descartes to this effect in his *Cartesian Metaphysics*, 215, giving as his reference AT, V, 164; again, from the *Conversation with Burman*. I have not been able to find this reference in *CMSK*.

12. See Secada, *Cartesian Metaphysics*, 215–25.

Therefore, we are not making an illegitimate substitution of one notion of possibility for another in this context. Nevertheless, to assuage the fears of those who may continue to balk at this idea, I offer yet another version of the argument, this time a *modal* proof in which God is conceived of as a merely possible being. The proof goes as follows:

Necessarily, God is a being in whom essence and existence are identical; this is a conceptual truth about God, like the claim that every triangle has three sides and thus true in all possible worlds. Therefore, it is true in every possible world in which God exists that God's existence is identical with His essence. Furthermore, God can only fail to exist in a possible world if God's essence fails to be exemplified or instantiated in that world. For the same reason, God's essence fails to be exemplified or instantiated in any world only if, in that world, God's essence is not identical to His existence, since this is a necessary condition for the non-existence of any being in any world. However, if it is necessarily true (hence true in all possible worlds) that God is a being in whom existence and essence are identical, there can be no world in which God's existence is not identical with His essence any more than it can be the case that, given that any world in which triangles exist is a world in which they have three sides, there can be a world in which two-sided triangles exist. As such, there is no world in which God's essence fails to be instantiated or exemplified. For the same reason, there is no world in which God fails to exist. God therefore exists in every world, which is to say that necessarily, God exists. But the actual world is a possible world. Therefore God actually exists.

If we read Descartes in this way, the Ontological Argument is nowhere committed to the views that existence is a predicate, property, or perfection; hence, the classic Kantian criticisms of the argument (oft repeated by others) miss the mark. Furthermore, the concept of God being employed here is one of a being evidently unique, hence not one open to Gaunilan "perfect island" parody arguments. It remains, then, only to consider the objection that the Ontological Argument achieves only a conditional conclusion, proving only that, *if* God exists, then he exists necessarily.

Could God's Non-Existence be a Surd Fact?

Considered literally, this objection is simply senseless. Whether or not God's existence is logically necessary can in no sense depend on whether or not God actually exists, so it is difficult to even formulate this objection as a serious challenge to theism. The best I can do, at any rate, is to suppose that what lies behind this sort of objection, as well as most of the classic objections to the Ontological Argument, is a fundamental but hard to articulate intuition that *God could fail to exist simply by not existing*, i.e., despite everything I have said, God still might not exist and that it is simply a surd fact that God fails to do so. It is also sometimes suggested that something or other has to be a surd fact and so the physical universe that we actually experience is just as good a stopping point in explanation as the existence of a deity and ought to be affirmed, therefore, on grounds of simplicity.

I do not know if I can shake this intuition among those who possess it. In a certain sense, it does not matter, since I do not treat the Ontological Argument as a stand-alone argument for God's existence, but simply as further confirmation of the apprehension of God articulated in the Cartesian Cosmological Argument. Having established that a perfect being exists using Descartes' analytic method, we establish that that being is logically necessary as well and thus could not fail to exist by employing his synthetic method involving conceptual analysis and deductive reasoning. In this sense, a direct response to the foregoing objection is to suggest that, even if it is true that the Ontological Argument only proves that, if God exists, He exists necessarily, we have already proved the antecedent, so that the proof of the consequent (Necessarily, God exists) follows from these claims by *modus ponens*. Nor is this result mere "icing on the cake": it allows us to argue for the explanatory depth and completeness of theism as against rival views. In particular, the concept of God as articulated and analyzed above allows us to provide what Swinburne calls (and believes we cannot have) *an ultimate explanation of everything* that accounts for every fact, including God's existence, without the need to postulate any surd facts whatsoever.[13]

It is often suggested that when we get to questions such as "Why is there something rather than nothing?" or "What is the cause of the universe?" we have reached questions that are either meaningless or philosophically improper. The universe (usually construed as the observable, physical universe) just exists, and that all there is to it. However, there are obvious and well-known reasons for being dissatisfied with this answer. First, as far as we know, the physical universe consists entirely of contingent beings and thus bids fair to be a contingent thing in its own right and thus require an explanation for its existence. Even Hume admits that there is no absurdity in the idea that the universe might cease to exist in the next moment. Further, even if (as seems unlikely given what we currently believe about the origin of the universe) the universe has existed forever,

---

13. Richard Swinburne, *The Existence of God*, Revised Edition, Oxford, Oxford University Press, 2004, 79.

the feeling that it need not have existed *at all* (i.e. could have failed to exist simply by not existing) is at least as hard to shake as the intuition that God might have failed to exist simply by not existing[14] Nor will the fact that the existence of each of the parts of the universe is explicable in terms of other parts of the universe that acted to produce it be sufficient to explain the existence of the universe as a whole, since if the universe could have failed to exist simply by not existing, as is thought by critics of the ontological argument to be possible in the case of God, none of those parts would have existed either.

Theism can do better than this. Assuming that the physical universe is a contingent, not a necessary being, there is clearly one way in which it could have come into existence, namely, through being created by God out of nothing. As such, the existence of God and His act of creation (*fiat*) would provide the necessary and sufficient condition for the existence of the world and thus explain the existence of that world in the sense that it exists rather than failing to exist by simply not existing. It is simply false, then, to say that we cannot coherently conceive of a cause or explanation for the existence of the world, no matter how much some may want to resist that explanation. The physical universe is not self-explanatory. Since nothing within that universe can possibly explain why it exists rather than not, nor is it plausibly thought of as a metaphysically or logically necessary entity, the question "Why does it exist at all?" is hardly an otiose question. Only theism offers even a ghost of a chance of providing an answer to that question and thus ought to recommend itself to all reasonable persons on that score alone.

Nor are we merely exchanging one mystery for another, as Hume and his followers aver. Theism can also provide an answer to the question "Why is there something rather than nothing?" as well as explain the existence of the physical universe in accordance with the reasoning expressed in the Ontological Argument. The theistic answer to the question "Why is there something rather than nothing?" is that God, being a logically necessary being, cannot not exist, and this fact excludes the possibility that nothing might exist. Further, as Peter Van Inwagen has pointed out, the fact that God's existence is logically necessary *does* explain God's actual existence, thus ending the series of existential "Why?" questions in an intellectually satisfying way. What the foregoing reasoning adds to this idea is an explanation of *how* it can be the case that God's existence is logically necessary (something that Descartes believed could be supplied but which he

---

14. As is argued by William L. Rowe; see *The Cosmological Argument*, 151–65, summarized in his *Philosophy of Religion*, 26–30.

himself was unable to accomplish) in terms of God's nature itself.[15] That explanation is as follows. Since essence and existence are identical in God, by His very nature God fails to meet one of the necessary conditions for non-existence, i.e. the possibility that His essence fails to be exemplified, on the grounds that this state-of-affairs, being extrinsically epistemically impossible, is not coherently conceivable (first version), hence fails to be either metaphysically possible or logically possible (second and third versions). Thus, the logical necessity of God's existence, which entails His actual existence, follows from God's own nature, providing an ultimate explanation for everything in the order of being.

Let me put this point in another way. When the atheist says that it is possible that there is no God, he or she intends to be saying something more than that God's non-existence is intrinsically epistemically possible. Instead, what he or she is claiming is that God's non-existence is a *genuine* or *metaphysical* possibility, i.e. that the state-of-affairs expressed by the negative existential proposition $(\forall x)$-Gx might obtain in the actual world in such a way as to make that statement true in the actual world. However, that this state of affairs obtain presupposes that the state-of-affairs in question be coherently conceivable, logically possible and metaphysically possible. If the foregoing versions of the ontological arguments are sound, however, none of these necessary conditions for the genuine possibility of God's non-existence obtain. The genuine possibility of God's non-existence, then, is ruled out if the ontological argument is sound. As such, it is perfectly senseless to suggest that, despite this, such a state-of-affairs could obtain *at all*, let alone be a surd fact about the world that neither has nor requires explanation. I conclude, then, that the suggestion that the Ontological Argument only proves that if God exists, then He exists necessarily is either false or (as I much more strongly suspect) simply meaningless. Until more clearly articulated, then, it is no more impressive than the other criticisms that have been offered of the Ontological Argument.

God and Explanation

In line with the foregoing, we might mention that many versions of the Cosmological Argument propose that we ought to regard God as a theoretical entity whose existence is to be inferred as the best or only explanation of the existence of contingent beings. Some of these arguments

---

15. Cf. Descartes' claim that God is "cause of himself"—especially the discussion with Arnauld, e.g., *CSM*, 170. What Descartes is angling toward, I believe, is the claim that the *fact* of God's existence is ultimately to be explained or grounded in His nature, but he is not quite able to work this out—or, perhaps not willing to try.

begin from individual beings (like myself) and others from the collective existence of such beings (i.e., the observable physical universe taken as a whole). In such arguments, appeal is often made to the *Principle of Sufficient Reason*: for every state-of-affairs that obtains or thing that exists, there is a sufficient reason/explanation for why that state-of-affair obtains or that thing exists rather than fails to obtain or exist. Given the PSR, it is *never* a reason or explanation of anything that its obtaining or existence just happens to be the case or is a surd fact that neither has nor requires an explanation. If we accept the PSR, then it seems incumbent upon us to accept the foregoing account of God as the cause of the physical universe, on the ground that the only alternative is the unacceptable one of supposing that the existence of physical universe is *literally* a surd fact, one for which there is no cause or explanation.

Many people have expressed reservations about the PSR in this context—although no one seems to have any qualms about this principle except when it is used to argue for God's existence—but there is no space here for a detailed consideration of those objections. The notion that existence and/or non-existence of anything (especially any thing) could merely turn out to be surd, inexplicable facts seems incredible on the face of it. For any metaphysically possible being in the sense defined above, i.e. anything that could or might actually exist, there is a set of necessary and sufficient conditions that could, in principle, produce that being and are such that, if they were to obtain, that possible being would exist.[16] Given the foregoing, if some metaphysically possible being exists, it is due to the fact that those conditions obtained; or, if it fails to actually exist, then that fact has an evident explanation in the failure of those conditions to obtain due to the fact, e.g. that they were excluded from obtaining by other conditions with which they were incompatible. In no case, then, is either the existence or non-existence of any possible being a surd fact. To Schopenhauer's objection that the PSR requires that God's existence, in turn, demands a cause we can point to the analysis just given to show that a sufficient reason for God's existence in terms of His own nature as Perfect Being is available to us, so that the strictures of the PSR have been met in the case of God. If my argument has been successful, the difficulty envisaged by Schopenhauer has been shown to be illusory even if, as is very likely the case, Schopenhauer's premise is correct.

The simple rejection of the PSR by some critics, or their ardent desire to restrict that principle solely to the physical realm, is a harder nut to crack. They will not be persuaded by claims that the principle is self-evi-

---

16. Zeno Vendler, "Causal Relations," *Journal of Philosophy*, LXIV (1967), 704–14.

dent, and, of course, if it is self-evident there is no prospect of its being proved.[17] However, perhaps this difficulty can be evaded by proposing that, instead of treating the PSR as a self-evident metaphysical principle, we reformulate it as a principle of intellectual inquiry, called the *Methodological PSR*, as follows:

> *MPSR*: It is always reasonable (hence, incumbent upon rational inquirers) to accept the evidentially indicated best explanation of any state-of-affairs unless there is some sound reason to do otherwise.

Surely this principle is sufficiently formal to be unobjectionable to any disinterested inquirer; indeed, it is difficult to imagine how serious intellectual inquiry aiming at rational consensus could proceed on any other basis. Neither can it be plausibly claimed that the principle is somehow stacked in favor of theism, since it leaves open the possibility both that there may not be any, or any plausible, explanation forthcoming for certain facts, or independent reasons for supposing that the proffered explanation is false. Were this to be the case, it would not be unreasonable to treat those facts as surd facts, apparently without explanation, though, of course, in accordance with the MPSR, such judgments would always be open to revision. At the same time, the principle is hardly toothless, since it rules out certain, theoretically irrelevant grounds for rejecting the principle. In particular, it would rule out as good grounds for rejecting an explanation for a particular fact that one did not wish to accept it on the basis of pre-philosophical commitments, or because it would upset a cherished theoretical belief by introducing hitherto unenvisaged entities, or because it is seen to have undesirable practical implications either for one's individual life or for society as a whole.

However, my claim, given the foregoing, is that the acceptance of theism on the basis of the foregoing argument and analysis is eminently reasonable and thus ought to be endorsed by all rational enquirers who are not—as Descartes would say—caught in the unshakable grip of "preconceived ideas," i.e., pre-philosophical commitments that make theism unpalatable to them. The MPSR, then, creates a presumption in favor of the reasonableness of theism and thus places the burden of proof squarely on the shoulders of the atheist to provide good reasons for refusing to accept it. It thus makes theism the *default position* in the debate over God's

---

17. For a recent, stout defense of the PSR against its critics, see Alexander Pruss, *The Principle of Sufficient Reason: A Reassessment*, Cambridge, Cambridge University Press, 2006. Although I am sympathetic to the position taken by Pruss, I do not feel competent to evaluate the complex and sophisticated case he makes on behalf of the PSR.

existence, a complete reversal of the view in force just a few years ago. The final subtopic of this chapter, then, will be a brief consideration of the prospects that such reasons might be found.

Is God's Existence Impossible?

Given all that has been said in this chapter, it seems to me that the only prospect for defending atheism against the ontological argument would be to demonstrate that God's existence is logically impossible after all. There are two ways in which this could be accomplished, in my view. First of all, one might argue that the concept of God is that of a being whose existence is *intrinsically epistemically impossible*; essentially, this asserts that the concept of God is ultimately self-contradictory, like that of a square circle. The other approach would be to argue that, despite what I have claimed above, that God's existence is *extrinsically epistemically impossible*, i.e. God's existence is ruled out when taken in the context of our entire stock of knowledge. Some people, for example, have thought that the hiddenness of God or the existence of evil have these implications. Since I hope to discuss both of these issues in another place, I will say nothing about them here. However, the specter raised by the first of these approaches does merit a brief response at this point.

Our concept of God arises, as I have argued, from the apprehension of God as both our *per se* and exemplary cause derived from introspective meditative reflection on our own existence and nature. It is thus an apprehension of God that is mediated by creatures or rather, the apprehension of God made possible by and reflecting the manner in which creatures are really related to God by dependence on Him and as His image and likeness. This apprehension of God falls short of an apprehension of His essence *as such* and because of this our concept of God as perfect being (hence our notions of His individual perfections) lacks any distinct positive content. They are best understood in accordance with the medieval *via negativa*, according to which to call God a perfect being and to say that He possesses perfections such as immutability, impassibility, eternity, omniscience, omnipotence, omnibenevolence, and so on is really to deny of God the characteristic limitations we associate in our own case with being subject to the limitations imposed by change, vulnerability to external affection, temporality, lack of power, knowledge, goodness, and so on. Because the apprehension of God fails—in this life at least—to terminate in a positive apprehension of God's essence, it fails to yield any positive theoretical conception of that nature or of the divine attributes or of their relation to that essence.

This does not mean, as many thinkers whose piety has the better of their philosophy have concluded, that no positive theoretical conception of the divine essence or the divine attributes is possible for human beings. However, it is only possible by means of the sort of *indirect apprehension* or *comprehension*, which involves the use of a different cognitive faculty, one that constructs theoretical models or hypotheses as a way of exploring realities that transcend our intuitive faculties of knowing. So, just as the physical world as such transcends our senses and lies beyond their reach, so that we understand it by taking information derived from the senses as data for which we construct explanatory hypotheses whose predictions we confirm or refute by a combination of observation and controlled experiment, so too must we attempt to positively characterize the divine essence and its component properties in conditions of reflective equilibrium using a combination of conceptual analysis, philosophically purified religious intuitions, and thought-experiments. Of course, in so doing, the results we arrive at are much less stable and certain, remaining open to revision no matter how apparently well confirmed they might appear to be, at least from the rational point of view.

I mention this because atheistic philosophers eager to prove that the concept of God is, despite appearances, somehow self-contradictory invariably attack some theoretical conception of divine perfection or some particular analysis of one of the divine attributes in an attempt to show this. However, the concept of God yielded by introspective apprehension is a very different thing from a positive account of the divine essence, or of one or another of the divine attributes arrived at through the sort of model building involved in theoretical comprehension. As such, even the failure of all such theoretical accounts would not prove that there is anything intrinsically wrong with the concept of God or reflect against His existence, any more than the failure of physicists to come up with any feasible account of the nature of gravity and the mechanism of its propagation and influence would suggest that there is either a problem with the concept of gravity or give us reason to doubt its existence—as it has not done in physics up to this point.

Given the foregoing, then, it is fruitless for atheistic philosophers to attempt to show that the concept of God is self-contradictory by showing that a particular theoretical conception of God or particular analyses of one or more of the divine attributes are defective. Indeed, as the atheistic philosopher Richard Gale has recognized, such objections are really best understood as reasons for theists to revise or abandon these conceptions or analyses in the same manner that scientific theories sometimes need to be abandoned or revised in the face of recalcitrant data.[18] Of course, if philosophical theology were merely a matter of theoretical construction, the failure of philosophical theologians to arrive at any substantive results would reflect badly on religious belief. However, as I have strenuously argued, I hope to some effect, that theological speculation arises from the data of apprehension as above described, no such danger obtrudes. It does not follow from this that the concept of God is free from contradiction; however, that this is not the case is likely more difficult to establish than it is sometimes taken to be. If this is so, then the apparent coherent conceivability of God's existence should be enough to justify a reasonable belief in both in the logical possibility of God's existence and that God is a genuinely possible being in the further sense that He could or might exist in the actual world. This, of course, will be enough to lay the foundation for the Ontological Argument as I have reconstructed it here considered as a stand-alone proof for the existence of God.

18. Richard Gale, *The Existence and Nature of God*, 1–11.

Bibliography

Abbot, Edwin A. *Flatland.* New York: Dover Publishing, 2007. (Originally published in 1880).
Adams, Robert M. *Leibniz: Determinist, Theist, Idealist.* New York: Oxford University Press, 1994.
Adler, Mortimer. *Some Questions about Language.* Chicago, IL: Open Court Publishing Company, 1976.
Alanan, Lilli. "Descartes' Dualism and the Philosophy of Mind." *Revue de Metaphysique et de Morale* (1979) 391–413.
———. "Cartesian Doubt and Scepticism." *Acta Philosophica Fennica* 49 (1990), 257–69.
———. "Some Questions Concerning Objective Reality and Possible Being in Descartes and his Predecessors." *Annals of the Finnish Society for Missiology and Ecumenics* 55 (1990), 553–65.
Aldrich, V. C. "Image Mongering and Image Management." *Philosophy and Phenomenological Research* 23 (1962) 51–61.
Alston, William P. *Beyond 'Justification'.* Ithaca, NY: Cornell University Press, 2005.
Anselm of Canterbury. *Basic Writings.* Edited by S. N. Deane, Chicago, IL: Open Court Publishing Company, 1962.
Ariew, Roger. *Descartes and the Last Scholastics.* Ithaca, NY: Cornell University Press,1999.
Ariew, Roger and Marjorie Grene. *Descartes and his Contemporaries.* Chicago, IL: University of Chicago Press, 1995.
Ariew, Roger, John Cottingham and Tom Sorrell. *Descartes' Meditations: Background Source Materials.* Cambridge: Cambridge University Press, 1998.
Armstrong, Hilary. *Augustine.* Garden City, NY: Doubleday Anchor Books, 1972.
Augustine of Hippo. *Confessions.* Translated by Rex Warner, New York: New American Library, 1963.
———. *On Free Choice of the Will.* Translated by Thomas Williams, Indianapolis, IN: Hackett Publishing, 1993.
———. *On the Trinity.* Translated by Edmund Hill, O.P., Brooklyn, NY: New City Press, 1991.
———. *Against the Academicians and The Teacher.* Translated by Peter King, Indianapolis, IN, Hackett Publishing, 1995.
Austin, J. L. *Sense and Sensibilia.* Oxford: Clarendon Press, 1962.
Ayer, A. J. *Foundations of Empirical Knowledge.* London: Macmillan and Company, 1940.
Beilby, James. *Naturalism Defeated?* Ithaca, NY: Cornell University Press, 2002.
Berkeley, George. *Principles of Human Knowledge.* Edited by Jonathan Dancy, New York: Oxford University Press, 1998.
Boghossian, Paul. *Fear of Knowledge.* Oxford: Clarendon Press, 2006.
BonJour, Laurence. *Epistemology.* Lanham, MD: Rowman and Littlefield, 2002.
BonJour, Laurence and Ernest Sosa. *Epistemic Justification.* Malden, MA: Blackwell Publishing, 2003.
Broughton, Janet. *Descartes' Method of Doubt.* Princeton, NJ: Princeton University Press, 2002.

Bibliography

Burnyeat, Myles. "Idealism and Greek Philosophy: What Descartes Saw and Berkeley Missed." *The Philosophical Review*, 91, 1 (1982) 3–40.

Camus, Albert. *The Myth of Sisyphus and Other Essays.* New York: Vintage Press, 1965.

Carriero, John. "The First Meditation." *Pacific Philosophical Quarterly* 68 (1987) 222–48.

Cicero, Marcus Tullius. *De Natura Deorum; Academica.* Translated by H. Rackham. Cambridge, MA: Loeb Classical Library, 1928.

Clemenson, David. *Descartes' Theory of Ideas.* London: Continuum, 2007.

Collier, Arthur. *Clavis Universalis.* Edited by Ethel Bowman, Chicago, IL: Open Court Publishing Company, 1909.

Cottingham, John. *The Cambridge Companion to Descartes.* Cambridge: Cambridge University Press, 1992.

———. *Reason, Will and Sensation.* Oxford: Clarendon Press, 1998.

Cottingham, John, Robert Stoothoff and Dugald Murdoch. *The Philosophical Writings of Descartes.* 2 Volumes, Cambridge: Cambridge University Press, 1985.

Cottingham, John, Robert Stoothoff, Dugald Murdoch and Anthony Kenny. *The Philosophical Writings of Descartes, Volume III: The Correspondence.* Cambridge: Cambridge University Press, 1991.

Curley, E. M. *Descartes Against the Skeptics.* Cambridge, MA: Harvard University Press, 1978.

———."Dreaming and Conceptual Revision." *Australasian Journal of Philosophy* 53 (1975) 119–41.

Dennett, Daniel. *Consciousness Explained.* Cambridge, MA: MIT Press, 1991.

———. *Brainstorms.* Montgomery, VT: Bradford Books, 1978.

———. "Are Dreams Experiences?" *The Philosophical Review*, 85, (1975), 304–24.

Des Chene, Dennis. *Physiologia.* Ithaca, NY: Cornell University Press, 1996.

———. *Life's Form.* Ithaca, NY: Cornell University Press, 2000.

———. *Spirits and Clocks.* Ithaca, NY: Cornell University Press, 2001.

Descartes, Rene, *Discourse on Method and Meditations.* Translated by Donald H. Cress, Indianapolis, IN: Hackett Publishing, 1980.

———. *Discourse on Method and Meditations.* Translated by Laurence Lafleur, Indianapolis, IN: Bobbs-Merrill, 1960.

Dillon, John. *The Middle Platonists.* Ithaca, NY: Cornell University Press, 1977.

Doney, Willis. *Descartes: A Collection of Critical Essays.* Garden City, NY: Doubleday Anchor Books, 1967.

Farrer, Austin. *Finite and Infinite.* Westminster: Dacre Press, 1943.

———. *The Glass of Vision.* Westminster: Dacre Press, 1948.

———. "Does God Exist?" In *Reflective Faith.* Edited by C. C. Conti. London: SPCK, 1972, 39–47.

Frankfurt, Harry. *Dreamers, Demons and Madmen.* Indianapolis, IN: Bobbs-Merrill, 1970.

Gale, Richard. *On the Existence and Nature of God.* New York: Cambridge University Press, 1991.

Garber, Daniel. *Descartes' Metaphysical Physics.* Chicago, IL: Chicago University Press, 1992.

———. *Descartes Embodied.* Cambridge: Cambridge University Press, 2002.

Garber, Daniel and Michael Ayers. *The Cambridge Companion to Seventeenth Century Philosophy.* Two Volumes, Cambridge: Cambridge University Press, 1998.

Gaukroger, Stephen. *Cartesian Logic.* Oxford: Clarendon Press, 1989.

Bibliography

———. *Descartes' System of Natural Philosophy*. Cambridge: Cambridge University Press, 2002.
Geach, Peter. *Truth, Love and Immortality*. Berkeley, CA: University of California Press, 1979.
Geisler, Norman. *Philosophy of Religion*. Grand Rapids, MI: Zondervan, 1974.
Gendler, Tamar Szabo and John Hawthorne. *Conceivability and Possibility*. Oxford:. Clarendon Press, 2002.
Gilson, Etienne. *Being and Some Philosophers*. Toronto: PIMS, 1952.
———. *The Christian Philosophy of St. Thomas Aquinas*. New York: Random House, 1956.
Grene, Marjorie. *Descartes Among the Scholastics*. Milwaukee, WI: Marquette University Press, 1991. (Aquinas Lecture 55).
Grisez, Germain. *Beyond the New Theism*. Notre Dame, IN: Notre Dame University Press, 1975 (Reprinted by Notre Dame in 2004 under the title *God?: Philosophical Preface to Faith*).
Hatfield, Gary. *Descartes and the Meditations*. New York: Routledge, 2003.
Haldane, Elizabeth and G. R. T. Ross. *The Philosophical Works of Descartes*. Two Volumes. Cambridge: Cambridge University Press, 1911.
Hook, Sidney. *The Quest for Being*. New York: Prometheus Press, 1991 (Originally published in 1961).
Hooker, Michael. *Descartes: Critical and Interpretive Essays*. Baltimore, MD: Johns . Hopkins University Press, 1978.
Howard-Snyder, Daniel and Jeff Jordan. *Faith, Freedom and Rationality*. Lanham, MD: Rowman and Littlefield, 1996.
Hudson, Deal and Dennis Wm. Moran. *The Future of Thomism*. Notre Dame, IN:Notre Dame University Press, 1992.
Huemer, Sidney. *Skepticism and the Veil of Perception*. Lanham, MD: Rowman and Littlefield, 2001.
Hume, David. *A Treatise of Human Nature*. Edited by L. A. Selby-Bigge, Oxford: Clarendon Press, 1960.
———. *An Enquiry Concerning Human Understanding*. Edited by L. A. Selby-Bigge, Oxford: Clarendon Press, 1966.
Jackson, Frank. *Perception: A Representative Theory*. London: Ashgate, 1993.
John, Helen James. *The Thomist Spectrum*. New York: Fordham University Press, 1966.
Jordan, Jeff. *Pascal's Wager*. Oxford: Clarendon Press, 2007.
Kant, Immanuel. *Critique of Pure Reason*. Translated by Norman Kemp Smith, New York: Macmillan, 1958.
———. *Grounding for the Metaphysics of Morals*, Third Edition. Translated James W. Ellington, Indianapolis, IN: Hackett Publishing, 1981.
Katz, Stephen. *Mysticism and Philosophical Analysis*. New York: Oxford University Press, 2006.
Kenny, Anthony. *Descartes: A Study of his Philosophy*. New York: Random House, 1968.
———. *Aquinas: A Collection of Critical Essays*. New York: Doubleday Anchor Books, 1969.
———. *Aquinas*. New York: Hill and Wang, 1980 (Past Masters Series).
———. *Aquinas on Being*. New York: Oxford University Press, 2002.
Klein, Peter. *Certainty: A Refutation of Skepticism*. Minneapolis, MN: University of Minnesota Press, 1981.

Lear, Jonathan. *Aristotle: The Desire to Understand.* Cambridge: Cambridge University Press, 1988.
Locke, John. *An Essay on the Human Understanding,* Two Volumes. Edited by Alexander Campbell Fraser, New York: Dover Publishing, 1959.
Lowe, E. J. *Locke on Human Understanding.* London: Routledge, 1995.
Machuga, Ric. *In Defense of the Soul.* Grand Rapids, MI: Baker Book House, 2002.
Mackie, J. L. *The Miracle of Theism.* Oxford: Oxford University Press, 1982.
MacDonald, Scott, ed. *Being and Goodness.* Notre Dame, IN: Notre Dame University Press, 1991.
Malcolm, Norman. *Dreaming.* London: Routledge and Kegan Paul, 1962.
Malebranche, Nicolas, *Dialogues on Metaphysics and Religion,* trans. David Scott, Cambridge: Cambridge University Press, 1997.
Maritain, Jacques. *Existence and the Existent.* New York: Pantheon, 1948.
———. *The Degrees of Knowledge.* Translated by Gerald Phelan, Notre Dame, IN: Notre Dame University Press, 1995 (originally published 1938).
Martin, Michael. *Atheism: A Philosophical Justification.* Philadelphia, PA: Temple University Press, 1991.
Matthews, Michael R. *The Scientific Background to Modern Philosophy.* Indianapolis, IN: Hackett Publishing, 1989.
Matthews, Gareth B. *Thought's Ego in Augustine and Descartes.* Ithaca, NY: Cornell University Press, 1992.
Menn, Stephen. *Descartes and Augustine.* Cambridge: Cambridge University Press: 1998.
Newman, Lex and Alan Nelson. "Circumventing Cartesian Circles." *Nous* 33 (1999) 370–404.
Nagel, Thomas. *Mortal Questions.* New York: Cambridge University Press, 1979.
Ott, Ludwig. *Fundamental of Catholic Dogma.* Rockford, IL: TAN Books, 1974.
Owens, Joseph, CSsR. *The Doctrine of Being in Aristotle's Metaphysics.* Toronto: PIMS, 1957.
———. *An Elementary Christian Metaphysics.* Milwaukee, WI: Bruce Publishing Company, 1963.
———. *An Interpretation of Existence.* Milwaukee, WI: Bruce Publishing Company, 1968.
———. *Cognition.* Houston, TX: Center for Thomistic Studies, 1992.
Pasnau, Robert. *Theories of Cognition in the Middle Ages.* New York: Cambridge University Press, 1998.
———. *Aquinas on Human Nature.* New York: Cambridge University Press, 2002.
Perry, Ralph Barton. "The Egocentric Predicament." *Journal of Philosophy* 7 (1910) 5–14.
Plantinga, Alvin. *The Ontological Argument.* New York: Doubleday Anchor Books, 1965.
———. *The Nature of Necessity.* Oxford: Oxford University Press, 1974.
———. *Warrant and Proper Function.* Oxford: Oxford University Press, 2002.
———. *Warranted Christian Belief.* Oxford: Oxford University Press, 2004.
Pontifex, Mark and Illtyd Trethowan. *The Meaning of Existence.* London: Longmans, Green and Company, 1953.
Popkin, Richard. *A History of Skepticism from Erasmus to Descartes.* New York: Harper and Row, 1968.
Price, H. H. *Perception.* London: Methuen, 1950.
Pruss, Alexander. *The Principle of Sufficient Reason: A Reassessment.* Cambridge: Cambridge University Press, 2006.

Bibliography

Quine, W. V. "Epistemology Naturalized." *Ontological Relativity and Other Essays*, New York: Columbia University Press, 1969, 69–90.

Radner, Daisie. "Thought and Consciousness in Descartes." *Journal of the History of Philosophy* 26 (1988) 439–52.

Reale, Giovanni. *Systems of the Hellenistic Age*. Translated by John Catan, Albany, NY: State University of New York Press, 1985.

Reichmann, James, S.J. *Evolution, Animal "Rights" and the Environment*. Washington: DC, Catholic University of America Press, 2000.

Rodis-Lewis, Genevieve. *Descartes: His Life and Thought*. Translated by Jane Marie Todd, Ithaca, NY: Cornell University Press, 1998.

Rorty, Amelie. *Essays on Descartes' Meditations*. Berkeley, CA, University of CaliforniaPress, 1985.

Rowe, William L. *The Cosmological Argument* (2ⁿᵈ Edition). New York: Fordham . University Press, 1998.

———. Philosophy of Religion (Fourth Edition). Belmont, CA: Wadsworth, 2007.

Rozemond, Marleen. *Descartes' Dualism*. Cambridge, MA: Harvard University Press, 1998.

Russell, Bertrand. *Problems of Philosophy*. New York: Henry Holt, 1912.

———. *Why I am not a Christian*. New York: Simon and Schuster, 1957.

Sarkar, Husain. *Descartes Cogito*. New York: Cambridge University Press, 2003.

Secada, Jorge. *Cartesian Metaphysics*. Cambridge: Cambridge University Press, 2000.

Sesonske, Alexander and Fleming, B. N. *Meta-Meditations: Studies in Descartes*. Belmont, CA: Wadsworth, 1965.

Schmaltz, Tad. *Malebranche's Theory of the Soul*. New York: Oxford University Press, 1997.

———. *Descartes's Theory of Causation*. New York: Oxford University Press, 2007.

Skirry, Justin. *Descartes and the Metaphysics of Human Nature*. London: Continuum, 2006.

Smith, A. D. *The Problem of Perception*. Cambridge, MA: Harvard University Press, 2002.

Smith, Norman Kemp. *New Studies in the Philosophy of Descartes*. London: Macmillan and Company, 1963.

Smith, V. E. *Philosophical Physics*. New York: Harper, 1950.

Stead, Christopher. *Philosophy in Christian Antiquity*. Cambridge: Cambridge University Press, 1994.

Stroud, Barry. *The Significance of Philosophical Skepticism*. New York: Oxford University Press, 1984.

Suarez, Francisco. *On the Various Kinds of Distinctions*. Translated by Cyril Vollert, S.J. Milwaukee, WI: Marquette University Press, 1947.

———. *On Formal and Universal Unity*. Translated by J. F. Ross, Milwaukee, WI: Marquette University Press, 1964.

———. *On Efficient Causality*. Translated by Alfred J. Freddoso, New Haven, CN: Yale University Press, 1994.

———. *On Creation, Conservation and Concurrence*. Translated by Alfred J. Freddoso, South Bend, IN: St. Augustine's Press, 2002.

———. *Metaphysical Demonstration of the Existence of God*. Translated by James P. Doyle, South Bend, IN: St. Augustine's Press, 2000.

———. *On the Essence of Finite Being*. Translated by Norman J. Wells, Milwaukee, WI: Marquette University Press, 1963.

Bibliography

Swartz, R. J. *Perceiving, Sensing and Knowing.* Garden City, NY: Doubleday Anchor Books, 1965.

Sweeney, Leo, S. J. *A Metaphysics of Authentic Existentialism.* Englewood Cliffs, N.J.: Prentice-Hall, 1965.

Voss, Stephen. *Essays on the Philosophy and Science of Descartes.* New York: Oxford, 1993.

Vendler, Zeno. *Res Cogitans.* Ithaca: NY, Cornell University Press, 1972.

Watson, Richard. *The Breakdown of Cartesian Metaphysics.* Atlantic Highlands, NJ: Humanities Press International, 1987.

Williams, Bernard A. O. *Descartes: The Project of Pure Enquiry.* New York: Routledge, 2003 (originally published by Penguin Books, 1978).

———. *Problems of the Self.* Cambridge: Cambridge University Press, 1973.

Wilson, Catharine. *Descartes' Meditations: An Introduction.* Cambridge: Cambridge University Press, 2003.

Wilson, Margaret. *Descartes.* London: Routledge and Kegan Paul, 1978.

Wolterstorff, Nicholas. *John Locke and the Ethics of Belief.* Cambridge: Cambridge University Press, 1996.

Wippel, John F. *The Metaphysical Thought of St. Thomas Aquinas.* Washington, DC: Catholic University of America Press, 2000.

www.ingramcontent.com/pod-product-compliance
Lightning Source LLC
Chambersburg PA
CBHW062017220426
43662CB00010B/1368